TRAVE D0581713

'For pictorial quality and for revelation of character, her own and others', Miss Stark's *Traveller's Prelude* is one of the most astonishing performances in autobiography in recent years.' *The Times*

Dame Freya Stark has become a legend in her lifetime through her travels in Arabia and her ability to describe them and this is the story of the upbringing which helped to shape her destiny.

She was born in Paris where her parents were studying art, and her travelling career began at the age of 2½ when she was carried over the Pelmo Pass in a basket. Her parents' matrimonial disharmony and the family's natural restlessness ensured that Freya and her sister had a cosmopolitan childhood spent between France, Italy and England. They received no formal schooling, although Freya read a great deal. She worked for a time in a carpet factory and kept house for her mother, but she succeeded in matriculating and gained a place at the University of London.

The Great War broke out before she took her degree and Freya worked at censorship in London for a short time and then became a nurse on the Italian front, where she was caught up in the retreat from Caporetto. After the war she studied Arabic and went mountaineering in the Alps which was to prove invaluable training for her later expeditions. A gastric ulcer with ensuing complications did not deter her from her subsequent determination to undergo the rigours of desert travel.

Traveller's Prelude is a lively account of Freya Stark's youth, with a rich cast of characters brought vividly to life with her own inimitable style and humour.

'Exquisite balance of humour and wisdom ... She is a great writer and this is a great book.' *The Observer*

'The book is everywhere rich in interest ... A most inspiriting book.' Raymond Mortimer, *The Sunday Times*

Traveller's Prelude

AUTOBIOGRAPHY 1893–1927

FREYA STARK

CENTURY PUBLISHING

LONDON

ISBN 0 7126 0274 7

Cover shows detail of 'Verona' by J. Holland

Printed in Great Britain by
Richard Clay (The Chaucer Press) Ltd,
Bungay, Suffolk

Contents

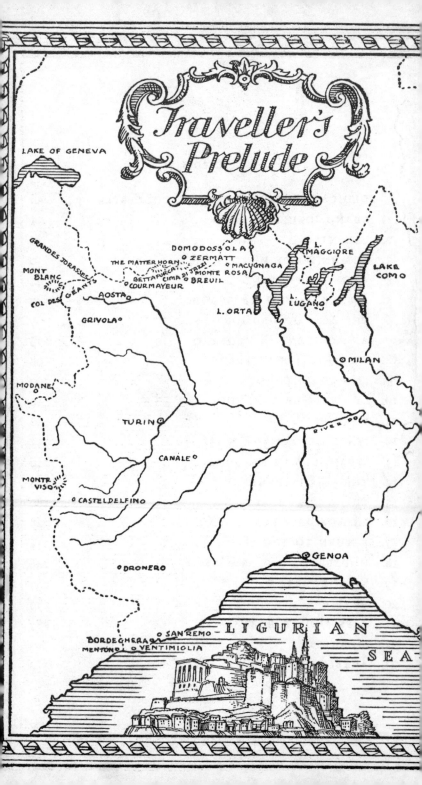

DOLOMITES

R. TAGLIAMENTO
CAPORETTO

BELLUNO

CASARSA UDINE
PORDENONE CODROIPO
S. GIOVANNI DI MANZANO CORMONS
S. VITO GORIZIA
CONEGLIANO
MONFALCONE

ASOLO
BASSANO
CASTELFRANCO TREVISO

VICENZA

PADUA
VENICE
CHIOGGIA
BRONDOLO
CAVANELLA D'ADIGE

MANTUA

LAKE
GARDA

CIA

RIVER

FERRARA

MAGNAVACCA
COMACCHIO

BOLOGNA
RAVENNA

A D R I A T I C   S E A

EGGIO

Scale of Statute Miles

10 10 20 30 40 50 60 70

My dear Sydney,

This is your book, written at your request in Arabia and in the pine woods of Cyprus. It was written during the war, and tries to render, in a small way, a war of its own, the clash and contrast of a human struggle, against a European background so different from ours as to seem already remote in time. This made it hard to write. Yet I hope that in its particular there is enough of the universal to make it interesting; in any case it has given me the pleasure of dedicating it to you.

Freya.

APRIL, 1950.

1

Grandmothers

My parents were first cousins, and the Stark family, to which both belonged, had lived in Devonshire for two hundred years or so, with the exception of a maternal grandmother, an old lady of such formidable ingredients that her character, more or less emphasized, reproduced itself in every one of her four daughters and in most of their children, and would go on doing so no doubt in their descendants if any were to remain. Her features were repeated, rather sporadically, in my mother, my youngest aunt, my sister and my niece, a face more square than aquiline, with thick eyebrows and a frown between them that showed itself quite early—with fine eyes, brown or greenish grey, and a violent mouth, not passionate nor voluptuous, neither pinched nor mean, but obstinate, with apparently an equal capacity for turning hard or gentle, according to the vicissitudes of life.

In my grandmother it settled with old age into benevolence of a determined sort, long impervious to advice and eventually almost independent of chance or circumstance. Her character, like her features, distributed itself among her descendants, with only a slight blunting of the outline as it passed from one mould to another. What strong hammering through the ages produced so enduring a core I know too little of the family history to tell. My grandmother's father was a court-painter in Aix-la-Chapelle —or Aachen as she preferred to call it. He came from a peasant family near Trier and was made Chevalier Schmid; while a *von* was added to the name by his brother, Minister to the Grand Duke of Tuscany. My great-grandfather's portrait still hangs, I believe, in the Uffizi in Florence among the other self-portraits of artists. He must have either originated or shared the family carelessness for anything like a fixture in space or time, for, having struck up a friendship in the small German court with the visiting Duke of Cambridge of that day, he transported his wife and a large Victorian family to Manchester Square, where my grandmother, as a growing girl, made friends with Harriet Martineau and acquired a habit of reading, and a rooted prejudice against the middle class virtues in England. Her own mother's outline is lost except for a fleeting vignette of a girl caught by a rainstorm in some German street where a young man gallantly protected her with an umbrella: they were pleased with one another, and she discovered his name to be Von Bismarck—but there the story ended and she disappears into her years—a vague figure struggling with cares of poverty and children. The great-great-grandmother too appears for a moment, a slim old lady sitting in black satins erect upon her chair, with a handkerchief all lace, complaining bitterly that her daughter's children are being brought up 'canaille'. She was French and partly Polish, of refugee parents—the Marquis and Marquise de Marneffe—who once belonged, I was told, to the household of the Princesse de Lamballe, and escaped across the Rhine. They sold their lands for paper republican money, and lost them for good, and set up in Aachen, the Marquis with a market garden, from which he went every day to sell his produce with his basket on his arm, while his wife gave lessons on the violin.

Into this mixed background, through which strains of painting and music run like a coloured thread, my grandmother was born, with a number of brothers and sisters around her: and—apart from the brief episode in Manchester Square—grew up in the old, quiet, liberal Germany that Matthew Arnold admired, and that has turned into a mirage in our day.

At the age of seventeen or eighteen she was sent alone to a friend of her mother's girlhood, the Princess Rospigliosi in Rome, to look after a small child there and to be treated almost as a daughter of the house. The family divided their seasons between the country estates where they played chess with the curé, and the palace in the city where King Ludwig of Bavaria complimented the young girl on her music. She once told me how, on her first morning at the country home, after a long drive the day before through the Roman Campagna into Tuscany, she came to breakfast and sat shyly down, and was non-plussed by the old Prince's polite enquiry: "Est-ce que vous avez accompli vos fonctions ce matin?" He was referring to early mass in the family chapel.

In their city palace, the Rospigliosi lived through Garibaldi's short republic and the French siege; neither of these things was ever mentioned, nor was any reference made to the explosions whose sound penetrated dimly through the thick walls; and my grandmother, who came to know medieval and ancient Rome better than any woman I have met, was almost entirely ignorant of the history in which she lived. The thuds of the explosions died away; Garibaldi marched out; and Pius IX was reinstated. My grandmother married from the Rospigliosi house, and frequently visited there afterwards; and my mother as a small child remembered being lifted on to the Pope's knees by young Rospigliosi in his parti-coloured uniform, designed by Michel-angelo for the 'noble guard.' But when Pius IX left in 1870 and the Italian nationals entered, the old Rospigliosi departed from the city never to return.

My grandmother was now married and settled in Florence, in a villa among the olives of Bellosguardo, which has since been turned into a nunnery. She married a young English painter, well-to-do and romantic, who saw her from a distance as she took the air in the Rospigliosi carriage in the Corso. He determined there and then to obtain an introduction and to propose to her. They were not very happy. My grandfather was bitten by a mad dog and died tragically in his early forties, leaving four growing daughters and a great many debts; so that I never knew him. But the tears came to my mother's eyes whenever she spoke of him, and he must have been impulsive and open-handed, and immensely gregarious—so that the villa was always full of guests, promiscuously gathered from all who came to Florence. The Brownings, the Thackerays, the Trollopes, the Landors were there at various times. They appear to have made no deep impression on my grandmother, who had a rather Teutonic blindness for the *variety* of life; she developed a Victorian delicacy after producing her four children, and spent most of her time on a chaise-longue studying Gregorovius and talking to a chosen and learned few, while the daughters were brought up wild and rebellious by a sadistic German governess. My grandfather's comfortable fortune, drawn from a brewery near Torquay, was splashed on the villa walls in huge frescoes—efforts to rediscover the ingredients and the mixing of Titian's colours. This of course he never did, but he painted happily, and enjoyed the flowing stream of guests at his table, and the villa and its overgrown neglected garden were big enough to allow husband and wife and the four children to lead their lives as isolated as ships on the same sea; nor was the German governess (in spite of her efforts with the household bills), ever able to unite them in anything but a general repulsion. My grandmother once told me the exact moment when the separation from her husband took place in her heart: he came in tired one evening, and took his boots off in her drawing-room, and she realized that she had married into the 'bourgeoisie'. Her next awakening to the facts of life appears to have been my grandfather's death, and the discovery that the villa and all inside it were barely sufficient to pay his creditors.

My grandmother then showed her admirable qualities. Her friends combined to rent her a small apartment in Genoa, and she gave lessons as her own grandmother had done before her. She had learning, and immense dignity and charm. In an age when it was derogatory for a woman to do almost anything at all, she never even realized that it could be other than a benefit and a privilege for her pupils to share the knowledge in which she delighted: Mommsen and Gregorovius, the German, French, English and Italian classics, were poured in a humanized stream into the ears of the young ladies of Liguria; and she kept herself and her daughters, and was received into the most reserved Genoese society as well.

All would have gone happily if prosperity had not immediately tempted her to abandon the small and suitable little house provided by her friends, and to sail out into one of the Renaissance palaces of the town. I can just remember its polished marble floors and gilt bases of doors and tables and mirrors whose upper curves and ornaments soared far above my four-year-old perspective. It was the last little bonfire of splendour in her life. The lease soon had to be sold; the daughters were now grown up and able, in a rather fluctuating way, to look after her; and it was felt, I suppose, that a person who never looked at a bill was not to be trusted far away from all control. My grandmother as I knew her came into being—always a little of a problem, living with this aunt or that, or in lodgings at the end of long tram or bus routes, in sitting-rooms of dark plush where all the pictures had heavy frames. Here, with small very wrinkled hands, and silk lace carefully and gently draped about her, she radiated her unchanging serenity and charm. She carried about with her that best of grandmotherly atmospheres—a taste of amplitude in Time. No hurry ever came near her. A whole series of episodes in my childhood show her peacefully reading, or dressing, or brushing the long white hair that still could touch her knees, while a babel of agitated voices urged departing carriages or trains. She always had a book in her hand and she was never busy; she would put it down and her arms would open to enclose any human being, but particularly a child, who needed a refuge there; what she gave was affection pure and simple, deliberately free from wear and tear of understanding or advice. She did this because she believed in affection as the panacea for all the evil in the world, and the essence of this simple love has wound itself in my memory with her scent of eau-de-cologne, and her blonde lace, and the wide silk folds and bits of warm satin that made up the black friendly labyrinth of her gowns. There one nestled for hours while she told stories. The book of Genesis, myths of Greece, the Siegfried Sagas, the Seven Kings of Rome, Tasso, Dante, Goethe, came to me in this good way, not arid noises from a mechanical cavern, or black and white deserts of print, but warm with the person of the teller, modulated with the inflections of a voice that meant safety and kindness, so that the childhood of the world merged with my own and lies there entranced in the same afternoon light that melted into twilight, and gradually dimmed the ivory face and left the voice almost alone to call up pageant after pageant, while one fondled the small hands, so soft and old, whose rings had taken the shape of the fingers and lost their lustre through more than half a century of wear.

This charm of fragile immobility was an illusion. Any physical exertion bored my grandmother, because it took her away from the meditations which delighted her: but when a necessity arose, such as a journey to Finland at the age of seventy-two to stay with an aunt and uncle, she faced it with no visible exertion—indeed scarcely noticed the outward break; allowed someone to pack for her as someone always did; and continued to read Dante on shipboard or train. On this occasion indeed she began to learn Russian and mastered it sufficiently to enjoy what interested her during the two years of her stay. Her gentle grand manner hid an unsuspected toughness which managed to resist—without a shadow of annoyance, and all through her life—the devoted efforts of friends and relatives to think for her good. No means were ever devised by which anybody's money could remain for even the shortest time in her possession: it found its way with unbelievable swiftness into the hands of the undeserving, and seemed to relieve my grandmother immensely by its departure. She not only gave away her own, but arranged for her wealthier friends to make gifts they knew nothing of to people they had never seen, or borrowed money to make presents to the people from whom she borrowed, which annoyed them.

A number of friendships gave way under this strain. She watched them depart with a serene remoteness, for she was quite inflexible; her humility existed in a general way, when she contemplated the Cosmos; when it came to her own dealings with other human beings, it was take it or leave it every time;

and she resented criticism in a passionate way which she bequeathed disastrously to all her children. "Your dear grandmother," in terms of reproach trailed through my childhood. But she remained untouched and free in herself; and no tinge of manner showed the dingy boarding houses to be any different from the palaces of her youth. "I have lived in every sort of state," she once told me; "and I find one much like another." To her it was so.

She lived to the age of ninety-three, and her eyesight failed at last and she could read no longer, but returned to Goethe, and the *Divine Comedy*, and the Epistles of St. Paul, all of which she had known by heart for many years. When she was eighty-four she spent a winter with us, and I put her into a sleeper on her way to London from Menton on the Riviera when her visit came to an end. As the train steamed out slowly, she stepped on to the seat to find something on the rack: and, in this independent way, the old lady who never took any exercise glided out of my sight for ever.

*   *   *   *   *

Very few people can dispense with the trappings of their lives and yet feel themselves secure; and these are remembered as victors, though they may be crossing-sweepers by occupation: they are seen independently of the furniture of their time.

My paternal grandmother was not of these. I remember her as small and fragile, a faded little flame for whose pale burning a whole household of Victorian bric-a-brac, servants and solidities, revolved in methodical plenty. She was born in Taunton in 1816 and lived, when I knew her, in a house at Tor, which is the inland half of Torquay. Here, in the housekeeper's room at the top of kitchen stairs, I used to join the servants in their daily amusement of watching the people who went to meet, and the people who came back from meeting the London trains. The last train puffed away in a coil of lights in sight of the drawing-room windows; it made for the West through the twilight and was the signal for bedtime. Until it flashed by, we were allowed to play with Grannie where she lay on a sofa,

[7]

her scented handkerchief in a bag of black ribbed silk, attached with black ribbon to her waist, the most alluring of all the delicate little odds and ends about her.

The house was certainly hideous, painted a congested brick-colour all over; but children do not see houses as things in which one lives enclosed, but rather as grown people see the world, a collection of openings and adventures, whose few familiar rooms are ringed with the unknown. The library, with its smell of books and tobacco, heads with antlers, family portraits, and the Murillo bought by my grandfather in Spain, was seldom visited: uncles sat there in leather arm-chairs talking to each other heavily. The drawing-room was opened only in the evening when people dressed for dinner, and our hair was brushed and tied with a new ribbon; someone gave a push, and in we went navigating between spindly legs of little tables and the stiff voluptuousness of female skirts, till we reached the sofa where Grannie reclined, in folds of black even more voluptuous but familiar, and with the firelight shining on china cabinets behind her. Those objects distracted from the boredom of saying good night so many times over, and it usually required a new propulsion to start one on the return journey, past other islands and pitfalls of taffeta flounces, to the red velvet curtain that hid the door and made all safe from dangers of publicity and circulating air. Such was the room in its hours of life, with the whist table ready in one corner, and the silver tea-tray beside it, and Kate Kegan the housekeeper ready to take a hand if the number of the ladies proved uneven. She too had surely become part of the furniture, though her frizz of rusty hair, her sharp elbows, her sharp nose, and features eaten by small discontents, seemed to lack the cordial polish of the other objects, which were dusted and petted every day with feather brooms and brushes by cheerful well-starched maids. But in the morning when no one was about, after a slide downstairs on mahogany banisters, I sometimes stole into the room in its private hours, and saw it fresh and airy; its innumerable knick-knacks, its miniatures and sketches, its water-colours full of good will, its cabinets of ebony and ivory or Buhl, its Dresden figures and Etruscan vases gathered in an age when honeymoons were combined with culture, all jostled each other in a life far more vivid, it seemed to me, than that of the old ladies at their whist.

Next to the drawing-room and the unknown, a china knob with flowers opened the dining-room door. This was our familiar world. Grannie's desk was in the window, with bundles of letters tied with pink tape beyond a boat-shaped inkstand of glass and silver; sealing wax and squeaking quill pens lay in the silver tray; and silver candlesticks with dunce-cap snuffers shone very bright. It was a corner we approached with caution; but the rest of the room was ours to play in, and all its details are clear up to the level of the table—the height of my head at that time. The chairs were red velvet, worn shabby in places and buttoned all over in lozenge-shaped fatnesses with buttons of the same; they were framed in solid ovals of polished wood crowned with carved rosebuds. An old Sicilian rug embroidered with bright wools and thrown over the sofa attracted me more; or the Sheffield biscuit box domed like a shallow temple on the sideboard, which produced sponge fingers when we had been buttoned into our overcoats, gaitered with small gaiters, and gloved with wool for our morning walk. The difficulty of not getting wool as well as sponge biscuit into one's mouth is still quite clear in my mind. The furniture was all shiny, and all the legs except those of the chairs were sheathed in brass and ran on wheels. There were books, out of reach: and a litter of *The Times, Country Life, Punch,* on chairs and floor. After meals, a maroon cloth with a fringe made up of solid little rolls like worms, was spread over the dining-table; Grannie then settled on the sofa with a rug over her knees, and we were allowed to sit with her—this was always a privilege and not taken as a matter of course as with the other grandmother —and we would watch blue-tits upside down at their swinging coconuts on the terrace outside. The English grandmother was the one for animals, which the German one treated with continental aloofness.

[9]

The lower garden spread there in sight, a small place with a level walk, a palm or two, a log summer-house pretentiously rustic, and beds of begonias above a sloping lawn. The upper garden was gravel with clumps of laurels. A wide low gate of fancy ironwork let the passing traffic of the station road show through. I once escaped from the nursemaid who was putting me to bed and danced behind this gate in happy nakedness under the gaslight of the street, with a still vivid feeling of emancipation.

Bedrooms opened on to a circus of a landing and all had flowered wall-papers. Their brass fenders were high and solid like parapets, their towel-racks loaded with towels, their beds piled with bolsters and pillows under curtains and canopies of chintz. The dressing-tables wore muslin flounces over a shiny white foundation. The beds had knobs of brass we could unscrew; we could sit for hours, silently unwinding knob after knob, working up to the crisis of destruction and collapse of the bed-head, while nurse—like governments and families and lovers in later life—went about in strange security, unwarned by the threat of silence.

There was a bathroom—a dull place I can scarcely recollect: but coughs or other ailments produced a round tin bath in front of the bedroom fire, and flickering flame-shadows on the ceiling whose memory still gives me happiness. The whole of life was one elaborate ritual of security carried out in the middle-class house as in a temple, where the inventions of the world and its ages were whittled down to routine pure and simple, devoid of dreams. At the centre of it all, in the inmost sanctum—a bedroom all white chintz with moss rosebuds, and high bay windows where the heavy lined curtains ran on rods of brass—my grandmother sat at her dressing-table, a fragile priestess, while Kate Kegan talked to her and a maid dressed her hair. This took a very long time, for it was like a tangle of fine silk, and bleached with age, not to silver but to straw-coloured gold; the maid piled it on her head with many little hairpins, and placed a small lace cap on the top—but not so as to hide it. And then my grandmother would be put into one of her silk dresses and descend, to write her letters or talk to my father—whom she loved best of her three sons—while the well-oiled wheels of the house revolved in their unchanging grooves, with no interest or interference of her own.

What she was in herself, beyond being this pivot of security in my childhood, I scarcely know. My grandfather was long since dead and even to my father was little but a memory of someone who took a small boy now and then to walk on the high moors. I have seen his picture. He had a sensitive free and receptive face, the face of a young man whom Socrates might have gathered round him among the less literary of his crowd, and he must have been one of the romantics of his day. His father, Robert, was of such independent mind as to make trouble in his diocese: he came to disbelieve in the apostolic succession, and laid various works and pamphlets at the feet of the irritated bishops of the west. A notice of the opening of the New Salem Chapel in 1839 announces that "R. Stark, of Torquay, will expound Galatians IV", and there is a letter extant which shows him likeable but stubborn.

His father, another Robert, wrote his will in the year 1764, and is referred to as "Robert Stalk otherwise Stark, yeoman, late of the parish of Cockington" (near Torquay). He leaves a fair substance, though his education did not include writing, for the will is signed with his mark only. After him, the family steps up among small squires and parsons who move without tremors among established things. Where the painter's streak came from which appeared so strongly in my father, and in my mother's father who was his uncle, is a mystery: there seems little soil for it in the solid prosaic background, and even less so in my grandmother's background, which was trade. My paternal grandfather was considered to have married beneath him, and when I was quite small, and taken to walk down the high street of Torquay, Kate Kegan would sometimes turn into a large shop full of white baths and enamels, in whose recesses an old jovial man with blue eyes who was my grandmother's brother, would make us welcome. After my grandfather's

[11]

death, I imagine that she saw more of her own people and less of his; yet there was a noticeable difference, so that even a child could feel that it was two worlds meeting and not mingling; and in her gentle reticent way she carried an air of authority, and was surrounded by a deference that came naturally, largely through the devotion of her three sons. The eldest of these, Arthur, was a doctor who was killed in Ladysmith and became a legend to our childhood; and the second, William Playters, was a rough man with a beard whom my mother disliked and we saw very little of. My father, Robert, was the youngest. He was born in 1853, and even in his schooldays showed his bent for painting and his love of country things; and whether this reminded my grandmother of her husband and the short happy days of their youth, their travels in Italy and drives over Dartmoor, whose memory still pervaded her house in little sketches and pictures and endless collected curios—or whether it was her own secret taste to which the Victorian life had never given passage—the fact remains that my father was indulged and educated in his own way. He studied sculpture instead of going to a university, and travelled to Italy as his uncle had done before him, and with the same result, for he met Flora, the eldest of his cousins, a girl of seventeen, in the Florentine villa, and married her.

Years afterwards he still came to the Torquay house as in his boyhood, and slept in his old turret room, up attic stairs. Nothing ever changed. Daily and punctually at tea-time, the yellow cat appeared and got its saucer of milk, and was succceeded by a younger yellow cat, and then a younger, in fullness of time. Among the crowded furniture, particular pieces were destined to a grandchild at its birth by name, and a label, written by my grandmother in blue ink, was pasted on the back: most of these objects have vanished now, but a black and white cabinet still remains to me, and stands like a little island of that lost solidity among the later chaos. The two grandmothers each bequeathed the permanence of their worlds; my mother's mother had not even a brooch or a trinket to leave us, but the ideas which gave their serenity to her old age have never lost their value, and she handed them to us in a familiar light: the Victorian house and the dividends it rested on have long since faded; they stand like a façade in the memory, and I wonder what living vitality it was that made them stand, and realize how brittle in reality are all the things whose permanence is never questioned, in a world whose flowing mortal nature is in itself synonymous with death.

When I was twelve years old, this grandmother died, and all the cocoon of furniture and ritual which swathed her showed for the lifeless thing it was and vanished. We were in Italy at that time, and the news came to the Tuscan sea-coast, and I took it with me and sat with it in the sun-warmed shadow of a wooden jetty, where carts drawn by many pairs of oxen brought the white blocks of marble from Carrara to load in tethered coasting vessels with furled yellow sails at the end of the pier. The sun lay like a cape of state, heavy and white, on everything around. The sea shone beneath it, a burning mirror with darkness in its depth. The sand was fragments, like everything in this world: bits of mother of pearl, shining mica, marble, white, green or black, could be recognized among the tiny particles that made it, and here and there a fluted shell lay dull and opaque, undigested by Time.

In the middle of this dazzling emptiness the fact of death first stood before me, the strange cessation of something that has been and is no more. "Never, never, never, never, never!" The house so intimately remembered, the rustling slow descent of the stairs every day in the middle of the morning; the face, like a pale Rembrandt above its ruff of black lace, with skin soft and loose; these things belonged to the only permanence we had ever known—and they had ended as a road might end with a wall built across it, and no clue to the further way. I sat a long time, I remember, not thinking, but contemplating the collapse; no one explained these things to us at that time; I sat till the thought of food made me run home—barefoot into the cool house with its tiled floors, where milk and dishes of grapes and figs buried in leaves awaited us at tea-time; and death was forgotten, though the first wrinkle on the face of the world remained.

NEEDWOOD PARSONAGE,
Nr. BURTON-ON-TRENT

8 *April*, 1845.

My dear Sir,

Your date inside is 5; outside, the dates are Liverpool 4, and Burton-on-Trent 7. To-day is the 8th on which I am answering your letter the instant after having read it. I have but a slender opinion of "quite a young man," altho' I recollect that Stillingfleet was *quite* so, when he wrote the *Origines Sacrae.* You think that "if 10 or 20 of the Clergy of the Estab' were to come out they would carry everything before them." No such thing, my dear Sir, on my conscience! Your matter must be carried out, if at all, not by numbers but by sound argument and the clearest statement, of which I should fancy you yourself more capable than half the young men in the United Kingdom, to say nothing of the Estab'; and yet you see you have not carried away even poor me, high as is the opinion I have most sincerely formed of you! We should never forget that we are uninspired men. I, for one, am more solicitous to recommend the Word of God than my own interpretation of that Word. But, let me not be deemed desirous of checking your ardor. The older I get, the less willing I am to become a ruler —or at least an overruler of minds; for I find that every year I become more conscious of my own liability to mistake. The best of us are as nothing compared with an inspired Apostle; and yet the giant of a man the American President Jefferson, deemed St. Paul what I will not write in words. I do not refer to Jefferson as an Example but as a Beacon. The ablest of uninspired men are poor creatures as Guides, but admirable creatures when led by the Word of God into the paths of Uprightness and Peace. Good Will towards men; Peace on Earth; what blessings!

[14]

You are downright kind in your wish to see me, and I would encourage you thereto by every means in my power, were I not confident you would be disappointed and greatly so. This is no high flight of humility, but thought and spoken in honest sincerity. I have been to no town in the vicinity of Railways above once or at most twice since Railways were adopted, and I am an entirely retired man of no note whatever, actually not worth your walking half a mile out of your road to see me, except that I am

Your cordial wellwisher,

H. PRICE.

2

Parents

I F we could make contours in hearts as we do in maps, to see
their loves, we should learn what strange unexpected regions
attain the deepest depth. Often we might discover that
a place rather than a person holds the secret. It was so with my
father. The wild country of Dartmoor, where he had walked
as a small boy, was to him a dark and refreshing well, from
which the water of his life was drawn. It gave him silent
serenity, and a sort of patient endurance, very like its own
high and gentle, cloud-receiving hills. It was a very remote
country in his boyhood, a long day's drive with pony carriage
or ride on horseback from Torquay; and even when he brought
my mother there as a seventeen-year-old bride, and in my own
childhood twenty years later, the train from Newton Abbot was
a shabby little country train waiting in a neglected siding like a
pony with a coat worn bare in patches, for the G.W.R. gave it
only old coaches whose velvet showed edges of wear. Metal foot-
warmers were laid down the middle of every compartment on
the floor, and my mother remembered an old farmer getting in
and squatting down on one of them on a winter's day, remarking:
"It's sartainly kind of the Company to think for'm comfort."

When the train reached Moretonhampstead, a pony carriage was waiting in the station yard; another footwarmer; feet
packed in straw; the rug tucked about one. The seven miles
drew out unending among hills with fields of turnips, grass or
clover, or ribbed loam, and in winter the shadows of hedges
wheeling across the snow. There was no asphalt, then, but the
road dried quickly, its puddles lined with pebbles whose glistening

granite edges never lose their sharpness; they shone with a clearness that I always associate with Dartmoor after rain. Ruts dipped in and out of them like ribbons, with a ruffle of curled mud at the edge: and when we had climbed to where Chagford spills itself on its hills, and had driven by whitewashed cottages under thatched roofs where only a notice in a window showed a shop inside; and had trotted down with the brake squeaking and the pony's neck well back and wrinkled under the tautened reins—then we began to ascend longer slopes and to dip less deeply, ever gaining on the brown fortress whose horizontal rocks lay wrapped in Atlantic mists or sleeping in the sun. Half-way up the last slope, where fields and cultivation end, rough walls of granite take the place of hedges, and a swing-gate eaten with lichen spans the roads to keep the cattle on their open moor. Here, even when it rains, the tilt of land is too sharp for mud, and runnels of clear water trickle through the turf. Trees lean away from the south-west wind, until only thorn and the mountain ash continue to hold fast where walls or boulders give shelter for their roots. The roads lead to some last lonely farm, or peter out into a deep-rutted soft track on the way towards it, while a great freedom of solitary breastlike ridges opens on every side. Here the farms and villages that had "moor rights" could put their ponies and flocks and the small tough cattle with blunt muzzles and flat foreheads, that flourish on moor weather, to wander at will. In the height of summer a rare cart would jolt across collecting the farmer's sods of peat, cut and stacked in small rows, two by two like tents, to dry in the precarious sun. A lark would hang over the silence, remembered as one remembers an aeroplane to-day, a filler of spaces; a lapwing fluttered from the wind-singing heather with pretended lameness to draw away the passing stranger from her nest; and rabbits made holes in dykes of short-bladed grass, boundaries of the moor.

My father knew this country and from boyhood went about it. He was a good rider and fond of breaking in his own horses; but he preferred to walk so as to watch the life about him more closely, and he knew plants and animals, and could find his way at night by the set of a star on a ridge where most people saw only the uniform pathless darkness of the moors.

He was well-knit, neither short nor tall, with a body whose muscles all were used and a face in which the grey eyes were remembered because they were so honest. He liked knee-breeches for walking. He had the slim beautiful ankles that many Englishmen have who live in the country, and wore easy shoes, and thick woollen stockings that Kate Kegan knitted in Torquay. Stepping behind him as we learned to do in our childhood across the boggy places, we saw his feet as easy on the moors as the heather they trod on, whose wiry tendons spring back and recover when they are pressed in passing; or as the pony that grazes at will and leaves the slant of its hoof in the peat to tell the direction in which it went. My father seemed always to make a harmony with these weather-beaten things. In his tweeds, shapeless and soaked with showers, he was at home; and my earliest English memories show him putting on an old Burberry to go for a walk for pleasure in the rain.

In the early time, before I was born, he had no house near Dartmoor, but used to stay at one or other of the farms where rooms were let to summer visitors. Their fenced gardens are crammed with flowers, and sedums blossom and mosses grow along the edges of their thatch. But it is safer to put all sheets out to dry before going to bed, for the whitewashed walls are usually wet if you press a hand against them; and though in the sitting-room some warmth can be coaxed round the fire when the wind is right and the chimney draws, in the kitchen the stone flags lead to a hearth wide and cold as a Druid altar, where peats smoulder as they stand on end, and hiss with raindrops in the chimney. You can make a chart of the winds and currents that eddy into unlikely corners and eventually wind into your spine. A wooden settle with high back and sides usually wards off the worst of the cold; and here my father would take his wet shoes off with a crowd of spaniels clustering about him, before he went into the tidy part of the house, where my mother was being acclimatized: for when he married her, he rented a

[18]

lodging in a Dartmoor farm called Berrydown, and brought her there from her Italian home.

At seventeen, my mother was tall, with red-gold curls and the dark inherited eyebrows; a gay, irregular and wilful mouth, and a mind and body both brilliant and alluring. I have met people who knew her at this time and spoke of her as a sort of Diana, a vision of radiance. Even the grocer at Chagford, many years afterwards, told me that "it was always a pleasure when your mother came to buy things, miss: she was a lady full of life: she made everything look bright when she came." The splendid presence, the buoyant confidence, were her charm.

Unlike my grandmother, she was never able to build herself an 'island of desire' away from the actual world, but lived without introspection, in every moment as it came. In the course of her long life I think she never realized what light and shadow of love come to most women in their youth. My father, eight years older, unobtrusively, inarticulately tender, was so deeply observant of her freedom and his own (he would not coerce even a plant or animal out of its natural path) that she took him for granted, and knew as little of him as she did of the sights and secrets of the country, which bored her to exasperation. I remember being surprised many years later to discover that she had no idea of the connection between a hazel tree and a catkin after living for years in a part of the country where hazels are the background of every copse.

The unexpectedness of life, waiting round every corner, catches even wise women unawares. To avoid corners altogether is, after all, to refuse to live. But most people learn by experience what may be coming; they keep themselves elastic, so as to swerve a little to left or right if an obstacle appears, and adapt their contours in some degree to the asperities of the surrounding world. My mother never thought of doing this. It was no strength in her, for she was uncertain of her direction and inclined to adopt the most promiscuous guidance as it came: but she could not realize that the object in the middle of her path was an obstacle, and would throw herself against it as I have seen horses (unreasonable animals) fling themselves against a van or doorway when blinded by some fright or fancy of their own. Just so, and with the same reaction of baffled injury, my mother flung herself against the adverse facts of life, and never I think, to the end of her days, understood how easy it would have been to circumvent them.

According to Dr. Johnson, it is "so far from natural to a man and woman to live in a state of marriage, that we find all the motives they have for remaining in that connection, and the restraints which civilized society imposes to prevent separation, are hardly sufficient to keep them together." The Victorians thought to manage it through a hierarchy of subjection, taking the Church as their analogy for wedlock—and a good many men still like to think of their wives as they do of their religion, neglected but always there. But the Church admits a short-cut to God for which the Victorian marriage provided no equivalent. A family hierarchy only works when unofficial relief is recognized and unofficial love, however tacitly, is allowed. To presume to carve up the human variety into parents and children, husbands and wives, and to cover these huge categories with a few general attributes to which every individual among them must conform; and then to make sin of all deviation —it is as if one parcelled the air and expected the plants to breathe in tight compartments, regardless of their roots. In such a dispensation, the feeble shrub may suffocate and die, but the tree will take its space and grow its height regardless, drawing its nourishment unseen as does the human soul; and only the most fearful unhappiness or perversion can come out of any *rigid* tampering with the particularism of nature.

My mother came to England singularly ill-equipped to deal with the Victorian order so uncompromisingly superimposed on the untidiness of God. Life in the Florence villa had practically not been domestic at all; and my grandmother's remoteness, buried in Gregorovius, and the unattractiveness of the German governess made any ordinary relationships of men and women more or less invisible there. She had seen no society except as a child before her father's death, and had never been to England; and now arrived like a young barbarian into the most stodgy, little-town, middle-class atmosphere that had ever been in the world.

Half the marriages that go wrong are destroyed by too much amiability at the outset; each human being has things that in the long run he cannot assimilate or forgo—and to try to do so only means a slow accumulation of disaster. It is far better to know the limits of one's resistance at once and put up as it were a little friendly fence around the private ground. Though un-Victorian, this would have been easy enough with my father, who was far too real and humble ever to wish to dominate another creature; but both were guileless and young, docile and honest, and the assumptions of their time destroyed them. My mother tried perseveringly to believe that marriage was for duty and not pleasure; my father demanded nothing, but took it all as a stability of nature rather than the false-solid façade of men, and continued to love in silence, never looking at another woman all the length of his life: and after many years, during which my sister and I grew up as it were in shadow, the human roots did their work underground, out of sight, out of consciousness even, and my mother's life shot out into its own sunlight, respectable but eccentric, and devastating to most of the lives around her.

This was all in the future, but the fact that I knew later times, and sadder memories, may have added a sober colour to my picture of the early years: to my mother's description for instance of the Dartmoor weather as it appeared to one accustomed to the delicate lights of the Tuscan hills. After three days of the unbroken south-west wind, when she had ridden or walked morning and afternoon, and had been soaked every time, and there were no more dry tweeds left in the house to wear, my father (who went out undeterred) came home to her in the middle of the fourth day to find the whole house shuttered up, the lamps and candles lit, and my mother savagely reading, trying to forget the existence of a climate.

The stolidity and dreariness of conversation chilled her in the same way. She told me how, at a first 'county' dinner party to which she was invited as a bride, she moved her hand suddenly—probably with one of those swift deplorably foreign gestures—and upset her wineglass. Of the eighteen people at the table no one spoke, while the little red stream spread and died among the begonias. In Italy they would have laughed.

It was a cold world, and a later generation would have eased it by allowing her to work or to travel: but such an idea never occurred to the solid middle class of the 1880's; and there was the further complication that she had no penny of her own. My father helped her to settle her parents' affairs in Florence with generosity so natural to him and so quiet that everyone else took it for granted as he did. He was partly supporting my Florence grandmother, as he continued to do for the rest of her life, and was paying for a younger sister's education at school. It never occurred to him that my mother would like pocket money of her own, and no one had suggested a settlement at the time of the wedding; the necessity of asking for every trifle entered with extraordinary bitterness into my mother's memory, so that her chief desire in later times was to earn enough to pay independently for herself. The fact that even a housekeeper is entitled to a livelihood never comforted her: she felt dependent and loathed it: and the intensity of this feeling was so borne in upon me that it has left me with a complex about money in family life, so that I would always keep it clear-cut, business-like and apart, to prevent it from intruding on feelings which it so easily destroys.

My father was very difficult over money. He would for instance gladly take us down the High Street of Torquay to buy boots which were good for bogs and kept the water out: a party frock when required was another matter and demanded weeks of diplomacy; and my mother's exasperation was not lessened when—in the very midst of remarks about extravagance —he would come home delighted with some new, small, and to her quite uninteresting daffodil or rhododendron, for which he had paid as much as would have kept her happy for a month.

She had, I think, a wrong idea, that came from the pride of her nature and a love of giving which was passionate. She was not feminine under this aspect, and lacked the wisdom of women, the receptive, listening wisdom, which is their part in nature and in birth. Not command and obedience, but giving and receiving makes the duet of male and female, and I believe there is something psychologically sound in the tribal habit of piling the family substance in bracelets and necklaces and anklets about the person of the woman in the home. The giving of gifts is a symbol of the profounder relationship; it is no empty prejudice that makes the gifts of a man to a woman more harmonious than those of a woman to a man. The Victorian reduction of all to a property basis has dimmed the fundamental relation; and even maternity, in which other generations saw the angelic messenger, the accepting virgin, is now contemplated, as is the whole life of women, in its most active light. The *dignity* of receiving, smirched and made sordid in the industrial age, has been forgotten.

To my mother it was radically antagonistic. It was an effort to her to accept anything even from those whom she cared for most. I think she was never sufficiently in love (even in the first few years) to fuse her universe and see the relations of things to each other in a light which transcends them: she was constantly being held up by their *separateness*, and her delight was to get everything into her own hands and give it away. Apart from base grabbing, love alone makes us happily receptive, and I suppose it was because she had never really been in harmony with my father that she found it difficult to understand the shy gentleness behind his gifts. Even a dog will bring some treasured useless object and lay it with endearing feelings at one's feet. Who would not be touched and softened? Yet I have read a description by Jane Carlyle, of a brown dressing-gown with spots, an obvious horror, bought for her birthday and received with not one scrap of tenderness, but coldly on its

[23]

defects alone. My mother was the opposite of heartless, but her feeling of dependence turned my father's presents almost into injuries. He would train the best horse for her with a care he did not lavish on his own. He would buy hunting crops, saddles and bridles, new palettes and brushes—all the things in his world he could think of as desirable. Later on, when my sister and I began to grow, these strange gifts so carefully thought out would come to us also at Christmases and birthdays, and I still handle some of them as if they had a bloom upon them, a never-fading freshness of affection. To my mother this double life of inanimate objects meant nothing. On one of her birthdays my father called me and put a white bicycle pump into my hand:

"Carry it to mamma on the sofa," he said. "Perhaps she will take it from you."

Yet there must have been many days when they were young and happy together on the moors, though only faint echoes come down from the thirteen years of marriage which passed before I was born. Long afterwards—turning things out of an old trunk in an attic, the sort of trunk that stood high, with a rounded lid strengthened with thick splints, shackled with locks, studded with nails, the indestructible Victorian trunk, too solid for what we now have left to put inside it—opening this trunk, I came upon my mother's riding habit, dark green with a long draped skirt, and many curving seams to model her fine young breasts, and collar and cuffs of velvet.

They moved to London after a time, and my father became a teacher in the Kensington School of Art, and was well thought of by the painters and sculptors of his day. In a tiny house in the Abbey Road in St. John's Wood they came to know them all. I have a picture of my mother, nineteen years old, sitting at the piano in the Alma-Tademas' house, at the corner of Grove End Road. The piano is built of carved light woods like pale gold, and famous composers who played upon it wrote their autographs inside the lid. My mother is sitting there with a little red cap on her short curls and a high lace collar like a ruff, and tight-fitting green velvet gown. She played beautifully. Her father had loved music passionately and made his little girls practise for five hours every day, creeping down the marble stairs of the cold villa before breakfast with chilblains on their hands. One day when my mother was doing exercises with her teacher, Liszt came into the room and watched her, and then sat at the piano himself, and played. She was soon asked out in London to perform for charities in drawing-rooms, and surprised people, in spite of being so young and unaccustomed to the world, by stopping even in the middle of a piece if there was talk or noise, and waiting for silence to be made. She never could bear to turn a great composer into a mere background for uninteresting remarks: and this uncompromising atmosphere about music, in which I was brought up, makes it difficult even now for me to sit with the wireless in a room where people are talking.

> "Does the fish soar to find the ocean,
>   The eagle plunge to find the air?"

My mother moved into social life as into a native element, and was extremely happy. She was invited into the St. John's Wood world which was that of artists prosperous and respectable enough for Victorian society, living in large or small houses walled in with gardens, with their year rising to a peak as the Royal Academy Private View and Soirée approached. There was a solidity about it, and the dinners they gave ran to fourteen courses, but it was lightness itself compared to the county shackles, and paradise compared to the bourgeoisie of Torquay. Among artists, every human being counts for him or herself regardless of birth or sex or wealth or age: to be once accustomed to this turns any other condition, however glittering, into a state of exile. My mother was a genuine person, and was at once accepted. She had learnt to make her own clothes (for she never would ask my father for anything even then); and she did exotic things with her appearance, such as winding swathes of peacock's feathers about her evening gown, which was remembered and told me thirty years afterwards, so that it must have been conspicuous at the time. But she could carry off this and a good deal more, for she had a royal generosity and radiance and the gift—the opposite of Midas'—of turning every dead object under her hand to life. She would not have made a *salonnière*, for like my grandmother she was strangely unperceptive of what happens in the minds of other people; but when she left London she was missed and remembered in a degree unusual in cities, for years and years.

My father too was liked in a quieter way by a smaller number, but he hated the pavements to walk on and the houses on either hand. He rarely spoke about these years, just as my mother hardly ever recalled the years on Dartmoor. One day, as he and I happened to be walking towards the Marble Arch, he remembered how he had once been in the same place with Gilbert, the sculptor of Eros in Piccadilly Circus, who suddenly stopped and knocked a man's hat off as they were passing by. They went on, leaving a certain commotion behind them, and my father asked what the man had done to deserve it.

"Deserve it?" said Gilbert. "It was his face that deserved it. One can't have a face like that."

If my father had been poor, he would have had to go on with his sculpture, and it and my mother between them would have brought him into the limelight of their circle. My mother would have been happy, and he would have lived in an unnoticed nostalgic atmosphere of his own until a time for peace came and he could retire into a garden. But he had means to live comfortably and, after a very few years—I never knew how many— had designed and built a house called Scorhill, on a steep high slope above the North Teign, where Dartmoor ends and woods begin. Here he came upon his real genius—the designing and laying out of gardens: he scooped his first little lake out of the hillside, and surrounded it and planted the whole slope with shrubs and rare trees, which have now grown into woods transforming that corner of the moors. In course of time, my parents lived in seven, and actually built four houses in this neighbourhood, and their woods and gardens still show my father's hand.

Scorhill and London must have gone on simultaneously, as the Dartmoor houses continued to do later, when the habit was acquired of spending half the year abroad. I never heard a single word from my mother about it, except that there were lots of dogs and that one day, after weeks of rain, as she had just begun to climb the steep ascent where the north Teign flows between two hillsides in a cleft—she saw a solid wall of water come down, carrying sticks and trees before it, and swirling almost up to where she stood.

In the year 1887 my father left the Kensington School and London, which he hated, and settled in Paris to paint seriously. They were both happy there. They worked in the Delacluse Studio, and lived among casual cheerful people of the left bank of the Seine, an international coterie, mostly poor, though sprinkled with a few well-to-do American or British amateurs— all living the same life of work, painters' gossip, and enjoyment of the unexpected. Artists are often criticized for being improvident, but it is difficult to be otherwise when one's income is by its very nature unpredictable, and perhaps their ability to enjoy the unforeseen is paid for by the fact that it is so often unpleasant. My parents used to go about among little inns where the insolvent painter could pay his bill with sketches; they learned the new and dashing sport of bicycling along the straight French forest roads (my mother a pioneer in bloomers, decent but emancipated for that time). They made friendships into which my sister and I later grew up and which lasted through their lives. And they both became very good painters. In the year 1891 a little boy was born who died in less than a year. And in 1893, on the 31st of January, in a studio of the Rue Denfert Rochereau, No. 37, in the middle of Bohemia, I was born quite unexpectedly at seven months, with not a garment ready to receive me.

My father went out with Herbert Young, a student friend, to buy some clothes, and they made their way to one of the big shops, and looked dubiously at what the young woman brought them.

"It is too big," they said.

She came again and still it was too big.

The third time she grew impatient. "How old is this child?" she snapped.

"Half an hour," said my father in a small voice.

The two poor males were provided for with all human sympathy, and my first difficulty with dress was surmounted.

LETTER TO FLORA STARK FROM AMY ATKINSON, AN ARTIST

VILLA ROMOLI,
FLORENCE,
6 Feb., 1893.

Dearest Flora,

"You know I ain't strong" and you really should not give me such shocks. I have been breathless with astonishment. Why did you not tell me? I had not the very smallest inkling of it. Still now I have adjusted my ideas I am very glad indeed. I congratulate you dear with all my heart. To have accomplished three Salons and all you wrote of—and this is indeed a feat to be proud of—and only you could have done it.

Freya Madeleine is a most advanced young person to have a card of her own at three days old—it is delightful to think that I have now really an interest in one who belongs to the 20th century. I want to know how you are and I want to know lots of things—which I suppose I shall have to want for. Who have you got to take care of you besides the German bonne of your own sex?

But what is the good of my asking questions which I shan't get answered? Though Mr. Stark if he is as charming as I think he is might send me a line.

You know, of course, that if I had known of this in the

autumn, I should have chosen Paris instead of Italy, on the chance that I might have been of some use to you—I wanted an excuse to choose you and Paris—instead of Italy and Trottie and that would have decided me. However I have no right to feel a grievance, so I will try not to.

It was good of you to write to me so soon before the event. I should have felt worried about you, if you hadn't described yourself as so well installed. I had old times vividly recalled to me on Sunday when I met Highjinks in the Uffizi. We embraced with fervour and he introduced a blue-eyed Mädchen from Berlin as his wife. He is stolider than ever and getting fat—looked terribly rangé and bourgeois—wished to be remembered to you.

Trottie and I have parted company for the present—not "incompatibility of tempers"—she had the signal bad taste to prefer good food to my company—so she has gone to the flesh pots in a city pension and I remain here and starve. It is so conveniently near my studio I can't be bothered to move. I expect to be here till the end of March anyway. I forget if I told you I had sold two pictures—one to a French artist at the N.E.A.C. and one (the old Lavoir) to a provincial gallery. I am glad the latter's travels are ended, poor thing. It must be quite worn out.

If you don't come to Italy I shall stay in Paris to see you on my way back. Do take care of yourself all that is reasonable.

I am so sorry Mrs. Stark has had a bad knee.

I hope you haven't made her too musical with all your concerted music. Keep the painter uppermost.

Your friend who thinks of you much,

A. B. A.

3

Beginning of Memory.   1893-1898

A VISITING card tied with white ribbon to that of my parents was sent around to announce my birth, and I was welcomed by the students of Delacluse and the left bank of the Seine.   Bachelors dropped in to advise on the rearing of children, on which I soon developed ideas of my own; my mother—late at her painting in school—would hear a voice from the far end of the street and find the young men from studios upstairs and downstairs grouped round the cradle, trying uselessly to distract my mind from its dinner.   They brought gifts, of which the strangest was a baby's 'biberon' for milk, a pretty earthenware object with a spout, that had belonged to Robespierre.

My parents were singularly mobile even for that age of easy frontiers.   Before I was a year old we spent ten days in the country near Paris, travelled to England (at four months), visited in Basingstoke and Torquay, and settled close to Dartmoor for the summer.   Scorhill had been sold, and we had a house called Yelfords, which I remember a few years later: at this time I naturally remembered nothing, but caused anxiety in the neighbourhood by being allowed to lie in my cradle out of doors.   At nine months I again travelled, visited in Paris, spent a first Christmas with the Genoa grandmother, and settled down for a year and a half of only minor movements (a certain immobility being induced by the birth of my sister Vera in May 1894) in the little town of Asolo near Venice.   My earliest and many later memories are collected in this small town, which my father knew before he married.

When he first came to the Florence villa, he was a young man doing the Grand Tour as his father and his uncle had done before him. He had already sailed to Spain in a coasting steamer, and had seen smugglers wind rolls of lace round their bodies before landing, to provide mantillas for the fashions of Seville. He had ridden from Gibraltar to Granada through the Andalusian spring, collecting botanical specimens with a brother, and watched a bull-fight in a town where the bull broke loose and charged maddened down the main street, which emptied in a trice. He studied in Rome and spent a winter there in 1876, when the cavalry of King Victor Emanuel bivouacked round camp-fires that flickered at night in the Colosseum. In the marshes of the Campagna, whose desolate stretches then strayed up to the city walls, he used to walk for days watching wild buffalo, and told me how the villagers would ride out and catch these creatures, and chivvy them into a compound and brand them with their marks; and how the animals would walk out quietly, not feeling the iron on their thick hide, until in a minute or so the heat penetrated and made them jump and bellow. In these wanderings my father picked up malaria, which never quite left him, though he learnt from an old Roman peasant to dose it at once with a whole flagon of red wine. And at his school he made a friend of Herbert Young, who as a student of art was more of a dilettante than he was. When the schools closed they travelled together to Venice, and, being caught there by the heat of summer were advised to visit Asolo by Robert Browning's son Pen.

The place has scarcely changed since they saw it, though motor cars have now taken some of its remoteness away. There was and is no railway nearer than Castelfranco or Bassano at ten miles' distance; thence you drove across the plain towards the hills in one of those loose-limbed fiacres with dusty hoods whose nodding backs can still be seen in quiet lanes about here. Many little towns are seated on blossoming slopes of the foot-hills, with a line of snow behind them and the wash of the plain in front; but there is a distinction about Asolo which dates back through centuries, ever since the last Queen of Cyprus received it from Venice in exchange for her island, and kept a gay and learned country court, and was painted by Titian and praised by Bembo, her cardinal, whose villa half fallen to decay is in the plain below, and whose invented verb, *asolare*, describes something that now scarcely exists—the purposeless, leisurely, agreeable passing of time.

There are two castles—Queen Cornaro's with a square tower at the head of a cobbled curve, and the medieval keep with pre-Roman foundations which encircles the top of the hill where the town-walls end. The roofs of the town are red, darkened and mottled by centuries of sunlight and rain, for this is the dampest and greenest corner of Italy. The piazza is shaded with chestnut trees and has steps, and a sloping road descending into it from an upper level; and the church—which possesses one Lorenzo Lotto picture—has a slim straight tower washed bright pink, in whose open top the bells can be seen ringing for even the most insignificant saint's day of the year.

Herbert Young decided to establish himself here, and within a week had bought from a local curé the house which is now my home: it had once been a gatehouse on the southern wall. Just across the way lived Mrs. Bronson, Robert Browning's American hostess, to whom he dedicated *Asolando*. Hers was a gatehouse too, and an arch across the road divided her from Herbert. My mother was once her guest on a carriage tour through Switzerland; and described the dreariness inherent in the coachman's back, always in the middle of the landscape. Before Mrs. Bronson came to die, she lay ill for a long while and my mother nursed her. She would ask for her pearls and lie caressing them wound about her wrist: and the sight of her transitory clinging, and the dead precious toys she cared for, cured my mother for ever of any great attachment she might have had to personal possessions.

Robert Browning's son Pen had various houses in Asolo, and came and went from his Rezzonico palace on the Grand Canal. He once lent this to my mother for the summer, together with his gondola and two gondoliers in white with crimson sashes, who stood on carpets whose fringes floated in the water on either side. He often stayed in Asolo and had made friends there. An old man now living told me how they went together one day to a fair, in a village, at the bottom of the hill, where a girl with three pythons was entertaining the country people, and Pen told the Italian that the possession of a python would make him the happiest of men. After a few days' bargaining, the snake was bought for three hundred lire. Pen Browning used to drape it round the two village girls he employed as models —the one for her face and the other for her figure; and he used sometimes to carry the snakes to and from England. On one occasion, when the case was opened by a suspicious French customs official, Pen and his cabby were left alone to nail it up again in a panic-stricken, deserted custom's hall.

Pen brought the Nerudas to Asolo: they were keen mountaineers. They became his enemies later, and stirred up a small city feud, until Mr. Neruda found his death suspended in a chimney of the Dolomites, while his wife sat the night through on a ledge unable to reach him, waiting for help. Mrs. Neruda is the first incarnation of wickedness in my mind, for I heard my mother telling a friend how she had seen her poking her hat-pin through my mother's bicycle tyre as it stood outside the post office (years after, when the Browning-Neruda feud was on). She also gave us a Christmas party when I was a year and eleven months old, and this is the first thing in the world I can remember—a shiny arm-surface on which I was carried (nurse's starched white overall); a dazzle of light; and annoyance with some object rattled in my face: the sensations were so vivid that I recognize them now, and would still react much in the same way I suppose, with a love for smooth surfaces and candles, and a resenting of intrusion.

I have been curious to note what other first things impressed themselves upon me. A little group comes in my third year, when we had once more been to England and back, with two bits of summer in the high Dolomites thrown in. My parents treated Europe with extreme nonchalance as a place to run about in. They took my sister and me home over the Dolomites when we were two and a half and one and a half years old. They had us carried over the Pelmo pass to Cortina in a basket by the guide. Nothing of this enchanting trip has consciously remained with me. It was said that I vanished when I could, wandering after flowers, and was lost at the end of a day in a high village, and found in the priest's house, sucking sweets; and lost again in the train across Austria, which had a corridor: up and down it my mother hunted, until she saw me through wreaths of smoke in a third-class carriage, sitting on the knees of a sailor.

All this, and the whole of the summer in England, went without leaving a recognizable mark: but the tall narrow *palazzo* in Asolo, where we lived at the top of the piazza, has produced several pictures, rather like Rembrandts, shadowy darkness with a bright central spot of light. One is a doll's house my father built out of boxes, swinging open with all its doors and windows and muslin curtains attached, and closing again on the dolls within, who seemed alive but less comprehensible than people and animals. They were not things to play with like a cat or dog, but malevolent: I disliked them, and poured tea into the mouth of one, with a secret pleasure over the ruin of its sawdust stuffing, not diminished by the fact that it was Vera's doll.

I remember the rough glossy feel of my father's head, as he carried me on his shoulder through the Saturday market (which still fills the town with creaking carts, and booths): where I saw, as from a height, two sheep tethered in a shady corner of the street.

I can feel myself pursued in a small garden, small even to me, with upright bricks outlining beds, and brick paths between them. This was an anxious tottering but not unpleasant feeling with an effort to keep steady at the corners, and a *bogus* excitement knowing that I was *certain to be caught or to fall*. Later, I have seen foxes sloping along, well ahead of the hunt, with an expression of prudent enjoyment, and have believed that they were feeling very much as I did.

[34]

I had at this time a tiny gold thimble that fitted my finger, and as I slipped it on and off some voice told me how it had come a long long way, so that I dimly connected distance with the shine of gold.

Then there is a shocking picture near the open raised hearth of a kitchen where servants (I suppose) sat at their meal on a bench. I know that I was no taller than their knees, which were covered with blue and black cotton and jutted out like promontories in a long row. Someone from among the arms and heads out of sight handed me a piece of food I took trustfully and bit into, and it was a slice of onion, very sharp. After the shock of the taste, a roar of laughter followed. It hit me, like a desolate wave, and I can still recognize this misery, the unexpected unkindness, opening a chasm where I had stood secure.

There is a roadside picture that still appeals to me. I must have asked to see it, for a carriage was stopped and my father lifted me out to look at a runnel of water that slipped away between two planks of wood—the feed no doubt of some small mill. The water scurried green-black with a bright ridge like a long wriggling animal with scales. My father tore up small pieces of paper for me to throw, and I watched them tossing gay and helpless into the unknown.

The last of these Asolo memories is more sophisticated and probably belongs to my fourth year. A circus was rigged up in a corner of the piazza under the chestnut trees: I was still small enough to find some difficulty in the steps that led down to it through the dark, and I remember pleasure at the sight of the tents and their ropes in the shadows. Under the light inside, a cord stretched from darkness to darkness, and a girl with a tasselled cap, or it may have been a boy, walked on it, parasol in hand. Pure devotion, a nirvana of admiration possessed me, a strange identification of myself with the object of worship. This often came, and with a sort of passion when stories began to be told. With real people it came much later and the next occasion I remember was in Paris when I was eight. Tired and dirty from some journey, we were being fed in a restaurant and a messenger boy in a green uniform, with two rows of gold buttons converging at an angle down his front and a round green cap clapped over one ear, sat at a table near by. I looked at him with admiration and wonder, a worship all humility, and surprise at the calm way in which a quite ordinary girl beside him seemed to take her privileges. I think there was no Freudian complexity in all this dedication; but a small stirring of that generosity which is the unity of love apart from sex or time, and is given to the world's excellence wherever it appears.

In all these memories, the thing itself has remained far less vivid than the feeling connected with it, which is as clear to me now as it was at the age of three—in fact more so because more intelligible: and I find that my memory still works in the same way, and evokes a scene or sight or conversation in the measure in which I felt it when it happened: so that when I think of writing, I rely on notes in part, but far more on having enjoyed and felt the things I write about, as completely as I could in their time.

Of the other senses, a long way behind this passion of feeling, sight comes first, and then touch and smell and hearing last. I imagine every human memory varies according to how these elements combine.

In June 1896, we moved to Genoa. A confused glitter of mosaic floors, consoles and chandeliers remains, and the snappiness of my grandmother's old servant who evidently disliked children. She looked after my grandmother with devotion, as people do with those who are too casual to attend to themselves. One wonders what unnecessary compulsion it is that makes us efficient? Perhaps artistry, or arrogance? The latter, I think, in the case of this treasure, who once did *too* well: for my grandmother dreamed three clear sets of numbers and wrote them down, and told the servant to register them in the state lottery which exists in Italy and is the only organization ever known anywhere to make a regular income out of dreams. The maid thought it a pity to waste her mistress's money, neglected the request, and was ill with remorse when all three numbers appeared and Granny lost a sum so large that it would have taken even her quite a number of weeks to spend it. The lottery is still popular, and there are books that interpret dreams and tell one the numbers to play: and I heard of another maid who *stole* her mistress's money for herself and won 31,000 lire. There was a law-suit as to whom this gain belonged to, and it was decided that the servant kept the profit of her theft, but went to prison for committing it.

In Genoa I remember little else, except the swirl of water in a river, its play of light round boulders, and the feeling of being alone: the first extraordinary sensation of being one thing when all the rest of the world is something else: a sad feeling which it takes us all the rest of our lives to dissipate. Adventure too I first remember in Genoa—creeping through a larder window for Parmesan cheese; the difficulty of the wriggle to get in, the joy of attaining, the whipping which followed and left me indifferent, puzzling over the omniscience of people who knew it was I without having seen me.

We were back at Yelfords this year and I was nearly four, and the joy of running away became conscious. I set out with a mackintosh over my arm, my toothbrush and one penny halfpenny in its pocket, walking down the road to Plymouth to get into a ship and go to sea. The early stages, and whatever tale led up to this exploit are lost: but the white road is there with a film of dust upon it, swinging downhill, and the open, high, cathedral feeling of the world as the latch clicks the home-field gate behind me. And then a rather small feeling as I walk down the road alone. At the bottom of the hill, Mark the postman appears coming towards me, and asks what I do so far from home? "Plymouth's a turrible long way," he remarks. He thinks a penny halfpenny will not take me so far. He is very sympathetic. He suggests we might go home and collect a little more cash and start again. And I remember a rather warm pleasantness in the holding of his comfortable hand, and a tiresome amount of surprise shown by a group on the lawn. Running away is the wrong word for such adventures, that go not to escape but to seek. The beckoning counts, and not the clicking latch behind you: and all through life the actual moment of emancipation still holds that delight, of the whole world coming to meet you like a wave.

I can remember no time, however early, in which I did not reason things out, with a certain detachment. Things were interesting to me in themselves. When my mother whipped me—on only one other occasion, after I tried to hit her with an umbrella—I went round among her friends and discussed the matter, leaning up to the drawing-room chairs and murmuring "My mama beats me" in an irritating way. I can see myself in an ecstatic hour tearing strips of dark red paper with flowers off a lodging-house dining-room wall. The tear began small and widened—an isosceles triangle with a curve—making a sort of white wave and a delightful noise: and I was put into a corner. There seemed no reason to stay: people are always remaining in unnecessary corners. My father had to bring up his sketching stool and sit holding me, and I comforted myself by the reflection that we were *both* in the corner together.

I had a surprising absence of pride, due always, I believe, and certainly now, to a genuine love of enquiry into things for their own sake. When I was being punished, I asked "Why?"

"Because you're naughty."

"I was: but I'm not any longer."

The punishment was remitted.

But my sister Vera, who was nearly always good, would 'bear it out even to the verge of doom' if she were punished, and once sat in her chair for twelve hours rather than admit defeat.

Our wandering life made us precocious and pretty tough. In a diary kept by my mother I find this description of myself at the age of five:

"Walked easily five and a half miles on a very hilly road and went for a second walk in the afternoon. Began to speak at 1 year and 3 months: at three spoke German and Italian: at five, German and English fluently. Recites in both languages well. Has an exceedingly good memory, a good sense of rhythm and rhyme and of the exact meaning of words. Is extremely observant and displays a good deal of tact, and great wish to please, also much self-control. Has become very neat and deft with her hands. To me her most noteworthy characteristic is her quick perception and grasp of any subject presented to her. Her desire for approval might interfere with her straightforwardness in time; at present she is quite truthful. Absolutely no ear for music, but decided one for poetry."

Making every allowance for maternal prejudice, I cannot help feeling that never again have I had quite such a creditable record as at the age of five.

We now stayed in yet another little house near Dartmoor, called the Log Hut, for it was built all of wood. Its kitchen was inhabited by old Jane, my father's nurse, and had a rocking-chair with patchwork cushion always warm either from her or the cat. A dog or two stretched by the fire. The walls were covered with postcards, pictures, Christmas cards sometimes three deep, from the wainscot to the ceiling; and old Jane moved about there fat and lame, with her apron tied askew round what might figuratively be called her waist, and never went further abroad than the kitchen porch. From her table, where there was a pastry board and rolling-pin I was not yet tall enough to see, I once reached down a knife, and ran my finger on its edge and cut myself, and remember that surprised little feeling of resentment against the impersonal unyieldingness of Things.

We came to this cottage only for short periods now and then, while some other house was building; and the winter of this fifth year was spent at St. Ives in Cornwall, where in an artists' colony and among the other odds and ends of their amusements, my parents played golf on the windy downs.

Here the seriousness of life began for us and a German governess arrived with lessons, and trees and flowers stitched in wools on cardboard, and those recitations which impressed my mother and which my father bore on his birthday with signs of embarrassment, while we apostrophized him with appropriate gestures and Fräulein stood by. I took it with a general zest, and my sister with groans and almost tears and the most torturing pauses. German virtues were laboriously sown. I spent an afternoon's play-time trying to put green cotton through a needle that refused to accept it: and can still see the thickened sucked end of that disgusting thread pushing itself finally in, sodden with tears.

The Fräulein was a caricature. Her mercilessly utilitarian features and tight straight hair did not prevent a perverted romantic heart and a passion for my mother which everyone found trying. My mother was casual with all adorers, and Fräulein frequently dissolved in neglected tears, or turned her glass upside down at table if the decanter had not reached her with proper alacrity; and she hated my father who took us away and forgot to bring us back in time for lessons, and made intentional German hash of the little poems we were taught to esteem. Us however she tamed, and we loved her; and were taught to sing *lieder* sitting on the floor round the fire; and had chocolates popped into our mouths with good night on the days we deserved them, which happened so often to Vera and so seldom to me that I eliminated chocolate from my dreams. Vera and I slept side by side in a big bed, and played a game we more than half believed in, which filled the darkness outside with danger if so much as a toe or hand stretched out and touched the ground. Long afterwards, in the desert, I have known the same feeling for the movement of shadows about me, though it had become awe rather than fear; and the childish sense of a human safety attached to my bed and circumscribed by it, remained.

Vera appears at St. Ives for the first time, intimate as a part of myself, with no single memory beforehand to prepare for her: our past is like a dark sky crowded with invisible stars which a stronger telescope might reveal in their forgotten places. Vera is suddenly always with me, chubby and serious, placid and independent, with brown eyes and pink cheeks. She was such a pretty child that an old Jewish couple asked to buy her, seeing her in some railway carriage, placed on the luggage rack to be out of the way when we travelled, absorbed in threading beads. She was rarely spurred to action, but never moved from her own secret freedoms, and this character—like all characters—lasted through her short life.

She was undemonstrative, quiet, sturdy and uncomplaining, with never a scrap of jealousy nor envy, and so loyal that loyalty ceased to be a quality with her, it was the very stuff she was made of. I had many loves; but she cared more for me than she cared for anyone in her life except her children; and died at twenty-six, though I think of her as a part of me still.

The tides roll in at St. Ives to a coast of smooth black rocks. They scoop out holes with black rims, green like the eyes of cats. There we played and patted castles on the sand. The horizon is very small to children and I remember no distances beyond the seaweed, swelling and ebbing in its pools—and bits of cliff grown with flowers—and sea-roughened, wave-bitten edges of small coves. Into these the tide washes and catches the unwary, pinning them with no outlet against the sheer cliff walls. We were so caught once, and knew nothing about it except that our playtime was extended, while Fräulein no doubt had some anxious thoughts of her own. We climbed from one rock to the other, three times, till the cliff rose sheer, and still the little waves came lapping to the edge. They hurried, harmless to look at, with a sucking noise. Then they began to retreat, and Fräulein took us home, commendably restrained.

The only other adventure in St. Ives was a surprise visit to the parents at Land's End where the golf club stood. It was a long walk, and it was my expedition, and Fräulein and Vera were a rebellious crew, stationary at intervals and Vera in tears. There were telegraph poles along an endless road with grey dusty ditches: and I suppose we went on because we had come too far to turn. But I remember the going on as an effort of my own, quite separate from the two jaded ones behind me. A year before, and the postman's hand had been held out too easily on the road: but this time we made our target, and were treated to a small triumph and a sumptuous tea at the clubhouse, and a charming man turned our thoughts from the pain in our legs by telling how Manx kittens are just ordinary kittens produced by having their tails threaded through a keyhole and pulled.

ECCLESTON,
TORQUAY
12 *Feb.,* 1898.

Dear Freya,

I have been wondering whether you have been over to Lelant again, to look for those shells. I am afraid not, for it has not been very nice weather. When you go, you must go there at ebb tide, and further on than we went, right beyond those rocks where we had lunch, then you will find those shells lying just about where the flood tide reaches on the sand.

Do you know I have been to London since I left you. I came in the train, the first day, as far as this house. Then I left again the next morning and went to Uncle Playters at Basingstoke and then from there to London.

One morning when I was there I went with Queenie to a place where a man named Jim keeps all sorts of animals for sale. I went to see if I could find a nice little one for you. He had all sorts in his house, but none I liked for you. There were two tiger kittens, who were so nice and tame, just as tame as Pips, and came up to the front of their box to be stroked and petted, but even when they are babies they are so big that I expect if you had one and took it out for a walk with you in St. Ives everybody would run right out of the town, and I don't know but that Fräulein would say she would rather stay at home. Then there was a baby lion, such a beauty, and a big panther who was very savage, so that no one dared go near his cage, and then there were monkeys and deer and little cows, much smaller than Flossie, and all sorts of birds. Some day you will have to go down there with me. Then one day I asked Queenie if she would like to go to the Zoological Gardens, and she said "Yes" so we took the omnibus and drove there.

The first place we went to was the house where they keep all the snakes, and there in one cage, all covered round with glass, so that it cannot hurt anyone, was a big cobra. He had just slipped off his old skin and had a new one on, so that he was looking so clean and his keeper was clearing out his cage, so he was rather angry and stood with hood spread out and head in the air as if he would bite him, but he never tried to. Then we went to the house where all the Lions and Tigers are, and then to the deer houses, and next door was a house where they had storks and cranes, all birds with very long legs, so they can stand in the water without getting wet. The sort of legs you ought to have at St. Ives.

There were five storks in one place all pretending to talk to each other at once, like visitors do when they come to tea: they all stood in a circle facing each other, and one would begin clapping his two bills together (that's the way they talk) and then all the others would do the same and so loudly that one could hardly hear anything else when they began talking, they throw their bills upwards and one twisted his head right over his back when he was saying anything and then they always like to stand on one leg. They think it so nice, I suppose. Then there was such a nice baby Elephant which I should so much like to have. Poor little fellow, he was so lonely having no one to play with him, and so he was trying to amuse himself by standing on the edge of his wash-basin trying to balance himself there. And after that we went to see a monkey who was so clever he could do all sorts of tricks, hanging on a rope, turn somersaults, stand on his head, and plenty of other things. I played with him a little while, he would pick up a straw from his house and give to me and then I would push it through the keyhole and we both pulled then as hard as we could to see who would get hold of it.

You must let me know what you are doing sometimes.

Yours,

PAPA

4

Roots in England. 1893-1903

My parents were moderately well off people of good taste, with a liking for the arrangement of houses, and yet it is astonishing how much of our childhood was spent in dingy lodgings, of the sort where the front door opens on to an umbrella stand that hits you in the face, and the vista of the staircase leads only to the w.c. Our own new, beautiful home was like Alice's jam, always yesterday or to-morrow, and we had to be near at hand, searching through the neighbourhood or attending to the building, while it became habitable.

My father now designed a house in Surrey, at Upper Hale near Farnham, which was as near to London as he would go. Here, when I was six, we settled, after months in a drab little Farnham villa where I learnt to read on my own account by picking up the letters off the hoardings. At Upper Hale we lived until the call of Dartmoor again became too strong, and a second house was built near Chagford: after which, in a very short time, we left them both and returned to Italy. This kaleidoscope, produced I think by my father's and mother's conflicting backgrounds, has no doubt made the idea of travel easy; but it also engendered in the children a passionate love for a stable home *somewhere*; and the fact that, since then, for the last twenty-one years we have not moved our *centre*, whatever might be happening to the circumference, has been entirely my own accomplishment, for even in her seventies my mother was disposed for a radical change at intervals of every few years.

Asolo lay anchored at my heart through all eastern wanderings; and when the war rolled it up in the darkness of its continent, and I could not feel it mine, I realized how spiritual is the life of the home inside one. The loss of it was a constant sorrow to me, though I had not been in it for more than a few months at a time for twelve years. My father too had the same rather abstract love of stability, which is natural to a gardener who watches growing things: but so long as he was allowed to have more plants than people round him, he little minded where it might be; the actual business of moving the human body from one place to another never struck either of my parents as a thing to make a fuss about; and a postcard would often arrive when we thought my father was in another country, asking to have his bed made ready for him next day.

In our two English homes I spent three practically stationary years between the ages of five and eight, and the Chagford one in particular has left a permanent love behind it, so that I never move into Devonshire lanes or towards the Dartmoor tors without the knowledge that my roots are there.

Upper Hale came first in time, and there was a sort of enchantment in its garden. In the house our bedroom had blue tits on branches of peach blossom displayed on papered walls, and a nursery below with window low enough to be easily escaladed. The drawing-room we knew, for we were made to dust it every morning, and that was always something of a voyage, among books, Chinese figures, paper-knives and boxes and brocades, with long pauses at pictures, whose subdued life seems to become animated when you look right into it. It was a good way perhaps to acquire the happy, neglected habit of looking at beautiful things.

I would creep into this room when my mother was at the piano. Though I never cared for music for its own sake as a real musician would, it yet led into an otherwise unattainable world, and made me feel, while I listened, different from myself. At the end, my mother would play Schubert's *Erl-König* for me, the thing I loved best. I then did more than listen: I *was* the rider, and the child, and the white wraith of the river king, and the horse galloping: I was annihilated in them; and this capacity of complete diffusion in delight has never left me, and is the reason I suppose, why I continue to feel young. My love for music, too, is still of the same sort, and it is only Bach who ravishes for his own sake and not for mine, like a lark in the sky. On the whole, I am more purely delighted by the sounds of nature, wind, water, and tiny rustlings, and waves and birds—than by the notes of art.

My mother at this time was wonderfully beautiful. She would come to kiss us in our beds, or tell a story before she went down to her guests, and we waited for her as if she were an angel, with her white shoulders and necklace of amber, and gown of grey satin covered with pink flowers, decorated with black velvet bows. Her word ruled absolute. Yet she remained very distant and there was a change in the atmosphere, a sort of temple feeling, when we passed through the green baize door into her realms, from the scrubbed bright kitchen and happy servants' quarters where the staff bore my new enthusiasm for reading aloud with patience, and listened to the Seven Champions of Christendom from a series of little pink paper-covered books. In the drawing-room all sorts of books lay scattered, and in a pause of the dusting I came upon a poem by Mrs. Browning far beyond my grasp. It was about a young knight, stretched on a tombstone in his picture, and, according to Mrs. Browning, 'pure as woman'. This questionable statement seemed to me obscure even then. I asked my mother what 'pure as woman' meant. "It means never smoking a cigarette," said she in her resourceful way (for women were not to smoke in public for years to come). I went off about my business. But some days later on my way back to the nursery, I stopped and lifted myself by my fingers on to the ledge of the dining-room window, as we did now and then, to see what the grown-ups were doing inside. There they were, with luncheon just finished, and quite a crowd of people : and someone was bending towards my mother to light her cigarette. Her purity, as far as I was concerned, was done for ; I felt it bitterly, and hid myself under an apple tree, and cried.

We lived in the garden, in that world which vanishes—
though I can still think of it as the real world now and then—
where there is no barrier between human and non-human existence, and even the inanimate object has its independent life, a
target for passions. My father taught us chess, and being
annoyed with the Red Queen I buried her under a holly bush.
The garden was our universe. It stretched downhill in a solitude
peopled with birds, frogs and tadpoles, and hedgehogs in the
twilight, which we carried home in a ball and waited to feed
with milk when they unrolled. The place had once been an
orchard and was filled with fruit trees of every sort; and its
gentle life busy with tiny incidents in the sun and dew—its
loneliness—with only an old gardener, usually out of sight, and
my father among the daffodils—and the careless abundance—
circles of fruit on the ground beneath their boughs—gave it an
atmosphere which I have never met again except in the descriptions of Eden in *Paradise Lost*.

We, too, had things forbidden: we each had our own cherry
tree, and once raced each other through a long summer's day
to see who could eat most (and I won, with 1100, honestly
counted, and no evil results as far as I remember); we could take
what we found on the ground, but to pick from other trees was
not allowed. More ingenious than Eve, Vera circumvented this
rule by shaking the chosen apples till they fell.

The garden gave that delight of something going on all the
time, which the world gives later to happy people. It *was* the
world, with a vagueness of chaos and the unknown beyond its
neat wooden palisades. Once only the wandering will o' the
wisp led me out, to look for Hans Andersen's Sea Witch—for
I had achieved the reading of his stories, and the Little Mermaid
was one of those many, and a peculiarly difficult one, whom I
longed with passionate admiration to imitate. I thought I might
follow the railway tracks from Farnham station, and enquire for the
Sea Witch when I reached the coast; and set out with sandwiches
in a box and a cousin whom I inveigled to come with me across
the Bishop of Winchester's park into the open world. We

stopped to say good-bye to the cousin's family in Farnham, and this was disastrous, for an angry aunt who disliked walking brought us back across the park in darkness and rain, with lightnings, like swords, shepherding us in the wrong direction back into Eden. This escapade left a certain bitterness too, for Fräulein had been honestly told beforehand, and, having probably paid no attention, denied all knowledge; her treachery humiliated me as if it had been my own. Our parents believed our word implicitly, nor did we ever deceive them, and it was a surprise and resentment not to be believed.

Joan of Arc superseded the Little Mermaid, and ruled so strongly that I asked to be given her name for the day if I had fallen and hurt myself and had not cried. And after that King Arthur reigned, and dragons inhabited the common land towards Aldershot, beyond our palisades. My father, never rude to one's dreams, would take me out to hunt for them in the dusk. They might look like railway trains, streaking with swift bodies of lighted carriages and smoke, but I remember *making* myself think that they were dragons, and dragons to all intents they were.

My mother kept us carefully away from anything that might contaminate—servants, nursemaids or other children: but my father believed in a barbarian foundation for the growth of human beings, and told us long stories of trackless forests and Siberian wolves. He took us sometimes to sleep out, on mattresses under the trees. The house was quite close; one had to turn on to the other side and think it away, and lie awake like cats with shining eyes in the dark, and listen to the night with all its noises. When our cousins came to live near by, and we met our own age for the first time, and began to build the Argo in our pine wood, I became a most insufferable bully and—as the idea was mine and I was captain—made them all walk behind me wherever we went. They made themselves into a little deputation to complain; and my father suggested they might mutiny and depose me, and fight it out as they were bigger, and four to one. They never did; but he found other ways to encourage toughness, and bribed us with double pocket money (twopence a week instead of a penny) if we walked across the pine wood to the far fence and back in the dusk alone. The wood was full of brambly hollows into which the evening slid. At the fence, before turning, I looked out into the bishop's park, and saw the deer grazing in open security and peace in the last yellow rays of the sun, and pulled myself together to return through the gathering darkness of the pines. The shadows seemed to settle between my shoulders. I dared not look round, or even walk quickly, for panic was ready there to pounce. I went very carefully and stiffly, till safety and the little gate in the fence were close in sight, and then I ran with all the Eumenides behind me, and clicked the latch upon the outer world of Fear.

Vera hated romance, of which she must have had to bear a very large dose. She watched with a stubborn expression of contempt at bedtime when I kissed King Arthur's portrait—painted with the dragon on his helmet by one of my many grown-up friends. When I called my cat Lancelot Vera insisted on calling hers Mrs. Belly. She was fond of few people, and when the cousins came and we neglected her, and she was the smallest, and we were unkind—she said nothing and wandered away and played by herself, in a world of which no one was ever told. I think of this sadly, as of one of the many little wrecks one leaves—and always for those one loves best. But when my father was by, in the world shared with all the animals in the garden, we came together. He would take us by the hand, quietly, to see the moorhen sail out from among the rushes in the evening with her brood. The bishop's fallow deer became familiar, who browse so tamely and yet never allow you to approach quite close, and we recognized the soft clashing noise of their antlers in autumn, when they fight for the does. He would visit the keepers, and place a baby bundle of long legs and frightened eyes and ears smooth as lily petals in our arms. Once or twice he took us to London to watch him modelling the rhinoceros at the zoo. He cast it in bronze and sold it to the Tate Gallery, where it stands to-day. He knew most of the zoo keepers, who would bring us sleepy pythons and baby lions to fondle; and he would tell us stories about the other creatures in their cages. He collected strange small beasts, and, when he went to America, disgraced himself with my aunt's New England family by forgetting a menagerie of little reptiles in a drawer in his bedroom. On a bicycling tour through Holland with my mother and Constance Fletcher, who wrote plays under the name of George Fleming, he put a whole village to flight on a Sunday morning because frogs jumped at intervals out of his pocket, as he wheeled sedately along. He was particularly fond of toads and salamanders, and showed us how beautiful and harmless they really are: we used to find them for him later and bring them back from the continent in biscuit boxes with holes punched in the lid, and had some little trouble with the customs. Along the smooth Surrey and Hampshire roads he took us for many drives, on a cushion made out of his Burberry and strapped to the bicycle bar in front of him: we would come back quite late when the light of our lamp made patterns on the dust, and the pubs by the wayside sent a cheerful red glow into the landscape through the curtains of the bar. I have always kept a friendly feeling for public houses from those nightly drives, though we never went inside.

The tidiness of Surrey soon became too much for him, and our last Dartmoor home was built. The loveliest of his gardens was created, in and out of an oak wood scooped in a curving hill. It was below the edge of the moor and out of reach of the south-west wind, that howled and tossed above but stirred no leaf around us. The wood was so sheltered that bamboos would grow. There were glades of azaleas, and rhododendrons now thick-trunked like trees, and daffodils beside wild bluebells, in dappled clearings. The house was stone-built with window-frames of the rough white and black spotted granite of the moor, and I still love to think of its pleasant mixture of horses and stables and tweed coats hanging near the hall, and dogs in the long low drawing-room filled with Italian and Dutch coppers and brass and pewter, pictures, and beautiful furniture, and casually thrown pieces of brocade. Sometimes later, in far more luxurious houses starched with upholstery and thick with photographs of ugly important people, I have thought of the beauty that grew like a flower under my mother's hand: what lies behind it, and from how many countries and centuries it comes, built like a coral island of the generations in the mind that at last gathers it together. This room was wainscotted, dark green, with a jutting corner that was all window, and books at the other end round a fireplace where a fire was usually burning. Its ashes were allowed to pile up and a small tree-trunk was pushed in to sizzle with sap day by day. A long room above belonged to my sister and me. Walter Crane's fairy tales ran round it in a frieze, and the toy cupboards and bedsteads were decorated by my mother. On each of them she painted what we wished for. I asked for sailing ships, so that I might look at them from my pillow and think of myself sailing far away; and I spent many early mornings before Fräulein called us, looking at the little white triangles doubling a cape round which I could not see.

From the bay of this room, with a covered balcony running round it, we looked over the granite boulders of a rockery and open lawn, across the pond or small lake my father had dug out and planted with lilies and miniature islands, across the crisp woods and the drive curving through fields, to where Meldon Hill, cone-shaped like a volcano, dreams in moonlight on summer nights. We could catch the last rise and dip of the road as it went to Chagford; and there Fräulein in carriage filled with trunks was seen departing, some time during my eighth year. She told us to cry till we could see her no longer, and the methodical German training held, for we did so, with howls that echoed and re-echoed, until the little black speck disappeared.

She was the only person I have ever obeyed from obedience and not from affection, but she had not troubled us much lately. We had the run of the woods and were let loose there, to climb every mossy tree we liked, and to live the Mowgli stories, until someone called to fetch us in to meals. I learnt the pleasure of moving among boughs, high above the ground through canopies of leaves; and only once came down, years later, with the broken branch beneath holding me, so that it was a gentle voluntary motion, like flying, pleasant to recall.

. At four years old we had been put on to Flossie, the pony. She was black with a long mane and tail, and lived till she was thirty-seven, having carried my father as a boy. We were now made to ride her bareback up and down the drive, with Tom the groom trotting beside us; and were soon taken out to the Mid-Devon meets when they happened to be near at hand. I remember them vaguely, with a mixed feeling, of anxiety about my relations with the pony, pride in my bright red woollen coat, and reliance on my father sitting there on his big stallion so straight and quiet like a tower. He used to breed and break in his own horses, and now and then would be lying for a day or two on the sofa by the fire, when they had thrown him. Sometimes he would take us out for picnics on the moor, jolting in a cart that met the heather as a clumsy creaking fishing-boat meets the waves, and would fry a pancake mixture from a jar over a fire of heather stalks which he built up with great delicacy and skill. We carried a little bottle of ammonia with us in case an adder bit our bare feet. The dogs' noses would get bitten and they would be doctored with brandy and nearly die, until they were bitten a third or fourth time and became immune. There is still a bend of the Dart which I think of as Pancake Corner; and a hilly summit covered with whortleberries where we listened to artillery at their targets on the moors. The heavy explosions sank and were bedded in thick summer air, and even then seemed threatening, though not as later, when American guns practised in the same places, training for France.

Sometimes we would drive out to watch the cutting of our peat. Neat squares were sliced with the sharp edge of the spade and leaned one against the other for the drying air to wander through them; for we had all moor rights by virtue of the 'newtakes', or half-wild grazing lands enclosed in rough walls of boulders, which have only recently been appropriated from the open moor, and now make a sort of border fringe to the properties about here. They carry with them the right of grazing, peat-cutting, and shooting, and indeed everything but 'vert and venison'; and as vert is the green oak, and venison the Exmoor stag, and neither of these exist on Dartmoor, there was no limitation at all to our rights until the Duchy of Cornwall to whom the moor belongs began to lay down grouse on the land and fish in the water, and tacitly obliterated the Norman code which favoured us.

Older than the Norman and his hunting laws, and far nearer to us at this time, were the hut circles and stone avenues of the people who brought their summer-grazing flocks up here before the Romans came. Some were on our property and many were scattered on the moors around. Even now, in the dusk, I prefer to ride round and not through them, from a feeling not of fear but of some privacy into which I seem to be breaking. Only rough boulders are left, often grouped in compartments in a circular form, gay with frilly lichen and half sunk in the sweet spongy turf. Thorn trees find a crack of shelter here and there between them and bend, knotted, over their ragged symmetry like the witches in Macbeth over the cauldron, and catch lost wisps of mist that drift about the moors. The circle huts were never roofed, my father thought, but covered over with thatches of heather or hides; nor did he think there was ever much forest here in historic times, though it is still called the Forest of Dartmoor. The circles and the piled rocks of Middle Tor and Kestor were our favourite playgrounds, because they were nearby. The granite, oldest of rocks, rounded by weather, wrinkled and rough to the hand as some old grandfather's cheek, has written itself into me so that it seems a part of my being, a thing like our bones that we carry till we die; and I can think of nothing purer and cleaner than the wind-whipped pools made by the whirling pebbles on the summit, where the rain-water keeps the rock creamy white amid the surrounding weather-darkened grey.

In this outdoor life of ours, my mother seems to have had

no share. She scarcely ever rode, and turned away from the moors, and drove us in pony-carts, tidily dressed, with brushed hair decorated with big bows, towards the amenities of Chagford. We hated this. A children's party at the vicarage, and return invitations through which we were made to be polite, were actively tiresome; and I have a vague but depressing memory of social picnics on the bank of a stream, under umbrellas, with knots of grown-ups and a dull little froth of children, and *foot-men* handing round sandwiches in the rain.

My father never had any abstract love of work for its own sake: he was drifting away from his art and settling down contentedly as a country gentleman; and my mother, who had a superabundant vitality, could not bear such a change for very long. My father now slept downstairs, in a small room filled with a chaos of seeds, and paints and papers; and sadness crept into the atmosphere indoors. From the woods outside, it was like entering a darkened room. I once came in suddenly and saw my mother sewing with a sort of rage over some dull domestic task; and she leaped up to escape, frightening me with a face like thunder.

By the summer of my eighth year a little Italian governess arrived, a timid, gentle *contessina* from an impoverished noble family of Vicenza: and in the autumn we were passing through London, lifted into horse-buses which you entered by steps at the back; lowered through subterranean shafts of the sooty old underground: until we crossed the Channel, and Paris, and woke with the St. Gothard snows about us; and reached Asolo again.

CHAGFORD,
DEVON,
15 *Feb.*, 1898.

Dear Freya,

I have come back again to Chagford, you see.

I left Grosmother's last Sunday evening and took the train to Moreton, but being Sunday there was no bus to Chagford, so I had to walk all the way in the dark and it was so muddy and slippery and as I could not see where I was going I must have stept into lots of puddles I know on the way. It was so late when I got to the Log Hut that Jane had gone to bed and the dogs who were asleep in the kitchen all woke up when I tapped at the door and made such a noise barking that Jane soon woke up again and got up and gave me some supper for I was very hungry after walking so far.

On Monday morning the foxhounds met at Leigh Bridge and I went out riding with them on Tim. He was so glad to see them once more as he had not been out with them for ever so long. He jumped about and did not know which legs to stand on, he was so excited (that's a way ponies have). Well we went all round by Frenchbeer and back by Kestor Rock but could not find any fox, but presently I said to the huntsman: "you try over in that long grass at Scorhill close by the river. I know Mr. Fox likes to stay there because I have often met him there and it is nice and warm and quiet there and he often goes there and has a sleep after dinner." So the huntsman called his hounds and they swam across the river and presently out jumped Mr. Fox under a bunch of grass, and he ran up across the hill and close by the Dartmoor gate where you and Vera used to go for a walk and if you had been there you would have seen h m pass. Then he went up over the Moor as if he wanted to go to Kestor Rock, but presently I suppose he got tired of running up hill so he turned and ran across the fields to Yelfords, and all this time the hounds were galloping after him and the people on horseback were galloping too as hard as they could and from Yelfords he went to Yeo and from Yeo to Miss Ormerod's, and then to Leigh Bridge and Gidleigh Park where he went into a hole in some rocks, which he knew of, so that the hounds could not catch him. And by that time the hounds were tired, and the horses were too and poor Tim, he no longer wanted to stand only on his hind legs to see how tall he could make himself but was glad to stand still on all four legs and see how fast he could breathe.

I hope the little sleep mice came safely to you the other day, did they and do you and Vera like them?

PAPA

5

A Background of Europe. 1901-1903

WE spent the winter in Asolo at La Mura, where Mrs.
Bronson, now dead, had left an atmosphere of cultured bric-a-brac behind her. A very delicate woman
called Mrs. Riley came to stay. She was always lying about on
sofas in lacey tea-gowns, and her husband adored her. I rather
think many husbands *prefer* wives whom they can leave safely
on a sofa, like the woman in *Diana of the Crossways*. Mrs.
Riley (for whom other women I now realize had very little use)
ruled everyone in a languorous way and then fell very ill indeed:
she liked being nursed by my mother, who dropped us into the
nearest lap, which happened to be that of Herbert Young next
door, while she devoted herself to the invalid. This habit of
flinging her family away at the call of the stranger caused nearly
all the sorrows of our later girlhood, but at this time we felt
merely the delight of staying in a new house where we were
spoilt. Mrs. Riley I remember no further except for one piece
of advice; she told me to "enjoy little things, for they are the
secret of happiness". I think she was right; but I have wondered
later whether her husband's devotion came under this heading.
Perhaps the people who enjoy the little things usually have one
or two big ones as a foundation.

Contessina now ruled our life, if such a verb can be applied
to anything so mild. "I shall have to punish you to-morrow,"
was her utmost severity; for she longed for affection, and we
gave it as one gives to a slave. She lived in a meek, unobtrusive,
unmistakable atmosphere of gentility and decay—the genuine
thing with no affectation about it. With her the neat blouses

[57]

and small belted waist, the straw boater tilted down at an angle with a veil and the scattering hairpins of that period, all took on an intense though humble femininity. Her grandfather, a nobleman of Vicenza, had ruined the family fortunes by the extravagances of his costume at the Venice Carnival (so she said). She described one of these suits as being made up entirely of tiny copper centime coins, like a coat of mail; and the thought of any more vigorous squandering of a patrimony would, I believe, have pained her. I think that, in her timid way, she fell in love with Herbert, and spoke to us of his goodness with a delicate warmth. She used to allow us to play in our bath with two china figures off the mantelpiece, one representing the Madonna, the other St. Antony of Padua with a sheaf of lilies and the baby Christ on his arm: the evening ritual was to make them dance to the sound of her alarum clock, which she set going for our amusement. I am sure it never struck her that this treatment of the Holy Family and saints was at all irreverent; affection and not protocol was what she cared for; and it has left me with a happy intimate feeling towards St. Antony ever since.

Herbert used to join the party at the bath, which was a round tin affair in front of a wood fire. It made him happy to have his house with children in it, though he kept an old bachelor aloofness which endeared him, and made us feel to him like an equal. With an arm round each of us he read aloud for hours. *Treasure Island*, the *Black Arrow*, *A Gentleman of France* and *Ivanhoe*, were added to King Arthur and his knights. Their mixed crowd built a world far brighter than that of the nursery, a world where everything was deepened as if seen through water. Vera, bored by chivalry, made her own lonely little games. She wandered away uncomplaining and uncommunicative, while I monopolized Herbert in dragon hunts. I had a reputation for naughtiness at that time, which seemed to make me unjustly popular, for all my parents' visitors were ready to come and play at my games. Yet I was possessive, envious, and full of rages. I remember still with a feeling of shame one of Vera's sea-shells, handsomer than any of mine, which I threw away among the laurels. Vera would gladly give me anything of hers. On any expedition unconnected with the Age of Chivalry, she trotted behind full of admiration unblemished by envy. She was a silent child, and quietly thought out plans which I put into action and got the blame for; and no one accused her, so unobtrusive in the background. She struggled stubbornly to the most difficult places in our unlicensed expeditions, and there, clutching some hand-hold in agony and miserable to be the cause of detection, declared herself unable to move, and gardeners had to rescue her with ladders.

An old Asolo doctor used to arrive every evening to call on my mother. He cannot have been exhilarating for her, but she was the most patient person I have ever known under boredom, and in fact was too vital and too simple ever to realize what it was. This old man had a white walrus moustache and a stick, and tottered about in an antique frock coat: and in one of its pockets kept chocolates wrapped in silver and gold. We were each allowed to draw out one handful only, and I remember, also with shame, how the knowledge that my hand was bigger than Vera's gave me an unworthy satisfaction.

We became devoted to Herbert, taking for granted his long-limbed, quiet manner and simple ways. Everyone spoiled us in his house—the termagant cook with meeting black eyebrows who ruled him like iron, put up a picnic if we asked her nicely; the meek old housemaid like a Dürer engraving, hands folded on so many skirts, petticoats and aprons that one wondered whether she ever got undressed at all, stood forgetting to serve the dinner, contemplating us with smiles. The house was clear and clean and sparsely furnished in a masculine way, with beautiful threadbare rugs on its floors and tapestry on one of its walls; and the garden was a spring garden, half wild. In the warm March days when violets, primroses and hepaticas were out, we used to play about there naked on turf which covers the old Roman theatre. Lizards ran over the stone seats; the moss and young grasses were fresh to one's feet; and a memory of the golden age has remained all about it.

My father must have been in England at this time, and wrote letters that are sad and touching to read now, asking about walks, and dragons, and robbers' caves, and telling us where to find salamanders or Christmas roses.

At the end of the winter, when we left Asolo, Vera was given a doll as a reward for being good. The promise of this desperate bribe had had no effect at all on my conduct and I had no hopes, yet there on the table for me was *Treasure Island*, not as a reward but as a present, with all the charm of injustice about it that still warms my heart; and I think the warmth and affection of this childhood lasted us all our lives, for we never became embittered in later sorrows.

At the beginning of summer we left for Belluno and the Dolomites, and took an 'apartment' in a long Venetian villa with pediment and wings, outside the town. I remember very little of it except an avenue down which we were sent every morning to fetch bread from the baker's oven—a little stone hut with a triangular door where a long shovel pulled loaves in and out. Behind the villa, Monte Servo was powdered with snow. A foaming stream poured down from him in a canyon, spanned by a bridge which shook in the spray and was called *Ponte della Morte*, the bridge of death. When Herbert came to Belluno to join us, I tried to make him climb down the cliff side, but the bridge of death was hastily put out of bounds. I longed already with a passionate longing to climb all hills in sight.

We were extremely honest children about promises, and very truthful, but we had a strange absence of feeling for other people's property. In the bare hall of our 'villa', common to all its apartments, where busts in stuccoed niches contemplated a mosaic marble floor, an old carved chest stood full of odd pieces of material; and we used to help ourselves and make clothes for dolls (I began to be quite clever and fond of this dressmaking) until one day our landlady said in a reflective way: "That was a piece of my wedding-dress." This vagueness in our sense of property was, I think, the fault of Contessina, who even after that remark never really investigated. The landlady was placid and stout and wore two long cigars, of the kind with straws inside them, stuck into the apex of the curve of her bosom.

One day Count Mario di Roascio, Vera's future husband, came here to stay. He had appeared as a week-end visitor in England, brought by an aunt, and my father invited him to Dartmoor, took him for long soggy walks over bogs and through mists, and taught him to box—all of which pleasures he looked back upon with shuddering admiration and no wish ever to repeat them. When he came to Belluno he was a short, bouncy, dictatorial young man of twenty-three, and we children both disliked him at sight. My mother thought he might take us out for walks and we laid careful plans leading him by rocky stream beds to walk on my favourite ledges; whenever he started in a panic to hold me, a wail from Vera "Please, I'm slipping," dragged him back, and he asked never to be sent out with us again. I cannot remember what made us so perspicacious as to dislike him.

We left Belluno and went on to a drab little summer 'appartement' at Le Touquet, then a modest place of garishly ornamented houses where the very minuscule but fat French bourgeoisie came for the plage. It was my tenth year and a lovely summer. Contessina, after some half-hearted attempts at geography, of which she was quite ignorant herself, had given up education altogether: nobody could suffer less from it than we did at that time. All day we ran about in striped red boy suits so that: "Est-ce un garçon ou une fille"? was almost the only French I picked up. The beach was scattered with shells, coloured rays that could be imagined as landscapes, sunsets, or almost anything you liked. We played with the fishermen's boats, waiting for the beating tide to come up around them, with a rising height of waves that gave a feeling of solitude and ocean. At night, the cones of light from the lighthouse swept through our uncurtained room. There were two of them, and I thought of them as turning round after each other perpetually in a chase which never ended, like Apollo and Daphne in a picture at Asolo. My mother was happy here. She spent most of her time at a studio in Étaples and painted for the Salon, fisherwomen with the poles of their nets held like banners on their shoulders, walking barefoot across the sands; and the whole place was full of artists who were her friends. To us she was remote, but still came like a vision in the evening to lie on our bed and tell us a story before she went to dine. In the daytime we saw her always with a background of groups of people sitting on chairs, drinking tea on the beach, with flounced parasols and immense hats; and we tried to slink by unperceived so as to escape the social duty of shaking hands with strangers.

In the later summer my father came out, and filled our life with incidents and imagination. He brought a Canadian toboggan to slide down the sand dunes. Our walks were no longer solitary: when we were tired of scampering about, there was always a big, very gentle hand—the veins knotted all over its outer surface and brown with constant living out of doors. All the feeling which my father could not put into words was in his hand—any dog, child or horse would recognize the kindness of it. He went away again and we were left to the nominal company of Contessina, a small bundle on a dune in the distance engaged in darning our perpetually worn out underwear. We were made to wear long stockings, widely ribbed, to reach the thigh; and a hole appeared every evening on the kneecap—a source of constant and, it still seems to me, unreasonable trouble.

Autumn drew on with gales; the bathing cabins were deserted. We made marauding expeditions to loot them through the small windows at their back. I stiffened myself like a ramrod, Vera pushed my feet, inserted me head first into the window, turned me horizontal, and gave another good push to send me through. I landed on whatever might be inside, reached out all sorts of toys, and trusted to fortune or a bench or stool to be able to escape again. Contessina, seeing these new objects in the nursery, enquired mildly, and seemed satisfied when we told her that "they came from the beach".

Whatever laxity there may have been in our geography, our physical discipline continued stern enough. There was a retired

English business man called Mr. Boddington who—when he and his wife must have been well over seventy—began to study art in Paris and filled the end of their lives with enthusiasm and fun. He liked us and used to bicycle over from his cottage at Trépied before breakfast every morning with two creamy cakes from the *pâtisserie* wrapped in white paper and pale blue string in his hand. With this bribe we were induced to put on bathing dresses still dank from yesterday, and shiver out in the wind across the sands to a cold receding sea where he taught us the elements of swimming. How we disliked it! The landscape of an autumn seaside resort, in the north after its season, has stamped itself as a windswept desolation in my mind. We left the deserted beach when this morning ordeal was over, and played in the woods in those untended places where the sands have ended and the real landsman's earth has not begun: or spent the rest of the day learning to bicycle. My father had promised a bicycle of my own on my tenth birthday, and it arrived, black and silver, shiny as Pegasus, when we returned to England.

This time the Channel crossing is clear in my mind because we had a Manx cat in a basket, and it squeezed itself out and was lost at Dover; and the whole business of the ship was interfered with by a hunt in which the sailors took part, until it was finally discovered, flustered and aloof, in the engine-room. This was the first occasion too on which I remember a conscious enjoyment of natural beauty for its own sake, the scattered discs of moonlight on a black sea. I remember also noticing with surprise as the hunt went on that everyone seemed to think of their own feelings and not of those of the cat. Some time before this, my aunt had put on her boots one morning and squashed to death my pet dormouse, who happened to be sleeping inside: everyone was sorry for the aunt. My father would have thought naturally of the small creature, but he was away, and I began to realize that most people care for the human side of life only, and that he was unusual in keeping a feeling for the wholeness of the world, which he shared with children.

We spent the winter at my grandmother's house in Torquay,

and I first learned to enjoy poetry by myself, through a book of ballads my father gave me. The Arabian Nights and the Greek Tales were superseded by Sir Patrick Spens, The Inchcape Rock, The Nut-brown Maid and Count Arnaldos; and the ballad of Count Arnaldos—which I have since known in Spanish—still seems to me the essence of romance. A book from my father's boyhood was on a Torquay table; it dealt with the Wild West, and opened a new landscape of buffaloes and prairie.

The best of our child life was now over, and I was never to have the real feeling of a home again until we settled in Asolo twenty-four years later. Next spring, in May or June, when I was ten, we were travelling, Vera and I with Contessina, to Dronero in Piedmont, the home of Mario di Roascio. We were to spend the summer there, and actually stayed for sixteen years, till after the first world war. My mother had gone ahead of us. I think we spent the interval in Asolo, but cannot remember. We were jolting in one of those old-fashioned train-trams that run along Italian country roads and clatter through the cobbled streets of little market towns, stopping at wayside halts; full of livestock they were and country produce, and burned cheap coal that filled one's eyes with smuts. The seats ran opposite each other the length of the carriage, and you read at intervals, strung up on placards, the fascinating notice: "You are requested not to spit outside your own pocket handkerchief." This antiquated affair became our only contact with the greater world until cars grew common, so we got to know it well. It belonged to a Belgian company, and as it was recognized to be dying out of the modern world, no one ever renovated it or provided a spare part; there was a corner where at intervals the whole thing derailed and turned over from sheer old age. Yet it went on right through both wars, and is probably going still, puffing out smoke over the white dust of the road and the rows of the peasant passengers who sit with their baskets on their knees. On market days we would see the local lawyers travelling to and fro, arranging the plan and duration of their lawsuits before they met and argued them out on opposing sides in court.

LOG HUT,

19 *Nov.*, 1901.

Dear Freya and Vera,

I do not know when I shall be able to come out to Asolo as I have so many things to attend to here about Ford Park and Frenchbeer; perhaps later on I may be able to come, but as yet I cannot promise quite.

I wonder Freya now you have seen Asolo again whether you remember any of the streets or places. Have you been to see the house where we used to live and the garden at the back where you used to tumble down the steps and frighten us so thinking you would get killed. Vera of course was too small then, she used to roll about.

What do you do with yourselves all day long? Have you been along the top of the hills towards Cornuda, there is a little path leads right along so you can look down over all the country, but the best side of the hill to go along is that facing the mountains; after going along it for about two or three miles you will very likely come to a place where Christmas roses are growing amongst the nut bushes, and some should be in flower by this time, only be careful if you go down over the hill as there are some precipices there over which you might tumble.

I daresay you will have some snow later on, so you had better keep a look out now and find a nice sloping place where you can go tobogganing when it comes. There is a very good carpenter at Asolo who would soon make a toboggan for you. We had some snow here and hard frost but it is all gone again. I think I have found a nice place for a slide here, for another Winter when you are staying here. The ponies are very well. Frolic is getting quite a hunter. The other day I put her in a field by herself but she was so unhappy being left all alone that she jumped three hedges to get to Festive and the little colt who were in the paddock at the bottom of the wood at Ford Park.

I saw Mr. Black Bunny rabbit the other morning just in the same place in the meadow where we used to see him.

Whose pony is Frolic? Because next year she will have to be ridden often to get her broken well. She is quite tame and quiet now and has not forgotten I think how you used to ride on her. The baby pony must please have a name given him when he is grown up, that is when he is four years old. He will be quite as big as Tommy, I think and will be quite strong enough then to carry either of you hunting till you are as tall as Mamma, so that will be for some years yet.

I was going hunting to-day on Blackthorn but the frost was so hard that no one could ride at all so I had to give it up and shall try to go out next week instead.

Have you seen the pudding stone that the Asolo hills are made of? The stones are stuck together with lime, I think just as plums are in a Xmas pudding. I went up to the top of the Grappa one winter about Xmas time. I think it was when there was so much snow on top that one could easily be buried in it, but such magnificent slopes of it for tobogganing just as steep as a house roof. I should like to take you up there some time, perhaps you have not much snow there yet.

To go there it is a long way; first to get to the foot of the mountain. I think we should have to drive there. There are two villages there of which I forget the names, but you can see them from Asolo. Then one has to go up a valley with big cliffs on each side worn out by the stream that comes down there, such fine hiding places for robbers it might be. After that in about an hour's walk you come to the mountain slopes, very steep and slippery, up which you have to climb perhaps for three hours before you get to the top, and perhaps if you find much snow you could never get up if you tried all day, and so if Mr. Noke or Mr. Young will not promise to carry you up I think you must wait till later on when I could go with you.

If you had your tent we might camp out for the night.

Addio,

PIPS

6

The Alps of Piedmont. 1903-1905

DRONERO is in the top north-west corner of Italy, and my mother had written that there were mountains around it. As we trundled along in the tram we could see their peaks edging the Piedmont plain. Their unaltered stability in the heart of earth, rooted below the happy life of climbing villages and vineyards, their high snowfields paler than the sky behind them, filled me then with a strange yearning, and has done so ever since. Perhaps the love of hills came in years before memory when I was carried about the Dolomites, for it seems to have been there spontaneously and always; every new mountain—if it is a real mountain unspoilt and unobstructed —still comes to me with a sort of ecstasy.

My mother had taken a house outside the town with a small garden full of brightly-coloured glass pavilions and a pond of croaking frogs: it was called by the strange name of *La Mal Pensà*—The Ill-Thought-Of. The town was in sight, in the middle of a broad and fine valley between two streams. It was grey and cobble-stoned, and had a cathedral with fine work in medieval carved brick, Lombard Gothic, unfortunately renovated and painted red by one of the pious noblemen of the place. It had a single-arched fourteenth century bridge with a little penthouse shrine in the middle of it where the devil was exorcised and leaped down, leaving only his name. The bridge, battlemented and immensely high, spanned the whole valley, which lay far below, filled with white beds of river-stones where shivering poplar trees and walnuts threw pale blue velvet shadows; and close to it was a creaky ramshackle old building called the Laboratory of St. Joseph. Here the priests ran a small business of coir-yarn brush mats, carpets, and wicker baskets, employing all the halt, lame, goitered and mentally deficient of the town. Mario Roascio, full of young enthusiasm, tough, round, and small, with a moustache that looked downwards and hair already melting off his forehead, took over this place and was beginning a business career—a thing unheard of at the time for anyone of noble family however poor. One of the differences most noticeable in the last forty years is the change in people's attitude to work: I never heard any reproach attached to idleness in my early childhood, and my parents had never thought it in the least immoral to spend an income without making one. Mario was the first person I heard talk of work as the end of man, and not a punishment as Genesis describes it; though it is common enough now to watch men make their joy out of the punishments of God. Mario's relations, looking upon his enterprise as a juvenile caprice, excused it with tolerant amusement which soon turned to disapproval. But my mother watched with sympathy and soon came to be interested in the struggle. For many years she had had too little for her active nature to do. From watching, from giving advice, and a few days' help here and there, she began to spend more and more time in the dusty little office; she began to experiment with green and red dyes and to take over that part of the business; until she was drawn in, and for the next fifteen years of her life this carpet factory absorbed her.

In Dronero we were still blissfully free of anything in the nature of education, except for Herbert Young who came to stay, and read book after book, and for my own passion for reading, now in full swing and deep in Walter Scott. For most of the day we used to be employed tying labels on to the baskets in the Laboratory of St. Joseph. It was a crazy building, almost derelict, with storey below storey joined by creaking outer stairs and sloping balconies and, far below, the wooden wheels that raised the water from where it flowed under dim arches, and the dye vats, and the tin letters that wrote *Salve* in green or red or brown on the little mats.

On Monday mornings my father took us round the market, rows of stalls and open awnings, packed and transferred from town to town on carts with the drivers asleep, and horses that knew the way in the easy days before cars. They travelled by night, plodding along the dusty roads of the plain under the stars, and began to pack again at noon, so that by the afternoon all of the market except a débris of flying papers and some drunken voices singing in the taverns had vanished from the square. But in the morning you could hardly walk among the shoulders of peasants in their long round capes—men who lived in the fields, slow to move out of the way; or the round baskets of the women used as battering rams; or bleating sheep, and cows with heads low down, full of anxiety among the city noises and bewildered while the absent-minded owner forgot them or pulled suddenly at the head rope. We would choose guinea pigs, that ran about in low wooden pens near the chickens in one corner of the square, for the peasants to eat in winter. They are unimaginative pets and we rather hated them, as we had to clean out their hutches, and they used to eat oleander leaves, and die.

Dronero was rich in walks. Chestnut trees clothed the two low ranges that hem its river, and, where they ended, the great Italian plain began, deep in corn and mulberries and maize. We could measure its tilt towards the mountains by the snow-line, which was always level and made the hills beneath it look lopsided on their bases as they sank eastward with the sloping plain. The Maritime and Cottian Alps surrounded us with a fan of valleys each with a glacier torrent from its snows. During many summers we went by *diligence* with jangling bells, five hours up our valley, changing horses twice or three times on the way in cobble-paved little towns that grew more alpine and poorer as we climbed, till we came to the end of the road, to a mountain inn with balconies, hanging over a torrent that became our own river lower down, whose constant roar was like a lullaby outside the windows. This inn was kept by an ex-carabinier from Monte Carlo called De Poli, very neat and slim in knee breeches and a jersey becoming to his svelte figure. He was a bachelor. He kept a few cowed women in the background, but ran the whole place himself, constantly redecorating the rooms with paper rosettes and strips of colour and burying us in our beds between rough clean sheets and counterpanes that seemed weighted with sand. A barrel-organ that played ten tunes if you turned its handle stood among the wooden tables, and oleographs—Othello and Desdemona, Rigoletto, and the Four Seasons—pre-Hollywood beauties—decorated the walls beside a Government decree in a frame forbidding the game of Morra (a fascinating competition played with the fingers of both hands). If the landlord liked you he took endless trouble; if he did not, he soon made it clear that the other and inferior hôtel was your place, and was said to have turned away a general once for coming home too late at night. To us he was a friend, and ruled our holidays easily, for our good.

My father used to go on into the highest hills and rented a little hut or *grangia* beyond the last village of the watershed, with the French frontier running through empty rocks by solitary tarns along the high pasture lands above. It was called *La Massigliera* in memory of some old massacre, and he would take his gun with him to shoot chamois which he never once attained or really wished to kill. There was no village here, but two little huts on a promontory jutting out over a valley, and a stable where the cattle came clanking their bells at evening, and meadows full of edelweiss around. He took us to stay there once by ourselves, but his Spartan cuisine, a diet of sardines and macaroni cooked on two stones out of doors, soon brought us back rather ill. He made us know the smugglers, who carried salt and silk and women's hair over the passes into France. The women's hair was a regular product in Piedmont: a girl would cut a long coil of it off from the back of her head where the loss scarcely showed, and would be given a new dress, and thirty liras in exchange. My father spent more and more time in the hills living a good deal with the family of the chamois hunters in the village below, who loved him with the sort of equal love he always inspired. He would sit in their kitchen brewing his tea while the plain middle-aged sister darned his socks, and would eat the rye bread they baked once in the year only, after harvest, and kept stored in their loft—rows of dark flattish loaves so hard that a small axe was used to cut them: this bread he took out hunting, and said that a small piece nourished him all day, and tried it unsuccessfully on us; and I imagine it is the same sort of stuff that the Turkish soldiers were accustomed to and gave to their British prisoners on the long road from Kut, of which seven biscuits a week were considered sufficient for a man's need.

In winter the stars grew brighter and brighter with the cold and I remember a comet, shining enormous in the sky. When the snow came, we tobogganed down steep and twisting hill paths that soon turned to sheets of ice and sent us home blue with bruises. In the high hills they used the solitary paths to slide their tree-trunks down, and I once, in a narrow place, would have lost my life through a hurtling pine tree, if I had been two seconds later on the path. The whole country froze and collected itself for the long cold months. My father would take us to visit the peasants shut up in their stables for warmth, their stoves and their beds of mattresses stuffed with maize-husks arranged on a raised brick floor. An oil wick or paraffin lamp threw shadows over cows under ceilings vaulted like cellars, cobwebbed and low. The women held small bolsters and bobbins on their knees, and made the sort of lace known as Milanese point; and a story-teller would often sit there to entertain them.

I have never known anyone with less 'class-consciousness' than my father; he never thought of people except as individuals, and had the same manner exactly towards all. He was completely truthful; I never heard even the smallest complimentary lie from his lips—and I think he gave to both Vera and me a feeling of almost physical discomfort in the face of any lie, which lasted through life. Appearances meant nothing at all to him; and I remember a little scene at table when my mother said: "We can't discuss this before the servants," and he said, "Oh, the

servants," with a sort of sigh as he rose and, leaving the world of
appearances behind him in the house, went to look at the things
that really exist and grow in the garden.

In autumn, on the feast of St. Antony, there was the blessing
of the animals. Everyone took their dog, cat, canaries in cages,
cows, pigs and horses to the square round the steps of the church,
and a benediction was scattered with holy water and swinging
incense over the puzzled congregation.

The only sort of education I remember during our first
summer was that we were made to wait at table: it may or may
not be a useful accomplishment, but we enjoyed it. It began
after a maid left us because, she said, we "changed our knives
and forks just to make work." So Vera and I did the waiting,
and Mario's aunt came to dinner, a rich old contessa with bright
eyes and a bony face, the only one of his family who was at all
kind about the Laboratory.

It is difficult to write an account of these years without giving
the impression that Mario was my mother's lover: and yet I am
quite sure, and the few people who remember her then are
sure, that this was not so. There is no excuse to-day for sexual
ignorance and it is hard to realize how casually informed our
parents were. In Italy the convent school prepared a well-born
young girl for life; the accomplishments were taught by the
nuns and the necessary knowledge was spread illicitly by the
girls themselves. Everything of the sort my sister and I ever
knew before we began to mix in the world was told us by girls
brought up in the so-called seclusion of convents, and when I
grew up, a Mother Superior, a charming worldly woman,
approached my mother to ask if she might not arrange a suitable
marriage for me. My mother, in the wildness of her Florence
villa, had been deprived of this sort of preparation, as we in our
turn were deprived: and it is almost unbelievable how ignorant
a normally healthy young woman can remain. My sister bore
six children with never one moment's pleasure in conceiving
them—which seems a terrible waste of the kindly gifts of life.
I spent years of doubt attributing every natural human desire to

immodesty if not to sin, until I came to consider the thing itself and not the names it is called by, and stood on firm ground ever after. But my mother was not only ignorant but extremely un-sexual: not ascetic, which implies renouncement, but unaware. Men admired, but I never saw them fall in love with her—nor, as we grew up, was she able to understand our troubles or advise. It would have been better for us all, even for my father, if Mario or anyone else had been a lover indeed; it would have created gentleness and understanding; and would have done away with that fatal materialism in morals which relies on facts more than feelings, and gives a smug unreal security.

My mother must have loved Mario, but without ever realizing it—he was a part of the Italy to which she belonged. Innocent by nature and incredibly uncritical, she was inclined to take any blatant temperament at its own valuation. She had suffered agonies of repression, long frustrated years, in the laconic solitudes of Dartmoor, mere negations of life to her mind. Mario gave her the active organizing climate she enjoyed; and she thought no harm. He soon dominated everything—my mother echoed his every word. The worst things were said about her, and they filled our growing years with a shame, discomfort and agony which no one who has not been a child, dimly suffering and only half understanding, can ever realize. My mother, however, went on serenely, devoting herself with extraordinary contentment to those mats of woven or brush coco fibre which are, incidentally, among the most ugly carpets in the world. Filled with affection and happiness herself, she never noticed that all our lives were heaping themselves in little ruins about her.

The Mal Pensà was too cold for winter and we moved into part of a great mansion in the town belonging to the Counts of San Martino. The drawing-room was filled with small chairs on spindly legs, blue and gold. The front of the house and tiny garden were sunny and warm, while the back—all marble tessellated floors—was icy. We were ostracized at this time, and no one came to see us, but, as they were our landlords, the old Count and Countess paid a formal call once or twice in the season: he had been Minister for War (his name was Coriolanus) and had to resign because, when answering a question in Parliament about a mutiny, he had said that it was silly to make a fuss about things which are bound to happen now and then. (How right he was.) They were a gay and charming old couple with a rough air of breeding like country squires. Otherwise we knew next to no one except an old self-educated major who had risen from the ranks and retired to a vineyard, where he dragooned his fruit trees as if they were defaulters and invited us to eat his strawberries. And of course we knew Mario's relations. His mother lived in one of the cobbled streets of the town —an old peasant woman with a round stubborn face, very red, surrounded by white hair. She made the most appalling scenes and had been married, as an afterthought, by the Count his father for her looks and other reasons. His elder brother Angelo came in summer only. He was placid, plump, very good-natured, and would do anything to avoid unpleasantness: he had a Neapolitan wife, also plump, pretty, placid, and unobtrusively intelligent and unselfish up to the Italian limit, which rarely goes beyond the family circle if as far; she once told my mother that all she had asked of life was an affectionate husband and fine jewellery, and she got them both, as well as a family of two girls and a boy, then quite small. They lived in Rome in a world of fashion which we were brought up to look upon as corrupt, and they came to Dronero only in late summer, to gather in the harvests of their lands.

As our first autumn here drew on, we began to learn French at the convent of the Sacred Heart. The nuns, exiled from France and dispossessed, had settled in an old house on the foundations of the medieval city walls above the river. We went there for an hour every day for several years, and two hours a week for sewing and embroidery; and it was the only regular schooling we had before I went to London. We walked down a poor almost empty cobbled street that sloped to a central gutter. A feeble-minded boy with a goitre lived there, and used to pursue us with unintelligible, terrifying mouthings. A stone beside an arched door in a blank wall just enabled me, by stretching, to pull the bell, and a nun with black meeting eyebrows came to open a little postern inset in the big door. Flapping huge low-heeled shoes under voluminous black folds of serge, she led us through a grassy court to an austere room with a vaulted ceiling, cool in summer but chilly in winter, with pictures of the Mothers Superior and saints alternate on the walls. The Sacred Heart was there giving, it seemed to me, a gay and unexpected view of anatomy. We learnt a page of French grammar by heart every day, rising from smaller to larger grammars with the passing years until we reached the classics and Racine. I still think it an excellent way to learn languages, and did it easily, reading my task two or three times at night and remembering in the morning, while Vera, who had the artist memory for shapes and not for meanings, stumbled along reluctant, helped by laborious promptings, line by line. Contessina was still with us, and one of her numerous platitudes at this time was that people who do things slowly do them well. Vera did everything slowly while I was naturally quick: I discovered with surprise that Contessina was talking nonsense—the first grown-up shibboleth to be disproved.

We became very fond of our two nuns, Mother Superior and Soeur Sainte Reine. They both came from the south of France, had been devoted to each other as young girls, and then having separated, had met to their unexpected joy in the convent. They spent many happy years together until the eye of Authority, seeing them so united in an earthly affection, sent the Mother away to some distant place where one letter a year was all she could ever send. Thus misery descended on Soeur Sainte Reine and it was pathetic to see the fight between obedience and the natural revolt of her heart. For years however we had them together—the Mother an excellent teacher and Soeur Sainte Reine perpetually delightful, plump, smiling, and charitable.

"It is wrong for *us* to sin," she would say; "but for *you*, Protestants—God does not demand so much."

[75]

Her reflections on French history were always refreshing. She had her ideas of progress.

"Men invent cures," she said, "but then God sends us a new sort of disease, to show that he is there."

The great works of literature she taught in selected pieces, with a description of the author to begin with, "so that when he is mentioned in a salon, you will know what it is appropriate to say." But she always mixed her selections and got them attached to the wrong author.

The fact that our French came to be inspired mostly by the works of Dumas, all of them on the papal index, was tactfully ignored. In the convent all we ever read was Octave Feuillet, *Roman d'un Jeune Homme Pauvre,* a dreary young man: Xavier de Maistre, *Voyage autour de ma Chambre,* which was quite unexceptionable as it dealt chiefly with the inanimate: and *Paul et Virginie,* whose slightly erotic flavour was overlooked in view of the fact that the heroine prefers to drown rather than shed her petticoat. Racine, whom I delighted in, was permitted merely, I believe, because he wrote two tragedies for "Les demoiselles de Saint Cyr": Corneille was too romantic and Molière impure.

The sewing was very thorough—days and weeks over samplers of plain stitches before we reached the excitement of embroidery, and a ruthless unpicking if a false stitch were detected ever so far back. As a reward, months ahead, we were promised the sewing of a shirt for *Papa,* every seam to be stitched by hand, counting the threads of the linen for each stitch: this colossal labour, which would not have been received with much enthusiasm, we made every effort to avoid. The darning of stockings, a delicate tracery almost mathematically exact, has prevented my ever doing any mending afterwards, from sheer inability to do it badly and the shortness of life for the doing of it well. Yet the benefit of that teaching I have often been grateful for; and while sitting by the wireless listening to the news in 1940, soothing myself with my embroidery, have often thought kindly of Soeur Sainte Reine.

They never tried to convert us. Indeed we had no religion

to speak of, except that our grandmother had made us familiar with the stories of the Bible. We were taught to say the Lord's prayer by Contessina, who nightly lamented the fact that Vera was apt to forget it, while she so easily remembered the song of the fifteen men on the Dead Man's Chest in *Treasure Island*. But Contessina was no disciplinarian, and allowed us to pray under the bedclothes in the cold weather, which is perhaps the reason why I still do so, though our observance then was so remarkably slack.

The winter was bitterly cold. The streets were thick with ice that never melted for four months; the eaves were hung with icicles—when one breathed in the early morning a pain went up one's nose. It was considered weak to have a hot water bottle: Vera and I lay like islands in a huge bed, trying to get one foot warm at a time and then sending it out into the surrounding iciness of linen while the next foot was attended to. We had a hot bath and fire once a week—otherwise a short and usually victorious tussle with Contessina as to how much was washed. We were poor by this time, and all the succeeding years were filled with economy. We had austere breakfasts: a bowl of milk-coffee-bread with sugar on top of it—no butter or jam. And chilblains all winter long, under the thick-ribbed woollen stockings, or the knitted mittens we wore on our hands.

When the spring came there was a sort of agony of returning life. The snow began to drip from the edges of roofs on to the street, making the ice transparent, until the cobblestones below appeared in the clefts of the plopping drops. The bite went off the air, and every day snow patches on the roofs grew smaller and the dripping melting noise louder, until with a rush the last soiled whiteness melted and the spring was there, with lanes deep in mud and the young blades of the autumn-sown corn battered from the winter, but green.

ASOLO,
20 January, 1903.

My dear dear Sir Percival,

Many thanks for your letters. I am longing to see you and Vera again, so I hope it will not be long before you come to Asolo—*You* have got Mamma, and Pips, and Norma, and Signorina, but poor I am all alone and have got *nobody* to play with! If Mamma cannot leave England quite so soon, perhaps she will let you and Vera and Signorina come here first and she and Pips could follow after. Then we would all go to Belluno again; would not that be jolly! You know that we two, Sir Percival, made a *VOW* to go up the Serva someday, and we *must*, don't you think so? Do you remember how last year we used to have tea in my garden, and what fine games of dressing up we had, and also the battledor and shuttlecock in the Studio? I hear that you have got an accordion-pleated skirt for dancing. How much I should like to see you dance in it. I must take lots of photos of you in that dress.

I expect that you and Vera got a lot of nice presents at Christmas. I am charmed with the pen-holder papercutter you sent me, and I admire the napkin ring from Vera extremely. Our birthday will soon be here now; I am sorry we are both of us getting so old, you especially—I like little girls better than grown ups and I should like you to stay a little girl always, but I will try to like you when you are grown up all the same.

I daresay you will get some more presents, and it would be very nice if you wrote and told me all about your birth-day.

Give my love to Mamma and to Vera and Signorina and everybody—

Heaps of kisses from your loving

GAWAINE

7

An Accident in Dronero. 1906-1907

ALTHOUGH we remained stationary in Dronero for some
years, a six-monthly move from one house to another
gave the family restlessness an outlet. We spent our
summers in a fine villa in vineyards on the slope of a hill. The
plain lay at its feet, and, about thirty miles away, planted majes-
tically, the beautiful Bismalda raised her truncated pyramid,
covered till midsummer with snow.

The house itself was old, whitewashed, square and half-
fortified; its walls must have been three feet thick, and the ground
floor windows were barred with iron. Three vaulted bedrooms
dropping with tattered damask led through each other to a
private chapel at one end. From the first floor we climbed a
long stair which we took lightheartedly three steps at a time,
and came out on an arcaded loggia with a floor of red brick, and
rooms like cells around it; and here we spent most of the day.
The house was scooped in the hill and the ground fell gradually
away to that stupendous view, of which my father has left many
fine sketches. He now spent most of his time in the hills, but
appeared at intervals and tried to teach us cricket—a game at
which we served so much by only standing and waiting, with
such short intervals of batting and bowling, that we became
bored and deplorable. Once he said: "Life is too electric for
me down here!" Otherwise he kept his troubles to himself.
At Mal Pensà, the year before, I had seen my mother sweep away
when they had been talking, snatch a flower-pot and fling it to
the ground: and I remember a sort of sickness of horror which
did not leave me for days—in fact has never I suppose left

altogether; for the first sight of any sort of violence is a thing a child never quite gets over—like the first sight of death. My mother would have been surprised and mortified if she had guessed what jolts her robust character gave her children. I remember travelling with her about this time—a small cross-country journey by trains through little hills—when she lost her purse. There was a great to-do, and she rated an official angrily; and as we sat in the carriage afterwards she noticed tears trickling down my cheeks. I could not bring myself to say why they were there, but explained that it was because a peasant beside me had smelly feet—an answer which filled her with astonishment. I have had to become tough about smells; but even now the sight of anyone angry is almost unbearable. Yet I had a violent temper myself and used to yell with rage, shut up in my room, turning over murder or suicide in my mind as a means of retaliation, up to the age of eleven or twelve, when I suddenly decided that I would stop—and stopped. I have hardly ever been *uncontrolled* in temper since, though I notice that if I do get angry it usually carries everything before it.

My mother was nearly always away now, walking down to her work at six in the morning, and again in the heat of the sun, a two hours' walk or so in the day; and she and Mario would talk about the factory right through luncheon and dinner. Friends from England came more and more rarely, unable to bear it. New factory premises were being built, the alliance with the priests of St. Joseph had come to an end, and my mother was at last happy and occupied, holding the fullness of her life in her hands.

This all slid by us, only to be noticed later on. Our grandmother came with the old stories, and the leisurely far-away thoughts in which we were at home. We had her all day, after a morning spent walking to our French convent and back at the bottom of the hill. The stretch of dull main road on level ground was enlivened by tight-rope walking along a parapet of rough-squared tree-trunks laid loosely in stone piers; there was a deep drop on the off side and we prided ourselves on *running*, and were luckily never seen. The road crossed a ravine with a shrine upon the bridge, and we reached the town and sped through cobbled side-streets always in shadow while the church boomed its strokes to tell us we were late. Italian church clocks ring twice, so that one is given a second chance, a pleasantly unpuritanical idea of Time. We dawdled back in the heat of the morning. What did we talk about? I have forgotten it all, except the sleepy heat and leisure, and Vera a part of me as much as an arm or a leg, and so missed when she went, as only a sister or brother can be.

Herbert Young visited us and gave me a small red pocket edition of Shakespeare; and I absorbed it and said "it was very well written" and felt hurt at the laughter which followed. Another influence of that time was a book of alphabets and their use in decoration: I treasured it, and loved the beautiful lettering and began to wish to make designs of my own. Ardently we sewed presents for all about us: and Christmas was a zero hour for months beforehand, with agonies over slippers and bags stitched out of remnants of peasant cottons, which we picked up from heaps on the market floor, where they were sold. Everything had to be bought with our own money, all earned and very scarce indeed. My father paid a penny a week for pocket money, and another penny for every hundred wasps we killed, and that took a long time and cost a few stings.

Either this summer or the next an old friend, Mary Androutzos, daughter of Alfred Fripp the water-colour painter, came to Dronero. She had married a Greek and been sorry till he left her; she was stout and full of fun and had a violent temper and next to no income. She had lived near us on Dartmoor, and adored my mother, and would have settled close to her again except for Mario whom she loathed. We loved her. She had a particular affection for Vera, and, realizing how much she needed to be encouraged, took trouble to do so. Though surprised at seeing anyone preferred to myself, I continued to be devoted to 'Aunt Mary' and indeed have never been much inclined to like people only because they like me. We heard her and Granny saying to each other how dreadful it was that we should grow up so untended (a new idea altogether); and she was the first person who thought about our religion, and read the New Testament with us, which suddenly made everything we knew in the world mean more. My parents had a theory— fostered perhaps by an agnostic age—that one must not be influenced in any direction until one can choose for oneself: as if a plant should be full-grown before it is straightened to its shape. Aunt Mary came luckily at the time when our spirit began to grope about with questions. Vera thought of her for ever after as her dearest help and friend. They went away for a short holiday journey of their own, so that Vera might blossom independently; and I joined them later in one of a series of villas rented in the little Tuscan town of Massa. No villa lasted very long, as it nearly always ended in a lawsuit with the land- lord; but she arranged each one charmingly as if for a lifetime, and filled it with paying guests to whom she soon took a dislike, and so made a fluctuating and stormy livelihood, eked out by the sale of mild copies of Botticelli Madonnas painted in water colours in a delicate old-fashioned way.

We used to go to her often for a month or so in summer. Massa was a pleasant town, its piazza surrounded with orange trees, a seventeenth-century *prefettura* palace painted a dark rich red, and a café with exquisite Swiss cakes. A tram started under the sycamores and rattled four kilometres downhill to the sea. Sometimes we bicycled, over roads worse than any I have ever known. The marble was still brought down from the Carrara mountains by ten, twenty or even thirty yoke of oxen, cream-coloured with wide horns like Pompeian paintings; they dragged the blocks on shallow carts whose weight crushed ruts a foot or more in depth and churned the hard surface as if it were dust. The sea coast was sandy, flat and wide to the head- land of Lerici, with solitary pinewoods at its back and vines where the good earth began; and it was intersected by streams stagnant in reeds, crossed by black wooden bridges on stilts as it were, sharp in the sunset. They were always dank and cool.

One of them I remember for its name—the Frigido—beautiful for a stream, and I looked at it one evening and realized for the first time, I think, that the two beauties, of words and of nature, are in themselves the same.

I cannot tell how many summers we came here. We learnt to swim; a huge fat man took us out, one under each arm; he walked on regardless of waves, which broke no higher than his waist, but submerged us: and if we tried to kick out with swimming movements we only hit each other. When my father came, we dived for pennies from his shoulder; if we hesitated, he gave a twist and in we went. It was here that we heard the news of my grandmother's death, when I must have been eleven or twelve.

An American uncle died too. He had been rich, squandered everything, and left my aunt with expensive tastes, a small income, three daughters a little older than we were and a younger son. She was very beautiful and silly and when they all came to us for the summer, gave us our first sight of Parisian clothes. We had children of our own age about us for the first time since the days of Ford Park. We never noticed our loneliness at the time, yet this summer was a holiday of laughter and quarrels and enjoyment, and everything took on a keener edge. Our nuns asked to teach us separately: we were too much for them together. After the morning studies, the whole day was free; the hill-sides were a playground without a boundary covered with fruit trees and vines to roam about on; and the two governesses scarcely ever saw us till supper time. A small miracle brought them along one day to interfere, as I was being lowered in a bucket into a deep well. We hoped to find a secret passage to the cellars whose huge vaults made all the foundations of the house; and I had volunteered, but felt a little sick with fright, for the well was so deep that it only showed a pin's head of light where one's face was reflected far down. In the late summer we went up into the hills and began to learn how to walk all day on stony tracks with the slow unvaried step of the mountaineer; and we danced at night to

De Poli's barrel organ. When the autumn came, the cousins left: we were alone again and missed them.

By this time the new factory was built and new machinery had been put inside it, and one day in January, a little before my thirteenth birthday, we went to see it. Mario took us round, and as I was standing with a mass of loose curling hair almost to my knees, the wind of a steel shaft caught it. I was snatched up, revolving, with my head ground against the shaft and my feet floating horizontal. I know that it seemed a very long time: at each revolution my feet struck a wall or pillar and I wondered if my shoes were coming off. I felt no pain or even fright. Then Mario wrenched me out and carried me away; I saw terrified faces; heard the machinery coming to a standstill; felt a warmth trickling down my neck; saw my mother meeting me with panic in her eyes that I noticed even at that moment; and next I was on mattresses in the office and some doctor was sewing my eyelid into place. Half the scalp was torn away. After a few days an ambulance came to take me to Turin, wrapped up, with the snow lying all about us. My mother stayed with me all the time.

In Turin we went to a famous grim old man who had a nursing home. Its snowy gardens, with never a soul in them, already looked like a cemetery: I got very little nursing or attention: they operated, grafting pieces of somebody's skin, and it failed: and I was gradually dying. Then a young doctor from Dronero spoke to the chief surgeon of the general hospital in the middle of the town; against all medical etiquette, he said he would take me; the nursing home let me go thinking they meant to carry me to England: but my mother saw me across Turin and put me into a private room in the hospital. The young doctor invented a new scheme: they grafted my own skin from the thigh on to the scalp and covered it with net, so that the dressings could be done through it without disturbing the new application, and it took. This is probably a commonplace now, but it was new at the time. The dressings of my flayed legs were more agony than any physical pain I have ever had to suffer: but I healed slowly, and had four months to grow accustomed to the hospital routine.

The head surgeon was a tiny little man, almost misshapen, with a deep sing-song Ligurian voice. He was the son of a peasant and a sort of saint, loved by everyone who came near him—his whole life given to his patients. He used to come walking round the hospital every morning, very stiff and small under his big head, like a Byzantine Primitive, and show me off as a remarkable object to an obsequious circle of students. The nuns fluttered around him with the wings of their head-dresses like doves; you had only to step an inch or two out of their straight line of vision to be unseen if you happened to wish to be so, and perhaps that is why these coifs were invented. I began to enjoy my life again. All sorts of people sent presents—among others a Japanese doll I was fond of, whose head the young doctor used to pull out of its socket and tell me that its anatomy was wrong and I was too old for dolls: but I have never grown too old for childish things.

I can still feel the warmth and delight of my mother's presence. She now devoted herself to me and I *discovered* her as it were. Her love, which now became greater for me than for Vera, probably dates from this time when I was nearly lost. After about two months my father arrived, and sat for hours at my bedside, showing his affection by rubbing my arm gently, till he chafed it raw: I was too polite to ask him to stop, and perhaps dimly conscious that it made him happy to think he was doing something for me.

The hospital looked out on a public garden and trams. It is a mistake to think that invalids like privacy all the time: I used to watch the gardens from a balcony and get interested in the dramas I could follow there day by day, an uninvolved watching of other lives I still think one of the best of entertainments.

When the spring came I began to be driven out or to seek in the parks of Turin some patch of ground to lie on, and smell the grass growing and feel the earth again, as if life itself were pouring back through the living season. My head was bandaged; and when I got tired my father carried me with a struggle of tenderness that he could not express. The words "underneath are the everlasting arms" make me think of those spring days whenever I come across them. At this time we heard of the San Francisco earthquake, the first public event I took any interest in since the fall of Ladysmith, and, strangely enough, the Russo-Japanese war: it shows how remote our life was from the world's business and talk. My father and Vera left and my mother came back, and we began to amuse ourselves during the long hospital afternoons by visiting cinemas: we waited, on severe red-plush benches, till there were enough of us to fill the hall, and were then sent in through a curtain to rather simple films, pleased with the sight of horses galloping and trains running, still silent, of course. I can remember very little excitement in the way of plots.

Four months in a hospital are very long, and we returned to Dronero at last. I wore white lacy caps to cover my cropped and torn head. The scars got much smaller, but have always remained, and were a constant trouble, making me self-conscious, and also no doubt spoiling such looks as I might have had. The only other damage was that for several years I could not see even a sewing-machine wheel turning without feeling a little sick.

My mother was now all my happiness. I adored her, and began to notice, indignantly but without understanding, that nearly all her old friends had left her, or if they came once, never returned. They could not bear the factory and its attendant Mario. Herbert Young was reluctantly faithful. Viva Jeyes, and Edwin Bale her father, whose friendship went back for two generations, continued to come and to write for love of her, but they disliked it all intensely and said so. "My dear, your mother talks like an angel but acts like a fool," the exasperated little round old man said to me once. I don't think my mother noticed: at any rate she did not care. She had no time to do so; she worked from early morning till dusk. She became someone not only to be admired but to be protected. I spent half my time thinking out things to please her, and waited for her when she came home in the evening, helping her to wash and change. She was so used to these adorations that she took it all very easily—a thing always dangerous for any human being to do. But our love went on for years, unquestioning, and gave that warm background of affection with which my life has always been happily provided in one way or another. Vera, far more independent in herself, looked on in a reserved way—as she had done with King Arthur, years before.

I now read French (largely Dumas) and long Italian romances of the Risorgimento by Guerrazzi, and Manzoni: and began to teach myself Latin, looking out Caesar's words laboriously from an old tattered dictionary. What started this I cannot think, for there was no compulsion on us to learn anything at all. I read and loved George Sand's *Consuelo*—which one could never possibly tackle again at a later age. The romantic and medieval have left me with a taste for old fortresses and 'Gothic' scenery; and my enjoyment of the eighteenth century and the 'civilized' life is comparatively recent.

My father now stayed in England altogether. Some of his money had been swallowed by our Moloch factory and of course could not be retrieved. Various people tried to arrange matters amicably, but it was all wretched, and my mother—like my grandmother before her—was "impossible to help". The factory was a nightmare; and so was Mario. He bullied us till we hated him; he was like the old man of the sea. We made efforts to extract my mother from his clutches, if only for a short time, now and then. She was to go with two friends of her Paris days to the Abruzzi: he arrived, uninvited, to join the party, which broke up painfully and soon. Again, Viva Jeyes lured my mother for a few weeks' holiday in the Alps. She appealed to all their old friendship, and my mother set out with a gleam of her old sprightly delight. We had Mario upon us like a storm-wind within a week of her absence; he sent her a factory-problem-telegram and got her back before a fortnight was out. Even at this time, when all our lives were dislocated, my mother never recognized her own feelings: she thought of it as business and the emancipation of woman; and went on serenely secure in a technical morality, so that I have looked with suspicion on technical moralities ever since.

The third effort to shake off Mario still remains like a gloomy little island in my memory. We had long been promised a visit to Florence and had extracted a solemn word from her that he was not to come (we made no secret of our feelings). The day before leaving, my mother told us we must put up with it, for he insisted on coming. Just that and no more. I think I disliked Florence ever after; the Pitti, the Bargello, even the picture of the Annunciation on the hill, are mixed up with Mario. We longed to go to a real opera, for I had seen *Rigoletto* in Turin and had told Vera about it and she had never been to one at all; but Mario said we would not understand opera and switched us over to *The Belle of New York*—which was unintelligible to us. The last picture of that miserable holiday is a brown-papered pension bedroom where, while Mario had taken my mother to some theatre, Vera and I sobbed the matter out in each other's arms.

In the autumn of 1906 Mary Androutzos took one of her little villas at Massa in pine woods close to the sea, and we travelled there with her and Contessina. The villa was just vacated by nuns, and when we arrived we thought the floor was dark brown, but it turned out to be a living carpet of fleas, which they possibly had accepted as a mortification: it took us three days to clean. Otherwise it was a happy place: we bought figs oozing with honey, seven for a penny, and paid one lira a day for as many grapes as we liked—a woman with bare feet and lovely walk came carrying them in a basket on her head, whenever we called her from the farm near by.

Contessina was to leave us, and returned to Dronero, but we continued through the autumn in a new villa on a hill-slope just outside Massa town; its garden was laced with orange trees and small walls and vine pergolas on pillars. We were very happy.

Even here there was an atmosphere of constant turmoil owing to the three or four feuds Aunt Mary used to carry on simultaneously; but she did it in a cheerful way, and her accounts of her battles were always gay to listen to. She had an old lady called Miss Leigh Smith staying with maid and companion, a charming old lady, sister of Barbara Bodichon, a founder of Girton College. She was white-haired, angular and dignified, and spoke familiarly about Tennyson and Browning so that I sat listening for hours. Every afternoon she hired an open carriage and drove into the country, and took us with her, flattered but sedate, and secretly glad if there were enough guests to make it necessary for us to sit beside the coachman.

During this short stay we again became a little anglicized. Aunt Mary taught us a few of the things which Contessina should have taught and never did—how to be neat and clean and look after our things, the elements of being what is called a lady, I suppose. We returned to Dronero travelling alone for the first time, were put into the wrong half of the train, and found ourselves at Genoa at midnight with no money. We chose the Bristol Hotel at random among the gold-braided caps at the station, and telegraphed: an answer came to take the next train on. We had no money and were shy, and could not even pay our bill. With Vera in support I asked to see the manager. I remember how difficult it was to get the words out, to explain. But he was all kindness, and the awful moment was over. Money, tickets, were provided: and the first independent journey securely ended.

When we reached Dronero Contessina was either leaving or had left. My mother had no money of her own; apart from sixteen hundred pounds of my father's, swallowed by the factory, she could only get more by asking, and that she would not do. We had been poor for a long time because of this reluctance, but now she decided to live entirely on what she earned, and we were going to be very poor indeed. Contessina, with all the delicacy of her feelings, was almost more inefficient than anyone I have ever known. She had to be dispensed with. We took a modest four-roomed house in a vineyard, and one maid, and at the age of thirteen I was given the housekeeping to do, on ten pounds a month, including wages and all.

I was delighted to be allowed to help in some way in the heroic struggle of the factory which was, and continued to be, in the most appalling deep water. I spent endless thought in improving our one dining-sitting room, sewing linen, and struggling with the cost of living. There were frequent domestic crises, because we could only pay so little to the cook, and I must have lacked authority with my short curls and short skirts. In the following spring I remember a blue cotton frock which could no longer be made quite straight and flat in front; and I looked in the glass and suddenly thought the picture pretty. But life was too real and earnest for dallying. My French was now good, and I was struggling with Catullus, with a dictionary and a few hints from Mario, who came for meals (also included in the £10) and sat with us in the evening: his head was massaged by Vera—for he was distressed by signs of incipient baldness—while my mother sewed. We had my grandmother for a time, and liked having her with us through all our solitary day. My mother cared little for her and once told me so; in most living creatures, a close relationship between parents and grown-up children seems to be unnatural. I remember thinking with gentleness on the happy difference between my mother and me. Mario was the only blot. When my aunt joined us, and Mario began trampling on her also, there were storms and she and Granny left. I am glad to say that Vera and I kept our sense of proportion through this time in rather a remarkable way. Our education was simply forgotten: *work* was to be our household god, and only people who worked like ourselves were of any use at all: and as nobody else *did* work like ourselves, the helpful part of the world was reduced to the four of us: Vera and I used to call it the Pedestal in private.

BROKEN HILL RANCH
CRESTON B.C.
14 December, 1921.

Dear Freya,

... Tom Leaman is going for the post this evening as it is too cold for me to turn out; something below zero; unhappily no snow on the ground.

Well: I got the will fixed up all right and it is deposited with my bankers here. (I hope they may perhaps look at it in the light of a credit.) I enclose you a letter covering its receipt from my lawyers so you have all the necessary information at hand when the time comes.

I thought at one time of adding a line or two, saying that: (I tell you now instead) "Further I left to you the memory of the most delightful friendship and more which has subsisted between us all these years, which you captured from me at the age of about six months, just when your fist was big enough to grip my little finger and we took walks together (at least I did the walking) round the lanes at Yelfords, you gathering the flowers from the hedges as you spied them. Delightful days. Delightful memories to look back to these rather drab days. A wonderful new experience and a new relationship established, the charm of which one may say "passeth all understanding". So of that you may be assured. ...

With all love and good wishes, ever the same old

PIPS

8

Two English Interludes. 1907-1908

DURING the Dronero years of our childhood we paid two visits to England, in 1907 and 1908. Both had a lasting influence.

We travelled alone from Turin for the first time in 1907 in charge of the guard, who helped us through the icy customs of Modane. In Paris he handed us to a grim woman with a yellow moiré ribbon across her chest inscribed: 'Protection de la Jeune Fille'. She took us to a little 'laiterie', where labourers and drivers were eating an early breakfast while the streets were washed down with hoses, and then put us into our train, taking name and address 'in case you drown in the Channel, to tell your parents'. It was depressing, for we had been looking forward to Paris by ourselves.

A hot, long and lovely summer on Dartmoor followed. At the time, with a priggish feeling of responsibility, I wished myself back looking after my mother and the housekeeping; but now the memories of those months in England are very dear. We had our cousin Mary (the eldest of the girls who had been in Dronero) and we picnicked in our house, lovely but forlorn. It seemed to have become smaller and the garden larger, with a neglected feeling of the Sleeping Beauty about it all. Honeysuckle clasped the veranda pillars; the lake was thick with lilies, red and white. My father would come walking up with three or four of them in his hand, to float in a green bowl on the table. He dug out new ponds to swim in and islands to amuse us, where the South Teign ran through our land; and we camped for many weeks on its banks, sleeping on a mattress of dried bracken in an old caravan, where the river dropped through woods from pool to pool. Buzzards lived there. We bathed naked in the early morning under the little waterfalls; or raced barefoot from rock to rock (the rule was never to step on a rock that touched the shore, and Mary always fell in). We could run along almost at full speed, never hesitating for a leap; my godfather later on described me, with the eyes of affection, as a "beautiful leaping creature". I first noticed here how the sound of water is like the talk of human voices, and would sometimes wake in the night and listen, thinking that a crowd of people were coming through the woods, like Comus and his crew. All really good sounds are composite—even the song of birds which is helped and varied by the air it floats in; and the noise of crowds, and voices of wind, with sobs and lighter squeaks and whispers in it; the single human being's speech, made out of all his ancestors and all his past; and the sounds of water, moorland streams and alpine brooks, the waves on sand or shingle, or the drone of the water wheels of Hama.

I read and read continuously through this summer and the following few years as I have seldom had the freedom to do since. Indeed what happened to me between the ages of sixteen and seventeen is vague in my memory in comparison with books. I read Plato and found, and still find, in the words of Socrates the answer to all doubts as to a life after death. I read Darwin, his *Life*, and *Voyage of the Beagle,* and the *Origin of Species*, and dabbled with a little experimental bed of seedlings—which pleased my father, who was interested in these things. I used to collect the fly-eating sundew plants in bogs and feed them with pin-points of raw meat, which they devoured in a few days—and once offered one of them a drop of whisky, which turned its sticky antennæ temporarily white. One day my father took me to luncheon with Eden Phillpotts in Torquay, who, hearing about the *Origin of Species*, gave me a book called *A Picture Book of Evolution*; it began with the stars and came down gradually to man, and the laws of creation filled my thoughts, and wound themselves into the summer murmurs of the woods. I read enormously, picking at random: Peacock, Fanny Burney, Spenser, Browning, Hazlitt and Milton, Jane Austen and the *Castle of Otranto* and *Frankenstein*. I read them on a rock in the middle of the stream, surrounded by brown pools, where the moss is harsh, like velvet that has been washed and dried. Among other things, a notion of sex came, evolved by pure reason, out of the books on evolution: I remember thinking the whole thing impossible and being slowly and reluctantly convinced; and no one then or afterwards ever troubled to inform us more specifically.

I was still delicate. My father moved my bed into the big window of our room, to let me watch the sunrise or the moonlight. The house, in an orphaned way, ran itself. There were only two maids, and one gardener in the huge garden, and I took no interest in either. I was only fourteen and would have been incapable of coping with an English home: and my heart was passionately with my mother in Dronero. My father must have felt it constantly and was often gloomy. Only in the early morning, when I slipped out to walk over the garden with him, would he seem happy—like Adam remembering his paradise for some moments in the fresh dewy light.

A few relations came but they looked on us as barbarians; and we thought them dull, and disliked the way they spoke about our life in Italy as if it were an Outer Darkness. My father never did this. Everyone knew and liked him, but of course no one called on a man alone. He played tennis with us, on grass honeycombed by molehills, so that a new artfulness was brought into the game—and he made Vera's life at it a burden, for she held her racquet with such agony and stiffness that it made her almost as immovable as Lot's wife, and my father was extraordinarily explosive, when it came to sports or games. I think he ruined my nerve for riding permanently by asking me why I was not jumping ditches which my horse refused to take. He got a village tailor to arrange his old tweed breeches to cover us. They came up to the armpits and I think our first self-consciousness was born when we noticed a lawn full of orthodoxly-dressed people turn round as one, to watch our arrival for tea.

We came to know more people as the autumn drew on with cubbing and then hunting: I rarely went, being absorbed in books, and much as I love it now I have always felt that a serious drawback to riding is the amount of dressing and undressing it entails. Vera never missed a day, and returned with pink cheeks and her thick pigtails wet through. She would have been happy to remain. But we were back in Dronero for the winter, with no tangible novelty in our life except my habit of reading English poetry and of writing poor poetry of my own. I had bought Grote's *History of Greece*, which opened the gates of Hellas for ever; and I wrote a few little prose fables: I found them years later, carefully kept among my father's things in a brown cotton case I stitched for him. I wrote short stories, clumsily, and thought vaguely of authorship later on: with little promise except a delight in words, which I felt and still feel, as other people feel music or colour.

Early in 1908 we travelled again to Ford Park. My father's solitude there had been broken by his new sister-in-law, whom we did not know. She came with all her family, and my mother, rather unfairly, resented it extremely and sent us to evict her. This seemed natural to me at the time, though strange to look back on now.

We travelled once more by ourselves, but this time the railway guard took a less paternal interest, and invited me to rest in his little room. I was luckily not tired at all, and said so, and have often recognized later the baffled look that followed our extreme natural sincerity. I had never any want of resourcefulness, and once at Chambéry, when in the middle of the night a man got into the second class carriage, where I was stretched along a seat asleep, and slowly pushed me into a corner by stroking my feet, I grew so angry that I devised a defence with my hat pin, which met his outstretched hand: he retreated, and I advanced, holding it like a battering-ram from under the protection of my pillow, until, in the course of half an hour or so, he was sitting back in his corner again, and I was again outstretched. It all happened without words in the darkness, and he helped me with my luggage next day with a respectful air.

In 1908 we were certainly met in London, probably by Viva Jeyes, but I have forgotten all except the end of the journey, a long winter's drive brushing the hedges of lanes in the bus from Exeter. It was the last day of an election. The dusk deepened between the hedges, and the bus, more and more empty, stopped at every pub, where the results of the voting were being hotly discussed. At last we became the only passengers and it was ten or eleven at night when we reached Chagford. We went to old Perrott, who was a great fisherman and kept horses. He warmed us by his fire while the trap was harnessed. The winter was in the middle of its coldest snap, the hills so iced over that we had to walk most of the three miles. When we reached Ford Park my father was just going to bed. He had no idea that we were arriving, and came down in a flannel dressing-gown looking furious.

The new aunt was installed with a small infant. She was a bony woman of middle age, with calculating eyes. Perhaps she thought of herself as a home-maker for my father in his loneliness, and there is no doubt that we were prejudiced against her; but she received us without a grain of kindness and as if we were intruders. She had taken all our toys and given them to her children, and after a few days, when my father was away on some business, remarked that we had better leave. She little thought that we would take her at her word. I was now angry with a cold deep anger, and wrote to my father and told him all about it; again got old Perrott and the trap; and went off with Vera and a suit-case to an old friend of both parents, the daughter of the rector at North Bovey. She listened, full of sympathy and kindness. I rather think she may have communicated with my father. Anyway he came to fetch us. We drove back— another long night drive through the lanes. As I told him the story he said "Oh God" and suddenly sobbed in the darkness. I embraced him, weeping also. Some idea of his unhappiness pierced through me for the first time, and the feeling of being ranged against him never returned. Next morning the new aunt and I faced each other in his presence; my anger was so intense that it had reached a *frozen* heat; I found to my surprise that she crumpled up before me, and I felt like a terrier with a rat, calm and deadly. My father said nothing while I was there, and she left the same day.

The rector's daughter at North Bovey drove over to see us fairly often after this, with George and two grey horses who could never be kept out late: a message would come when tea was barely over to say that, "George says, Miss, that it'll be cold for the hosses," and Miss Thornton obediently rose to go. She asked us to North Bovey to stay, and I remember a happy summer week-end reading Cardinal Wolsey's Life in the shadow of a beech tree on her lawn. Her father was a hard-riding old hunting parson well-known and liked in all the county. He managed his parish and his large family of daughters with genial absolutism, and when only one out of the seven daughters remained at home, continued to order the same huge joints of meat as before, so that one sat at luncheon at his table in the shadow of beef, as at an altar where the sacrifice was far larger than the congregation. I lost the old man's good opinion by riding in breeches: for he came out to his porch some years later to help me on to my pony, and I was already half mounted and saw him standing with his white hair and fine old face, watching my departure with a bewildered air, as if it were the world rolling away while he stood still.

My mother's sense of values was now for some time strangely deranged. She began to write asking me to pack this or that of the things in the house which belonged to her, to bring to Dronero. It was not done all at once, but every little while a new letter would come with an afterthought—a new list. She was unimaginative about people at a distance, and never had the faintest idea of what horror this meant. I used to screw myself up to talk to my father, usually in the garden, or after dinner by the fire, and present these dreadful lists. It was bitterly painful to both, and I think the sight of my misery prevented his feeling any anger. When the ordeal was over I crept to bed, my feet cold as ice, and Vera would slink in to cover me with blankets. The pictures, copper and brass bowls, books, etc., were packed away and the house began to show bare places. I never can bear to think of this time, though it may have been useful later on. It made me realize that one can make oneself do almost *anything* in this world, however painful—and not so many people have been unhappy enough to understand this: but the cost of the learning was far too great. Many years later a feeling of resentment would come over me when I thought of it, as of an advantage taken of my ignorance and devotion, and I realized how dangerous it is to take from those who blindly love you *all* that they are ready to give. At the time there was never a question: I went on stubbornly packing the things away, with misery in my heart.

We were back in Dronero by the summer. We found Mary there. She had come to do work in the factory and had been at it a year, and was growing more and more unhappy. She was docile, untidy, dreamy and gentle, and would have done well in an office run on very methodical lines with a watchful eye upon her. The factory was a sort of tornado, where only a very steady sailor could keep his feet. Mario used to bully or tease and Mary came home in tears: some time during that autumn or winter she left. Mario began to talk about time wasted on education: the best training, he said, is *practical*—to type, to keep accounts, to run an office—better, he said, with a look at my shelf, than to read Grote's *History of Greece*. He talked in a loud way that was never meant for conversation and waited for no reply. Unfortunately, I was ready to be convinced, and was taken on in my sixteenth year in Mary's stead, with £1 10s. a month in wages.

I have sometimes wondered what our life might have been we had remained in England now. I was beginning to grow into girlhood: for the first time I took pleasure in a little green tussore gown; and I must have been rather attractive, though plain. I was not a bit shy at that time, and so entranced with life in general that that alone must have been engaging. On our way out to Italy we spent a short time in London and it was like a little sprouting of wings. Viva Jeyes had no room for us. We stayed with an old lady, Miss Francks, in Elm Tree Road, fat and serene and kind over a past full of love and human interest and understanding. Every morning we walked in Regent's Park with Harry Jeyes; he took out his rough terrier and an airedale, and talked about politics and books and the world. Even two years before, when I was ill and only thirteen, he used to write charming grown-up letters that went to my heart. He was a brilliant man, assistant editor of the *Standard*, and I believe practically ran it; all sorts of politicians came to him for advice. He and Viva were curiously assorted; she never suspected the existence of his intellectual world, but they were extremely happy. She had a delicate beauty, with hair like fine gold, and wore the sort of gowns that we had forgotten. I remember what a surprise it was to see Harry put his arm round her one evening and seat her on his knee: we had never seen a caress between grown-up people before.

We spent all our days with Viva and she gave a party. Sir Chartres Biron was there, with a subtle air of conferring a benefit by his presence but of being too well-bred to make it felt; Anthony Hope, and a wife all paint and feathers; Violet Hunt with the profile of a pre-Raphaelite gipsy and great blue eyes; Cope Cornford who became a great friend later on, and W. P. Ker who was to mean more to me than any other person for many years of my life.

And now this was all shut away again.

9

End of Childhood. 1909-1911

My mother believed, and we believed with her, that in Dronero she was rescuing us from the narrow life of the English country and providing a civilized continental atmosphere: I think it gave her immeasurable joy to maintain us by her own efforts. When she came home at night she would cut out our clothes—even suits—and sit over the sewing-machine running up the seams with a tired face: and we wore these garments loyally for years, with only a very slowly dawning perception of peculiar tightnesses and bulges. My mother, when they were brought to her notice, put the blame with characteristic confidence on to our own hips or waists or shoulders. She worked all day like a slave, and was responsible, I am sure, for such success as the factory achieved.

When I worked there I entered very little into its general affairs. I soon saw that I must stake out a field of my own or be submerged, and I took over the correspondence, kept other people out of it, learnt that I must do things myself and not wait to be told, and—unlike Mary—never wept. My mother gave me a piece of advice:

"If you are wrongly blamed," she said, "never say that it was not your fault: let it be discovered later, when people are calm, and you will get the credit for your silence."

It was excellent advice, though not what she followed herself. Of her hard struggle, triumphs, difficulties—of all her real life during this time, I cannot write, for we scarcely knew it. We heard about it, but it was in Mario's ceaseless monotone which slid over us like the sound of water: my mother's voice was scarcely ever heard. In winter we dressed, or at any rate breakfasted, by lamplight; went off at half-past seven, and all came back to lunch. I worked only half the day in the office, but my mother stayed till late, and then talked shop with Mario for the rest of the evening. She asked what we had been doing, but we discovered this to be a matter of form and gave up answering the question, and no one noticed. On Sunday mornings only did we see her alone, and we lay for an hour or so on her bed with her arms about us, feeling united against the world. In the whole town we had one friend at this time, an Italian girl who had written to ask if we might not meet and know each other. Mario made a great bluster and said: "One must not get involved", but for once my mother had not supported him and we were allowed to go for walks, with mutterings and a feeling of precariousness whenever the poor girl's name was mentioned. We soon came to know her sister—a beautiful creature married to an officer of the *Alpini*. Even Mario's own relatives we were not allowed to see much of, and they came very little. They had a family house in the plain—square and thick-walled and vaulted like a fortress, with farms attached to it on either side. Five buildings were joined so that there was one wall only, rising from a cool uneven country road. We sometimes went there, and loved the dark rooms and ceilings painted with lace canopies and roses; the four-post beds curtained with red damask and the atmosphere of daily business in the farms; especially when the threshing machines droned in their yellow dust and everyone helped to feed them, tossing the waisted sheaves into their mouths, till late at night: or when the cocoons of silkworms were gathered from the faggots where they had settled to sleep, and the women sat in long rows singing while they pulled at them and filled their baskets, in a sickly sweet smell I still remember.

Mario bought a motor car and we began to know all the mountain valleys well. They come down like spokes of a fan on to the Piedmontese plain, and all are beautiful, deep in snow in winter, with passes kept open by the snow-plough, or impassable till May or June. Each has flowers of its own, sometimes unknown in the neighbouring valley—sheets of snowdrops or narcissi. The little towns that sit there all have red roofs and cobble streets. We came to stop in many accidentally, as the car was an early model made by a friend and often broke down; and the Sundays would have been delightful if we had not been bullied all the time. Mario turned everything into a conducted tour, and there was always misery at the start. Instead of the happy leisure of the year before, a sort of tropical storm swept over us between breakfast and the time of departure. And our sins of the week were discovered and the untidiness of cupboards laid bare. My mother was working far too hard and had begun to be strained and nervous. Vera and I at this time were delighted when Sunday was over, and we returned to six days of almost unbroken solitude except at meals.

Early in 1910 we moved into a new home of Mario's own. It was an old mill, called *Tetti Camosci*, and it lay in flat fields between the river and the town. He had bought it for the mill race which would give him the electric power he needed. The water ran under the house, making it bitterly cold and filling its corridors with a rushing noise as if it were a train. A dynamo was installed, and gave power to the factory and light to the house; and I learned to turn the power on or off, and loved the feeling of managing those huge machines, willing and shining as the necks of horses. The house was very long and narrow, and the green water went under with a smooth curve. It flowed down between willows yellow in winter, from a distance where mountains closed the valley in the west. Gradually my mother painted, beautified and furnished all the empty rooms, but they never had the charm of our old villa on the hill and I still feel repulsion towards them—filled with so many unhappy things. I continued to do the housekeeping: Vera had been supposed to take it over when I began to work in the factory, but this caused so much misery all round that she was soon exonerated by general consent, and acquired a reputation for being non-domestic which I often envied her.

During all this time we resented the factory, and the continuous presence of Mario who was never away. But in my seventeenth year a change came. He looked upon me as his wife in the natural course of the future, and began to take a particular interest, shown by increasingly long disquisitions about himself. When I went to shut the front door after him at night he would keep me longer and longer. I knew nothing of what all this meant: no one now would believe how innocent we were: but as the months went by it began to dawn on me that I was expected to marry him: I thought it my mother's wish, and tried hard to think it mine also.

At sixteen one is awakening very delicately to love—a thing ethereal and elusive as a rainbow. I lived in a sort of languor: the lengthening days, the boughs of blossom against the sky, the long shadows in the cool grass, filled me with happiness that got itself mixed with sadness, so that I hardly knew which was which. I lay long hours on a grassy shelf of the vineyard, with cherry blossom hanging over me and the sweet scent of budding vines about me; the Peloponnesian War would drift away in dreams: the music of the Alpini's band from the square of the town across the stream seemed to open out rapturous, intangible, inexpressible distances. Into these thoughts, where Pericles and Alcibiades wandered vaguely, I gradually tried to introduce the concrete presence of Mario. I never succeeded very well, for I really did not like him; but he was the only man in all our field of vision, and I was awakening like a plant or flower, taking whatever sun was there. He was a terribly jealous man, and I think felt my remoteness, and would be angry or sulky for a few days. This made me miserable: we were reconciled: I had been "inattentive"; I tried to become as negative as he wished; it was a whole year of fluttering feelings. There was never the happiness of two equal human beings meeting, the only happiness in love, if men would know it.

As we drove one day through the lanes and the cornfields I remember that I thought of my life lying before me in that Piedmontese landscape, with children growing up and my mother and him to care for. I followed it with tender feelings into a long long vista of age, looking at the back of his head with its thin dark hair. But on other days I felt more and more that I *could* not. I wondered if it would break my mother's heart if I refused. My mother was my passion, an object of adoration: when she came home I took off her shoes, fetched her gown, watched the tired lines on her face with an agony of tenderness. She had the gift of inspiring this ardent love, and took it without surprise.

I made up my mind to ask her about Mario but always she was too tired to be spoken to, or Mario was there. At last, when this had been going on for over a year, and I was seventeen, a chance came. We had all gone for two days to a little inn in a mountain valley, and she and I shared a bedroom; we lay in a huge bed, in sheets of rough linen, smelling very clean. A barrel organ was playing in the yard below and peasants were dancing, and the moon came in at the window. I asked her if she really very much wanted me to marry Mario. It was a complete surprise. He had made love to me for over a year and she had never noticed! I felt astonished, but relieved too at the freedom it gave me. Some weeks later Mario came to join Vera and me in a long walk and he asked:

"Would you like us always to be like this—together?"

"No," said I, nothing if not truthful. "I think once a week would be enough."

He became very silent for the rest of the walk. The factory must be worrying him, I thought, and tried all I could to amuse him. As I undressed that night, it suddenly came to me that I had been refusing a proposal of marriage: a surprising feeling of relief showed how right I had been.

Mario's rejection came at one of those moments when the decisions of one's life, that have been working up gradually, are made—so quietly, one is not even aware of making them. My work in the factory came to an end and I had added a correspondence class for the London Matriculation to my housekeeping. I had a hunger for learning which seemed to come entirely of itself. Many years afterwards Vera told me that she could never forgive my mother for not educating her: she liked reading and showed a genius for modelling, first in breadcrumbs and then in wax sent by my father; but we were never made, or even actively helped, to do anything. For myself, I am grateful now for this emptiness of our youth, and especially for the habit of solitude, which is so hard later to acquire, and is to the spirit what a private room is to the mind, giving it space to grow. But unlike my sister I was gregarious by nature, and needed no encouragement. After the discovery that my mother would not mind my not marrying Mario, I set my heart on going to a summer university in Grenoble. My father alone could pay for such a scheme, and refused. I suppose he thought we were foreign enough already; we spoke English with a decided accent. Anyway he refused, and I turned to the correspondence course and struggled with the elements of algebra and English grammar. Our childhood was over.

My father too had made decisions. We joined him for a month or so at Massa by the sea, and he was already planning to leave England and go to Canada: he was silent and depressed. We had one or two happy expeditions—to Lucca and to a half-ruined castle in the hills. But the season was late and everything was sad; cold, long waves rolled like shrouded bodies on an empty shore; the only cheerfulness was Stella, our cook, who had an illegitimate baby of which she was so openly proud that it puzzled me. Immorality loomed large in our minds just then, because Mary Androutzos had adopted a niece brought up in the tropics and this girl, aged fifteen, after several years of care, let a sailor into the house who stole the silver. I was therefore surprised to find Stella not a monster, but warm and living and likeable; and concluded, apologetically as it were, that babies are attractive in themselves, however come by.

It is extraordinary now to realize how Victorian my moral reactions always were: and it sometimes makes me wonder whether these conventions are not more fundamental and less artificial than we take them to be. At thirteen I had longed to be good, and kept a note-book for my faults--about three or four a day as far as I can remember: it was a poor experiment, for Vera told me later that it made me intolerable. Now there was Stella's baby, a shock to all respectability. And then I was eighteen and we visited Herbert Young in Asolo, and the surprises of grown-up life came all together. Vera and I went very early in the year. Of the three places we chiefly lived in, Asolo is the only one that has no sad memories. We came into the hall, with a view through to the garden beyond; Herbert was there with his arms open to receive us, and every unhappiness vanished. We had seen him all these years at Ford Park, and at Dronero, where he came for our sake and listened to Mario's talk about himself with a glum expression, and suddenly, in private—with a fork or something in his hand to gesticulate more forcibly—exclaimed: "I don't *like* that man." But we had not been to Asolo since our childhood and this visit was almost the best of all. Contessina lived next door, teaching some American children, and we had a joyful reunion. Snowdrops and hepaticas were out; the garden was lovely; and it was blissful to be in a house where every human being was given *living room* so to say. We all became politicians. Herbert received the *Spectator* on Saturday and the *Nation* on Monday, and was liberal through the week and conservative at week-ends. He had his pianola and played Chopin's waltzes on it for us to dance to: I made him give a small dance. I wore a pale-blue frock of my mother's, soft wool and white lace down to the ground; and had put up my hair. There were various American families, and everyone friendly. I read all day—the book that ever remained with me was *Marius the Epicurean*. I read history at this time—Gibbon, Buckle, Lecky, a dreary scientist called Lubbock, and tried Herbert Spencer, but he was too heavy even at that age to go down.

The American neighbours were called Sullivan, and are still friends to-day. "They have had a terrible scene in their house," Contessina told us. "Mr. P——(a guest) was seen by his wife kissing her secretary." We were to dine there that evening, and I saw with a shock that I was placed next to this man.

Unconscious of the reprobation with which I regarded him, he made himself particularly agreeable. I forgot how wicked he was, I thought him charming. I realized it afterwards with pangs of shame. What could there be in me, I asked anxiously, that could take pleasure in such company? I prayed a prayer of penitence, and knelt outside my bed, instead of inside it as usual. Looking at that poor little thing across the stretched years I cannot help feeling how much happier it is to enjoy the reprobates as I do now.

LETTER FROM VIVA JEYES

11 *GROVE END ROAD,*
LONDON,
16 *July,* 1910.

Dear Freya, dear *budding genius,*

Please forgive my long silence, but I know you will because you understand what it is to have more letters to get through than it is humanly possible to accomplish! Also I am now able to enclose you the long awaited letter from that excellent critic who, I must now tell you, mislaid your precious MS when he was moving house and only discovered it after much hunting through his books and papers. The letter is so interesting that I do not like merely to quote from it and therefore send it on to you, believing that you will not be unduly flattered by its praise or cast down by its strictures! and that you *may,* just out of feminine contrariness, in this instance accept and follow the advice contained in it. I thanked Mr. Low [later Sir Sidney Low] and told him that when you were in London *next year* I would bring you to see him.

I also met your other friend, Prof. Ker, at a party, and reminded him that he had never written as he said he would. He made no excuses! but asked after your studies and feared you found studying alone very difficult. He is a pessimistic gentleman. I told him that you *did* find it difficult but that you were going to succeed.

My writing is more than normally bad as my hand is over-tired. I have addressed hundreds of envelopes in the last week—and written dozens of letters—usually up to midnight—and Harry says I have passed most of my days hanging on to the telephone! We had a very exciting meeting (Anti-Suffrage) in a big hall—Queen's Hall—last Monday—and the Suffragettes interrupted and screamed and behaved foolishly, but there was much enthusiasm on our side. To-day our Men's League hold a meeting in Trafalgar Square to which I am *not* going. Next week I give an Anti-Suffrage party so you see I am busy. Papa is better and going down to stay with Mrs. Olivier and the children next week in the country.

Much love to you both from

VIVA.

N.B. I fear Mr. Low is often sarcastic—what do you think of "Budding Genius"?

TO MY MOTHER

ST. MARGARET'S BAY HOTEL,
Nr. DOVER,

28 *Dec.,* 1910.

My own Mother,

It was a great joy to have your dear letter—the best of all Xmas presents for me. I wish I could think of you with less work on your hands. My dear one—another year we must get away somewhere and have a real holiday together and you must have nothing in the world to think of but amusement.

We had a lovely dance here and Mr. Beaumont and I invented a new one-step: I offended one elderly gentleman by cutting his dance and had to be so sweet and amiable to pacify him: but there were no programmes and I always had about seven dances engaged ahead, so that it was very confusing—the real reason however was that a more attractive partner had come along! . . .

We are returning on Tuesday. Do you think I shall be able to have some money? Mine is all gone alas!

A ball dress will be the loveliest present: I shall want one badly, and I think blue or white. Viva says I might be going to a naval dance at Chatham later on, and in that case it is better to have white so as not to clash with the uniforms.

I think I had better have it made by Miss Reid: it really suits me better than the ready-made and the price is about the same.

The Lows are still here! Elsie is rather silly, but he is very nice and a good talker although he talks too much. He enjoyed it very much and would stay on till Tuesday so as to be at another little dance we are having on Monday, but Elsie says he must be in town—it is always women who have this painful and unnecessary sense of duty!

Mr. Beaumont went out for a walk yesterday and came back with four ladies who had apparently fallen on him in the dark on the steep little pathway up the cliff: their cab had deposited them at the top with one heavy bag and a little Pom. dog and they had been wandering about the downs in search of a hotel. It turns out that they are friends of the Lows, so that we are a happy family party now. Mr. Beaumont is really very reprehensible: he flirts in the most outrageous manner and singles out all the prettiest girls to talk to; on Tuesday he is going to meet his wife and tell her what a quiet dull place St. Margaret's is.

Love to my dearest, from her

FREYA

10

The Last of Dartmoor. 1911-1912

THE summer of 1911 was filled with a great happiness, for my parents were reconciled. How it was done I cannot remember, but our life, so trickling and divided, seemed to be flowing again in one caressing stream. Perhaps the best function of parenthood is to teach the young creature to love with *safety*, so that it may be able to venture unafraid when later emotion comes; the thwarting of the instinct to love is the root of all sorrow and not sex only but divinity itself is insulted when it is repressed. To disapprove, to condemn—the human soul shrivels under barren righteousness. My parents through all their divisions had not killed or perverted this fountain within us. I watched them walking up and down at Ford Park, side by side, talking, and a sort of cloud of tenderness spread from me towards them, so that it seemed strange they should not actually feel it, for it was stronger in me and more vivid than all the world outside. My mother was young again, and lovely to look at, with leisure in her heart and on her face to receive the affection she had scarcely had the time to notice in all these years. She gave a party; the whole county came; it was a sort of Prodigal's celebration, and everyone showed how fond of her they were. My father was not happy so much as contented: it would have needed time and much affection to heal it all; and he was now leaving England and selling Ford Park, and his place in Canada was bought as far as I can remember: but I think it gave him great comfort at his going. Bygones never are bygones: they have become a part of ourselves; and perhaps it was lucky that the reconciling came so soon before a parting. Yet my mother was surprised and baffled to find a sort of reserve where she had expected to take up the threads as if unbroken, for she had a genius for forgetting her own mistakes as well as other people's, which is in its way a form of generosity.

I was to stay with Viva Jeyes in the autumn to work for my matriculation at Bedford College, and I spent the summer months before term started with my father at Ford Park, separated from Vera for the first time. The aunt and the cousins were there, and some Canadians to whom my father had lent money in his unlucky way, never to be seen again: and Grannie came and worked with me at German.

The chief pleasure of the summer was a family of neighbours who had recently moved into the moorland estate of Thornworthy beyond ours. Our one road ended on a naked hill where their uncle had in his day perched a small citified house and self-conscious garden over which the south-west gales and the encroaching moors and growing ivies had gradually cast their charm. The old people were nonconformist coal merchants. They were honest, fearless and delightful, and looked with amusement at their four children all bothering about sophistications they found unnecessary. The children had been sent to good schools and were Church of England. It took them years to change over from town to "county" and chapel to church, and I watched the process, and realized disgustedly what a lot of unhappiness is caused by snobbishness in the English country. People would sit for years in the scattered properties of our neighbourhood patiently waiting to be called on. My father liked the son, a young man in the Irish Rifles. He was so smart that I thought it a privilege to be of the party merely so as to look at him.

Dorothy, the elder girl, used to come out riding with me before breakfast. I had a pony called Whiskey, who tossed anyone else off out of jealousy and devotion, if I happened to be on some other mount within sight. We raced our little mares to a lather and crept into the stables from the back, unseen by my father, who was strict about bringing horses in slowly.

Dorothy was a socialist and wanted to be a sanitary inspector. Philanthropy and social services still seem desolately arid to me, but they took on rosy colours in that enchanted summer and dressed themselves in the loveliness of the warm moors, brown before the heather bells come out. This was my first friendship near my own age; the first time I talked with someone who looked at the world as I did, and there was no subject we dared not tackle. We would ride quite far, skirting the bogs, avoiding Princetown and the gangs of convict faces: and would canter by the old avenues and monoliths of graves, and Grimspound with its Stone Age gate and walls and houses, tethering our ponies to the pillars where the Britons must have tied theirs up before us. In shallow valleys below us, tin mines where the Phoenicians traded still spat out gravel and water with old and clumsy wheels. Sometimes a convict escaped and the Prince-town searchlights swept the moors at night; we would keep a look-out as we rode—and I left the larder door open without my father's knowledge, thinking of the hunted creature alone in the tussocks of the bogs.

This year, when the cubbing began in autumn, I enjoyed it. My father got the Chagford tailor to make a smart black riding coat for me and white buckskin breeches: I was proud of them and unconscious of being remarkable in the hunting field, except when I heard people asking: "Is it a girl or a boy?" I believe my father liked to think of us as boys. The M.F.H. was a pleasant colonel who—I once heard someone say—"hunts as if he were a bishop", because he liked the inland country away from bogs: the foxes I am sure came to know this and retired to their central fastnesses when they felt tired, and we got few long runs. But cubbing is agreeable in itself: the fields are small, and one dallies about, training the young hounds, and it is all informal. I think those were some of the pleasantest mornings of my life.

Now and then we would go into Exeter, and buy books; now and then, very rarely, to Torquay; but most of the time was spent on the moors. My father made us an allowance of forty pounds a year. I overdrew mine by ten pounds or so and at last, after sleepless nights, made up my mind to tell him, and found him in his little chaos of a bedroom, his desk inches deep in papers. He pushed a small island among them to rest his cheque book on and write my debts off for me. It was almost as overwhelming as a revelation of omnipotence.

My father had decided to sell Ford Park to the Duchy of Cornwall. They did not buy it till 1912, but he had already found his land in Canada and he left at the end of this summer. An ancient tin mine in one of the moor farms, unusable since the days of the Phoenicians, had caused our land to be taxed under Lloyd George's law of 1909, for 'unexploited mineral wealth'. My father was a thoroughgoing Tory; England, he said, was given over to the Radicals; it would have been easy to appeal but he never thought of doing so; and the Liberal Government of the day uprooted him as all his years of solitude had not succeeded in doing.

The Duchy of Cornwall were not as good landlords as we were and put corrugated iron where we had kept the old thatch at great expense. Of course our four little farms never paid; but the tenants remembered my father, and how he sat up all night with a farmer's sick wife while her husband rode to fetch the doctor across the moors; they cherished his memory. Before he left we went together over all the moorland pieces of our land and chose a small plot, seven acres, where the hills folded one into another to a far distance, and a little private stream tumbled into a few yards of fishing on the Teign. This was kept out of the sale and I still have it. I have often been there since, staying at Thornworthy, and have walked through the woods where we camped, and where my father took me with him one afternoon when he placed my grandmother's ashes in a mossy cleft of rocks: no one was ever told the place but I. He was a pagan at heart, and practised the Christian virtues under other names. I never saw him in a church except at my sister's wedding. But when I last went to the moor, I found his name remembered everywhere; he seemed to become an integral part of the places he inhabited. The trees he planted now cover many miles and have changed the whole look of that region. The people who live in Scorhill, the earliest of our houses, told me that one day a storm pulled up a tall rare pine, and under its roots they found a horseshoe, placed by my father when he planted the little sapling.

We visited Ford Park once after his departure, before the final sale. My mother, with Vera, and Mario and his mother, all came over for the Christmas vacation after my first term in London, and a last and rather peculiar spurt of gaiety filled the neglected house. It had been taken for granted for some time that Mario would marry Vera; I think he wanted to hurry it on lest she should slip away from him as I had done; and my mother, who had been treated for years in a coldly casual way in Dronero, was pleased to show his relatives that he was marrying into a suitable family. So they all came over, like a foreign invasion.

It was a very funny Christmas. Mario, resilient like a small tough ball made of very thick leather, untrammelled by self-consciousness, tried to run the house-party as usual, but was swamped and gradually subdued by the accumulated ritual of English country life. We hired three hunters for the three weeks of our stay and took him out with us, blushing when he turned to strangers and remarked: "The dogs are barking," or things like that. When the pace grew hotter we left him to his fate: we were not going to spoil a good run for anyone, and pretended not to hear his calls, and Vera was more lighthearted than I about it. I can remember her emerging from a peat-hole where her horse had gone full in, covered with black bog from top to toe, and round-eyed with surprise over the fuss Mario was making. She was fearless both in swimming and riding: I went where she went, but always with a rather sick feeling inside me: but she would take anything that her horse would take. Her long heavy brown hair, which reached her knees, floated in the wind behind her, for no pins were ever found strong enough to hold its thick smooth coils. "Let's lose him," she said. We were miles from home after the hunt, on winter moors with a drizzle descending: Mario, a forlorn speck, calling faintly. We took care not to look round and cantered in happy solitude—and had to be painstakingly pleasant for some time after.

It all ended with a few days in London, showing the future mother-in-law shops and taking her to *The Miracle* one day and to *Fanny's First Play* the next. I did my best to translate them into Italian as we went along, and left her with a bewildered notion of English life.

In June I took the matriculation at South Kensington. Viva saw me to the door. She told me I was very pale: when the signal came to go in I almost fainted. People have the same sort of feeling before the start, they tell me, when they ride in races, It seems the wrong way to deal with matters of learning: but it must make it less of a shock and be a great support to have school years behind an examination. I passed—second class I think, but anyway I got through; and, by the time I heard of it, was travelling out to Dronero with Dorothy on my first long vacation. We thought that by travelling all night we might save the day for Paris and leave again in the evening for Turin. We arrived in early dawn, when the shops were still shut, long before anything was awake except Notre Dame. We lingered there till we could see the Sainte Chapelle, which is like the inside of a ruby. After that we felt very jaded. We went out to the Bois de Boulogne and fell asleep on the grass, and made friends with a gendarme and his family. I cannot remember what happened next, but by early afternoon we were so sleepy that we took refuge in a room at the Hôtel Edouard VII, the only hotel Dorothy knew. It was an uneconomical way of seeing Paris.

Our minds were made up to take Vera to camp for a few weeks in the high alpine pastures, in a *grangia*, or shepherd's hut. My mother was always enthusiastic about plans till Mario killed them, and she had found a hut already. Mario threatened trouble and all hung in the balance for days; yet he loved mountains in his emphatic way: it was one of his nicer qualities: and a shepherd's hut seemed far from dangerous contaminating influences even to him. So we succeeded. We took our woolly mongrel dog to protect us, and a faithful Tuscan servant called Carlo to cook. Our hut had two rooms built with loose stones; in the evening the smoke oozed through walls and roof while Carlo dealt with our supper on open slabs that served for hearth and table. Pointed summits and sloping meadows were all around, and a stream fell, steep and narrow, into the pastures and widened there and wandered by our door. Then it steepened over the edge again to the next shelf below. In the distance was a *Santuario* where people came in pilgrimage for a three days' *festa* every year; its cloisters made the hills even more lonely, but kind. We lived three weeks here, and read, walked, talked and lay in the sun. *Anna Karenina* and *Sartor Resartus* were the two most absorbing books of that year. Vera was growing up now and blossomed into talk and gaiety; perhaps she was never so happy again. She was pretty, but careless about it, nor ever enjoyed clothes as I did. At night the stars hung over us enormous and dazzling in a sky that seemed very close. They swung in their orbits and we felt that the earth was only one among them; and the stream padded through the grass in the darkness as if it were shod with wool. When our time came to an end, we hired mules and moved all our belongings across the high passes patched with snow, a long day's march of twelve hours or so to the head of our Dronero valley, and De Poli's hotel. We were getting to know these mountains fairly well. They are little visited because of the greater Alps near them, and few hotels and no guides—so there are no tourists; but the Alpine regiments, who wear an eagle feather in green hats, moved about them because of the French border so near. We found some of them billeted at De Poli's, and a friend's husband among them, and were made much of because of our adventurous journey.

Dorothy was one of few visitors who did not mind Mario. She refused to be bullied and he liked her. She would sit in my room and watch him and my mother as they walked back to luncheon every day from the factory; they appeared a long way

off along a country road with the mill race beside it, Mario small
and rapid, two steps to every one of my mother's—gesticulating
as it were on tiptoe: he scarce interrupted himself to say good-
morning, and the saga went on—about himself. He had some
amiable qualities, apart from the one of not being shy, which my
mother liked so much but other people found trying. He liked
the country people and wanted to help them; and was vehement,
sometimes in admiration though more often in quarrels. Anything that was *his* became perfect at once. He enjoyed his own
truculence and spent years fighting the local M.P., Signor
Giolitti, who was also Italian Prime Minister at that time. Mario
flouted him and, with my mother's help, succeeded in safe-
guarding the water power of our valley from the hands of a
big company which the minister protected and which would have
deprived the villages of irrigation and of light. This epic struggle
took years, and Mario never got tired or discouraged; my mother
was dazzled, absorbed, and felt herself really useful; these adventures gave drama and colour to her life. She scarcely noticed
that he was impossibly egotistical, ruthless for the feelings of
others, and unprincipled about their rights as soon as they were
individual and not collective. Any happy peaceful life was
impossible near him. His Italian relations felt it as much as we
did; and my mother's complete abnegation made him much
worse than he would otherwise have been. I remember once
standing up to him on some forgotten matter in the factory; my
mother asked me to apologize; I laid the case before her, and
she admitted I was right but begged me to ask his pardon 'for
her sake'. I did so, for there was nothing in the world I would
not then have tried to do for her; but a dim revolt was in my
heart, impersonal but enduring, like that roused by Fräulein's
deceit in my childhood. It was the *existence* of injustice that
rankled. And the things my mother asked for in these years
were hard later on to forgive. As for Vera, she never did forgive
until just before she died, when my mother begged her to do so,
and all things had become indifferent.

Dearest Dorothy,

You have been so long without writing that I am beginning to wonder whether you got Joan's little cap: I sent it rather recklessly in a letter, and have had misgivings since.

We have had a most fearfully agitated time since you left: there has been a sudden revival of political quarrels; Mario tried to get a letter published in the local paper here, and was refused and had to rush off to Cuneo to get 500 copies printed. We had a high time folding and addressing them to all the magnates of the city and the valley and sent factory men on bicycles all over the countryside to distribute them before morning. It was most exciting and I enjoyed it immensely: I should like to be an M.P.'s secretary I think: one could write all the nasty things one liked to people and not have to bear the consequences.

Bosia took the most surprising interest in the matter and laid down the law with such torrents of words that Mario had to knuckle under and listen. Bosia is still here by the way: I think he is soon reaching the stage when we shall give him a hint that we have had enough of him: the picture went away almost a month ago, and looked fine, but we are agitated because Bosia is reduced to milk diet: he says it is because he dips his brushes in varnish and then sucks them, which seems foolish. How men love to talk of their insides!

I have been busy trying most inefficiently to replace Mama in the factory and as Materfamilias here. It was considered incorrect to leave two innocent maidens alone with three creatures of the other sex, so Olivero's mother was invited as chaperone, and Bosia, together with the other two, was herded in Mario's side of the house. As Mama forgot to tell him to change rooms, we left that delicate task to Mario, with the result that Bosia was most extraordinarily ceremonious and correct with us for three whole days; I should like to have heard the explanation.

Write to me soon, my dear: Pips says you are having nothing but rain, so you have not even that useful excuse of irresistible fine weather. Not that you need really make an excuse: I have a list of names in my writing-table, and I look at it when I want to feel melancholy; one is a letter of condolence too; it is gradually becoming a sort of nightmare to haunt me.

I believe I shall be in London in November as it is necessary to attend at least part of each term so as to be qualified for the exam. It is a great pity as I wanted to spend Christmas at home: the prospect is still beautifully vague however.

I send you a symbolical vine-leaf to remind you of Italy and bring you back soon. You can't think how often I miss you here.

FREYA

11

London. 1912-1914

I ENTERED Bedford College as a day student, and felt strange enough among so many girls. I was accustomed to people about twenty years older than myself, and my formal, elaborate Italian manners made me unpopular (I was told, soon and candidly, that it was affected to say "I beg your pardon" instead of just "sorry"). This was hard, for all my longing, rather pathetically humble, was to be exactly like everyone else and to be liked. After about six months I lived myself down and began to have friends, though I still continue to feel like a stranger in large gatherings, and hesitate with reluctance on the doorstep of a crowded room. They were a dull lot of girls on the whole, interested in jobs and exams, and as I was there only for lectures, I saw little of them. The school shibboleths, the team spirit, all the things that had no direct relation to the individual, met a mere blank in my mind. The meals were noisy and untidy, and I used to go to a little restaurant down the street, or to a French café where I lunched daily on two pâté de foie gras sandwiches and a cup of chocolate—a lunch fit to make anyone liverish one would think. I was much happier with the teachers, and particularly devoted to Miss Strudwick, who taught Latin in an inspired way so that the loveliness of the second book of the Aeneid, the silent ships moving out from Tenedos in the moonlight, are still woven about her memory.

Later I became devoted to Professor Allen, the history professor. He was tall and loosely made, and his hair tangled up like his moustaches. He would ask where he had left off, collect himself for a moment without notes, and wander down every fascinating by-way. His knowledge was immense and he never lost the proportions of a general idea. I was enthralled by these lectures, and he naturally thought well of me. He told me that he never reckoned on more than two students out of sixty understanding what he was trying to say. He used to invite the favoured ones to his house, where an elusive little wife seemed a part of the 'domestic arrangements'; she had been a former student and I felt that perhaps she had married him in historic admiration, a warning, it seemed to me then, on the importance of not getting things mixed that are separate by nature. These evenings were delightful, and he would sit clasping his pipe and go off at a canter down any path one chose. He was by far the most exciting person in Bedford College.

Mr. Thomas was a pink blond young man with a small peevish mouth terrified of all his female pupils: I suppose he was shy, but he made Anglo-Saxon duller than it need be.

We had Miss Spurgeon for Shakespeare, interesting but not inspiring as she so easily might have been, for she repeated her lectures year after year, and showed a feeling of relief when the hour was over. It is strange, and comforting too, how even with quite a dull class these intangible essences are felt; the spirit bloweth where it listeth, but it has to be blowing about *somewhere* if there is to be any result at all, and the good teacher cannot give less than his best. Most of these people only came into my view during my second year and I can hardly remember the first year's classes. I found them very little trouble; languages I was far ahead in; Latin and English I loved; mathematics I said good-bye to for good. We had to do Gothic, and walked across the park to University College as we had no Gothic of our own; a language which has nothing left to it, except a few bits of the Bible, which can be read far more beautifully in English, seemed to me a dreary waste of time.

The centre and gain of all my life at college was W. P. Ker. Since the age of fifteen, when I met him privately at Viva's, I had recognized his silent quality. I liked him so much that Viva asked him again; he became my adopted godfather, and I used to go to his lectures for the pleasure of it. He taught me all I know in English literature and corrected one of my essays by writing underneath it: "Too many words." He used very few himself, but always careful and good ones. He would come late to his classes, with a pile of books in his hand, his head a little forward as if it were stretching over a chasm, his pince-nez dangling by their black cord in one hand. He would tiptoe down the theatre at University College with the same step he used on a mountain path, looking neither to left nor right, while a gentle stamping of students' feet showed him how popular he was. He told me that he disapproved of more than three-quarters of an hour for any lecture and came late on purpose. No one missed if he could avoid it. He would say what he wanted in the shortest way and then open his books and read out of the authors themselves the things he wished you to remember. Many pieces live with his voice in my memory, but most of all the bit about the Oxus in Sohrab and Rustum and some bits of Dante which he would quote and suddenly look up at me, after we had climbed in Italy in the hills. He never insulted his classes by under-estimating them: you could pick your treasures out from his three-quarters of an hour: but if you missed them it was your own affair—he never underlined them, and you had to do your thinking for yourself.

I began by studying for an English literature degree, but then switched over to history because I found that the first meant too much reading *about* people, while for history I spent my time with the sources themselves. It made no difference to me; the war came before I got a degree, and I went to both W. P.'s and Professor Allen's classes apart from any idea of examinations. Once a month or so W. P. would be at home to all the students in the library of University College and we had tea out of a huge brown enamel tea-pot: I went, and never talked to anyone, but stood, shyly adoring him from a corner: when he spoke to me, a strange little voice crept out to answer, suffocated with shyness, and making me desperate afterwards over the chances of

conversation I had missed; but he had this effect on a great many
people, perhaps because of his slow speech, every word weighed
and meant, and then a sudden look, shafted like a spear, from his
blue eyes. Gradually he came to invite Viva and me to dine
now and then in his house in Gower Street, where no electricity
but only candles were allowed to light the branching Morris
wall-papers and piles of books on every floor and landing: if he
wanted a quotation, he would go with unerring aim, dip into
some heap, shoulder-high, and bring out the volume required.

I had become very gauche in the last few years, and must
have been depressingly unattractive. The clothes we wore
were hideous—white mannish shirts and unbecoming suits, and
I had no notion of how to put them on and was small and podgy.
My nose was too big and I was serious, with no small talk at all.
Viva herself had been an only child, and knew no young people.
She soon came to the convenient but mistaken conclusion that
I cared neither for youth nor gaiety, and though I longed for
both, I never had the indelicacy to say so. I was happy enough to
be with older people, nearly always men and writers: Sidney
Low, David Hannay, Cope Cornford and a few others all became
friends.

Viva's father thought of me as a second daughter, and I stayed
twice to look after him while she went to visit her American
relations. He was small, neat and pink with a little white beard.
He had made his own way, first as a painter and then, when he
fell in love with and married the expensive and fascinating widow,
Viva's mother, he took to business so as to make money to keep
her, and became a director of Cassell's. His painting was
reserved for holidays, and he made this greatest of sacrifices a
man can make, of the work he loves, without a regret, as if it
were a mere trifle offered to the beloved Julia, who must have
been charming, and kept a sort of salon in London in her day,
where Oscar Wilde dandled the little Viva on his knees, and talked
for hours and hours. Mr. Bale had that pleasant English mixture
of commonsense and imagination; he worked hard for the
Artists' Benevolent Society, the law of copyright, and such

things, and as my father had now given Vera and me two thousand pounds each of our own, he managed my funds for me and taught me the principles of financial prudence (not very adequately learned). It was wonderful to have a hundred pounds a year to pay for college fees, journeys and clothes: the feeling of great wealth soon passed away, but I am sure it was excellent training to manage my own capital.

On Sundays I put on a silk dress and waited for visitors: if I came in late I could see how many were there by counting the top-hats in the hall. They must have been stodgy afternoons but I never found them so, for I badly needed a quiet and well-ordered life, and it was pleasant to feel a ritual to which I belonged. We had to be punctual and dress for dinner; and Viva's puritan conscience was strict over promises, engagements, or even casual remarks: it all brought out something that had been struggling inside me; I was becoming passionately English.

My first dinner party was at Sir Chartres Biron's house: he had liked me two years before and now tried nobly to make me talk: but I was paralysed by my first décolleté, and yes and no were all I could utter. I never recovered in his eyes.

The first dance was a greater success. It was managed by a friend of my mother's, a painter from her Paris days called Amy Atkinson, and she was gayer, more casual, built on an altogether bigger model than Viva. She lived with a friend in a Chelsea flat, with seagulls on the balcony, and would have liked to adopt me as a daughter. I was nearly sent to her instead of to Viva and have often wondered what difference it might have made: like mountain paths, it seems a toss-up which to take, and they go down different valleys and never meet again.

With Viva, the smallest pleasure had to carry some ethical burden that was only too apt to snuff it out altogether, but Amy organized my first dance on principles of pure enjoyment, and surprisingly enough it was all that a dance could be; my dress white and spangly (long gloves); two perfect partners, one gay and dashing, one quiet and devoted: I said yes to everything, so that there was a moment when three people brought ices simultaneously; I was so excited that I forgot to be shy, and I went on dreaming of the night for months after. There were not more than four other dances before the war came and, owing to my shyness and constant feelings of humility, only one of them was really enjoyable. That was in Chatham, a Sapper dance in scarlet, and an Irish partner talked about road building on the Khyber pass. I remembered him, and he me—I heard a long time after: and he was killed, like most of the men one met that year, in the retreat from Mons. But such things were not yet possible to imagine in the spring of 1913 or 1914. Girls told me they liked dances only for the sake of the dancing; but I never believed them, and felt it was a waste of time if someone in the course of the evening had not been able to carry off a small piece of one's heart. I was ready enough to lose mine, though the world was full of a great many other things as well.

Viva and I spent Christmas in an amusing mixed company of bookmakers and golfers at St. Margaret's Bay near Dover, and a pleasant barrister, now a judge, flirted, admitted a wife on the day we left, and lent me Seeley's *Expansion of England*. I was led on to read the history of the Mutiny, sitting up half the night in tears over Lucknow.

I read Cowper, Crabbe, Pope, and all the poets I could find, and saw and heard Pavlova, Mrs. Besant, Adeline Genée, *John Bull's Other Island*, Scriabin, *The Importance of Being Ernest, Lohengrin*, Maeterlinck's *Death of Tintagiles*, Galsworthy's *Silver Box* and Shaw's *Pygmalion*. I went to *Parsifal* as to a ritual and heard poetry readings at Harold Monro's bookshop in Southampton Row. On Sundays Viva and I would sometimes creep in by the back door of the Berkeley (the front door being closed for religion) to luncheon with an Irish Colonel—a charming old Roman Catholic who said you could eat quails on Fridays because they were caught as they crossed the sea before they landed, and therefore counted as fish. I no longer felt envious of anyone at all, but gave a humble, uncompetitive worship to the brilliant and gay. The academic, which everyone seemed to think me destined for, I thought dull—a means to enter a world of imagination, but not an end in itself, and felt at home only with people who treated it in this subordinate way, like W. P. But across our road a young woman called Miss Raiguel lived with her uncle and aunt—rich, pretty, fascinating and exquisitely dressed; well set-up young men in the twilight after tea—impeccable top hats and beautifully tailored shoulders—would leave her doorstep with smiling eyes and an expression of ravishment: and I would now and then sit among her court, modestly adoring. When the Academy Private View came along, Viva chose her as a guest instead of me; and though it had been promised to me and I was disappointed, I remember watching them drive away with no protest in my heart, but sadly and impersonally, as one watches the Unattainable.

Such loves as I might have had I never noticed, and lost a conventional young man's proposal because he found me absorbed in *Don Juan* under a cherry tree in the garden. It was a tiny London garden surrounded by a sooty wall, but it had an old double-flowering cherry tree, a miracle in spring. W. P. used to appear now and then with a packet of books under his arm; the eight volumes of Lockhart's Scott are those I best remember.

I canoed in Regent's Park in term time: at Easter there were visits to Thornworthy on the moor. We walked or rode all day, and drove in to church on Sundays; and sat in the evening round a peat fire. The guest had a hard time because all the family talked at terrific speed at once, expecting answers, and even the dogs moved about asking for attention. The rifleman was there, and I looked at him with the disembodied admiration of the moth for the star and began to think what dress to wear for dinner, a thing I had never done before. One dressed with candles which scarcely lit the darkness of the mirror and made one's eyes look bright and shining, as if out of the shadows of a picture, while the flames bowed and swayed as the winds tossed and wailed round the corners of the house.

Nineteen-fourteen came and I was twenty-one; and I woke

[126]

that morning with a melancholy of age greater than I have ever felt since. Apart from this weighty feeling it was a happy time. My parents sent me a fitted dressing-case, a period piece of lovely morocco meant for a maid to carry. Viva gave a dinner party. The spring that followed I spent alone with her father while she went to America, and I enjoyed independence with someone so pleasant, easy and kind to look after. I had gained much more confidence, and had a number of friends—all much older than myself. The Easter vacation on Dartmoor was even lovelier than usual. My mother sent me a black velvet dress with lace ruffles, luckily not made by herself, and suddenly, for the first time, as I dressed for dinner I thought I looked pretty. The lieutenant in the Irish Rifles now asked me to ride and we had many good mornings on the moors. He went through the war from beginning to end, and wrote at intervals, one letter just after he had left the last boat from Suvla Bay—describing that quiet morning and the hush of the coast abandoned with so many dead. I little thought that I too should come to know that hush of war.

Viva gave me a dance party at the Savoy, and the few young people I knew and invited made a queer mixture. She had been lovely when young, with London at her feet, and never guessed at the difficulties of anyone as insignificant, shy and foreign as I was. (I still spoke English with a roll in the r's and an Italian accent.) She put it all down to a want of interest in anything but books and I was far too diffident to explain. I suffered for our childhood, so segregated from its own generation. My dance party, however, was happy in its result: no one took any interest in me, but Dorothy met a friend of Viva's, a commissioner of police in the Home Office, and they talked till 1 a.m. about sanitary inspecting—so she told me—and eventually became engaged.

In the summer I took my intermediate examination, paralysed, as ever, by the clock that ticks one on, brainless and distraught, towards the irrevocable. W. P. was one of the examiners. He set a question for me particularly, he told me afterwards—to describe the Golden Age in heroic couplets; it would have taken me a week in some Devonshire dell to do it. He said I wrote well, but very little; and he, and various people, urged me to continue. I thought about it, vaguely.

There was a fullness even about the fringe of life in London that year. As I walked home with my books I could watch lines of shining cars like a Druid avenue outside Lord's cricket ground; men in grey top hats and cut-away coats stepped out of them, and women in narrow skirts slit to the knees and hats with many flowers. I coveted one, glossy black, with a flat crown raised up on a little bank of rosebuds, and I bought it too, deliberating for a long time over the price of twenty-five shillings. I began to like many people. Mrs. W. K. Clifford took a fancy to me and I planned to go climbing with her daughter in the Carpathians another year. Margaret Jourdain with her quiet biting sparkle of wit I was devoted to. Mrs. Corbett lived in St. John's Wood near us and wished to paint me, though I was a plain little thing, still dressed in the clothes my mother sewed, and made very long when everyone else went short, because of a theory of her own that long skirts suit small people. I therefore looked nearer thirty-five than twenty, and never told her how little I liked it. Now and then a real dress was bought, and I can remember every one of these and the fine feeling of wearing them.

The great Russian ballet came that year, and Granville Barker's production of *Twelfth Night*, and fairies with gilt faces in *A Midsummer Night's Dream*. The Russian Operas came. Viva managed even in public life to find something negative to work for, and became Honorary Secretary of the Women's Anti-Suffrage League. I canvassed for her, and went from door to door down Harley Street in my new hat, finding doctors who seemed on the whole easily persuaded. I enjoyed this, and particularly the amusing diplomacy necessary for getting past the butlers. Mrs. Humphry Ward was an Anti-Suffragist and would visit Viva's office now and then, and I was introduced to her one day—a squat majestic figure, whose skirts looked as if when she left them they must stand rigid and empty like a dictator's court when the dictator has gone. Viva's League had a great meeting at the Albert Hall. F. E. Smith spoke and—I rather think—Lord Curzon, and as we came away we met Lord Cromer, and Viva introduced me: his blue eyes looked as if they saw no surfaces, but pierced through to what was there inside one.

There were many parties and garden parties. Violet Hunt's I remember best: her marriage or no-marriage to Ford Madox Hueffer was being talked about and he used to call with her on Sundays, with a sulky air and soft and flabby hand. Mr. Wells was at these parties, always with a circle round him, but I never spoke to him. Dorothy Stanley I was taken to visit, the widow of the explorer, a matronly Rubens figure, warm, intensely living and happy. She was married to Dr. Curtis, who moved about like a contented little dinghy in the wake of his frigate. As a child, I had seen a rough granite monolith for Stanley's tomb being dragged on a sort of sled by horses from our land on Dartmoor. Dorothy was very kind to me and asked me to see her in London whenever I went there, but the war and her death closed this possibility of friendship.

We knew most of the artists who lived in St. John's Wood, and in this my last year I was taken to the Academy Soirée and saw Frank Dicksee, the President, at the head of the stairs pretending not to notice that a policeman was carrying off a screaming suffragette.

I knew St. John's Wood well from walking out with Nipper, our rough terrier. We used to hand him to the crossing sweeper for his daily walks when we left at Christmas, and when I returned and once more took him over he would trot ahead of me, with one ear up and one ear down, into every public house in our neighbourhood. There were quite a number and I had to push open the swinging doors and whistle—a thing which, Viva told me, was barely permissible for a female when in serious need of a taxi, and under no other circumstances at all.

One late spring evening Nipper and I took Viva to the door

of the Edmund Gosses in Regent's Park. She was dining there and they were one woman short for their party and asked me to stay, and so I went in my day clothes and watched Yeats, Sickert, and Robert Ross on the opposite side of the table. I cannot remember who else was there, nor who it was who took me in and, when I launched some poor little conversational effort, said very sensibly: "Hadn't we better listen to what the others say?" How often I should like to follow this advice! But unfortunately I have forgotten what they did say: only a pattern of talk remains, dancing to and fro across the table to my delight and wonder, easy and effortless. Viva was bad at her dinner-table and would crush a conversation in its infancy by some sudden irrelevancy about the fish, or fruit, or wine, and I had already noticed that people stayed longer at my little dinners for her father than they did at hers: but here was the real thing, the Art of Conversation, with Edmund Gosse, pale and, as it were *bleached*, shoulders, hands, moustache all gently drooping, guiding his team with a voice of silky suavity which disguised the cutting edge. Beyond Yeats' dark hair and heavy chin like that of some prelate not too ascetic, and Sickert's aquiline profile, the open windows showed the heavy garden laburnums pale in candlelight against the sombre leafage of the park.

A week in Oxford ended the spring. We lunched with the President of Trinity, walked with W. P. through the alpine garden of St. John's, and were taken by him over All Souls, where his window trailed red geraniums against the grey wall of the quad, and he reminded me that Dr. Johnson noticed All Souls and Trinity as good for dancing. Our rooms, overlooking Oriel, were filled with roses, and I was invited by a young don to tea in his rooms and was rebuked by Viva for accepting. She was old-fashioned even for her day, and deprecated Bond Street for me in the late afternoon if I was alone. The Burlington Arcade was of course unheard of for a delicately-minded young female. Yet with all its shackles the world was easy; the English version of civilized living gathered itself in that last pleasantness before the war. And when the vacation came, and my departure for Italy, everyone I cared for most was at Victoria station to see me off. The boat train slid out, filled with ice-axes and knapsacks, and W. P. told me which side to sit on so as to see Mont Blanc across the Lake of Geneva. It was the first time I travelled by Simplon, for I was meeting my mother in Venice to walk down the Adriatic coast.

When next I reached London the battle of the Somme was preparing.

LETTER FROM MY SISTER VERA

19 Dec., 1912.

Dearest Freya,

I know Bumps [my mother] has already written you the grand news and I should have been with the first. Well, now I am writing with the engagement ring on my finger. I am very happy now that it is fixed. I broke the news to Pips and he seemed very pleased.

Mario is very nice now that I am a little more intimate with him. I hope that I shall be a good friend to him and I hope I shall grow bright enough never to let him get bored with me. He is very nice and always keeps Pips in a good temper when we dine together. It is very nice having an engagement ring. We are now getting to a better understanding of one another and it will get better still always. We really are fond of each other.

I wish you were here. I could tell you such a lot and I can't write it. Anyhow the grand event can't take place without you. That couldn't be allowed. It may take place in England some time next spring, before Pips goes to Canada but you will have to be there to dress me. I wish it was over. This preparation and warning of people is a bore, besides such a lot of fuss strikes terror in a way. It's a very large affair and I somehow had not realized it possible so soon: I don't know that

I have yet, and I feel disgracefully unprepared and ignorant. I shall be very glad when it's over and I am with Mario and fixed. We shall be very happy. He is very generous and good tempered and I hope I shall grow into a help and companion to him. I feel I should have such a lot to do in these few months to prepare. I wish I could get rid of housekeeping during them as it has got formed into a gigantic figure of which I can't get rid. One of those things you see in dreams and they go on growing and growing as you look at them. I know it's important but B makes me feel it's the whole of life. I'll take to it more kindly when it is for us two however. To get over the feeling of opposition to it is a comparatively small thing.

I do so wish you were here for this Xmas. It shall be a very nice one. We are preparing a tree for the children.

My Xmas present may be a little late as it won't dry. My best of friends, I wish I could tell you more but I somehow can't write. I shall see you in this spring then I hope and we shall have such a long talk. It was expected but somehow comes as a surprise, a very nice one. You shall always be the same dearest to us. To me you shall still be the person in whom to have full confidence and of whom to be really fond.

Give us good wishes. I so badly want you. Au revoir,

VERA

12

Italy before the War. 1913-1914

Two holidays and Vera's wedding fill my Italian memories of the two springs before the war. Vera was married in the Easter vacation of 1913. When she wrote to me in England to announce her engagement, I took a little gold ring which Mario had once given me and slipped it inside the envelope, and put it away with a contented feeling of finality. Everything was settled happily for all, and I heard little more until we met again.

Vera had inherited my father's gift for modelling and had developed it unassisted (except for a little advice from him). During the last year or so her only wish had been to go to an art school, and that was refused: Mario was not going to run the risk of losing a second bride. When I reached Dronero a week or two before the wedding, I was distressed and surprised to find her unhappy. She told me the whole story. She had seen that it was useless to try to persuade my mother. House-keeping, at which she had taken my place, she loathed: it was better, she thought, to marry. She was only eighteen. What distressed her most was that they had arranged to baptize her as a Roman Catholic and she had no wish to enter that Church.

I was now sufficiently emancipated from Dronero to be horrified, and I begged her to put her foot down at least about the baptism, if she did not feel strongly enough to break the engagement. We tried to talk to my mother—it was my first difference of opinion with her and it did no good. I tried also to get Vera's two thousand pounds settled on her (as, in Italy, everything not settled at the time of the marriage then went to the husband), but this too very definitely failed. Vera, like my father, was curiously passive: if they made her a Catholic against her will, she said, she would go on privately believing what she liked: all we obtained was a special dispensation to allow her to read the Bible. The whole thing was already arranged. Mario's relations arrived from Rome, friendly and kind. There was a religious ceremony, baptism and wedding together, in the private chapel of the Bishop of Saluzzo, small and dark with crimson damask, and Vera surrounded with flowers; then, a day after, the civil marriage in Turin. We slept the night before at an hôtel, where she and I shared a room and she lay awake sobbing in my arms.

They went to Naples and I returned to London. There had been a second difference with my mother, for she now quarrelled with Herbert Young, having taken it for granted that Vera might marry from his house, as we had no home of our own in Italy. She had written to suggest it; but he disapproved of the marriage strongly, and said so, and for years that old friendship was closed. It seemed to me that he was right not to lend his own house for what he disliked; and I decided to continue my friendship independently. His affection, steadily growing since childhood, increased more than ever from this time onwards to his death.

I think this was the last time that I arrived in Dronero with an easy mind. Always, from now on, a numb feeling of trouble to come would settle on me as I drew near: one's heart going to one's boots seemed a real sensation. And I never had the same faith in my mother again. What happened to my father had, I suppose, never really penetrated, but nothing could make me forget Vera's misery.

*   *   *   *   *

In 1913 you could still choose a holiday from the map of Europe, and when the long vacation came round we decided to try new mountains in the Val d'Aosta. The two girls from Thornworthy were coming and W. P. promised to be walking up the valley. We took rooms at the inn at Cogne—7/- a day and all included. My mother and I met in Turin. We stopped off to look at the Lombard façade of the church in Chivasso, and travelled to Aosta; slept at the Hôtel Mont Blanc; and set out in morning dew across the bridge, past Aymaville, by a zigzag track with Grivola smooth and white at the valley's head. Few pleasures are cleaner than the delight of the first morning's walk when one has reached the hills. The bitterness of the spring was forgotten and I remember the joy of the mountain road, my mother walking in splendid health and freedom, the blight of Mario's presence far away. We sat for luncheon on a warm boulder, and dipped our cups in glacier water from the stream (which was supposed to give one a goitre) and discussed life in general, which my mother found happy and I thought sad. Now that I have reached her age I too think it happy; but for her the years of insouciance were numbered. In a day or two W. P. arrived, leaning forward under his haversack: he had a stiff and old walk, misleading for the toughness and seasoned gaiety within. In the afternoon we strolled through deep meadows and uncut flowers towards Gran Paradiso shining with facets of glacier in the sun; and were caught in a small shower and rescued by the page boy of the inn with a huge umbrella and a St. Bernard dog, to W. P's amusement.

Here for the first time in my life I climbed with a rope; and it was W. P. who taught me: the happiness was almost frightening, for it seemed more than one human being could manage. The rope was only for six minutes or so at the top of the ascent of a small excrescence called Le Petit Pousset—but the feeling was there, the extraordinary sensation of safety, the abyss held in check, the valley with its life of everyday, bridges, tracks, fields and houses, seen from a narrow ledge which made it exciting and remote; this sense of *double life* is, I think, one of the main ingredients of the mountain sorcery. We sat for an hour while W. P. drew the horizon with all its peaks in outline: he did this on every new summit. We packed the snow thinly on a sloping boulder in the sun and the drops trickled into our cup down the granite. The layers of air and the little winds below ate up even the sounds of the streams: the great ones, the giants of Alps, stood about us here and there in a cloudless sky, a burning serenity. Their immobility never seems to me static; it has a vitality that seems to us repose, like that of a humming top at rest on its axis, spinning along its orbit in space. I had always loved scrambling, but from now on I became a mountaineer, and thought of each peak as an individual, with a character to be studied and respected. I used to dream of hills; and once in a dream climbed through powdery snow to a summit and saw a view that I had seen before; yet it was none of the hills I knew: I went through them one by one and realized at last that this landscape was indeed familiar, but only because I had visited it in a previous dream: I am still waiting to find it.

As we climbed down from Le Petit Pousset towards the woods below, the black hill crows veered round us: they call them 'corneilles', and W. P. said he preferred them to the racines, for we had been slipping on rhododendron roots all morning. This slight nonsense is all of the day's talk that I remember, but the golden atmosphere remains.

Our party grew. Vera and Mario arrived and I climbed the Grivola with them. W. P. disapproved of more than three on one rope and refused to come. Mario thought he could treat the mountains as he treated the rest of the world, and jumped on to what looked like earth at the top. It was ice at that height: his feet slid, and he lay like a beetle the wrong side up, suspended by the rope from Vera's waist and mine. We were on a six-inch ledge and were nearly jerked away, and clung to the rock above by our very nails, with the tautened rope trying to pull us in two until the guides hauled him up on his back, far less boastful than before. We had another bad moment in an ice 'couloir' that slid in a shaft between two steeply tilted walls of rock: the guides had cut steps and we were halfway across when a train of boulders came bounding from above: they leaped from their invisible sockets towards their unseen bed below, hitting and bounding at intervals from the precipitous ice; and we could see them coming but could not move in time out of the way. Vera and I both leaned in as close to our slope as we could, and the whole shoot leaped over us without touching—and over Mario too who had done nothing reasonable at all. The day made him lose his taste for climbing and Vera was made to give it up also. The guides, perturbed, took us down by a longer and safer détour; and W. P. wrote:

> One shouldn't be frivolous
> On places like Grivolas.

on the menu at supper.

The Thornworthy sisters arrived, and two young men who had come with introductions and were learning Italian for a consular exam. We climbed the Grand Serz, Herbetet and Tersiva, and began to grow familiar with outlines of the valleys as we saw them from different angles day by day. We took our luncheon and ate it by various streams; one of the young men fell in love with me; my mother sketched in the villages. W. P. wrote me an Italian sonnet; and I had learned to be a real mountaineer.

The Thornworthy girls and the consular student returned with us to Dronero for some weeks of autumn. One of the few concessions obtained at Vera's wedding was a promise from my mother that we should live in separate halves of the house and have our meals apart: but all that happened was that Mario brought Vera to our side—and while the house was full this did not matter; indeed it would have been a pity for her to miss our gaiety. The girls, however, left, and Mario became jealous of the young student and slammed a door whenever he was about. He lodged in a little hill town nearby and my mother—torn between her desire to encourage him and her inability to contradict Mario—kept him away by suggesting little expeditions here and there, so that we might meet and yet not contaminate the home. She always came too. I was so purely brought up that this seemed natural: what the young consul thought of such chaperoned outings I never heard. Perhaps if he had been eloquent about it I might have married him: as it was, he went away and wrote to ask if I would wait till he had made himself a career—and I was far too taken up by life in general to reduce it to the particular so soon, and answered that I changed my mind about people once a month or more. Yet we wrote to each other till the war and my engagement came between us.

Mario was the most jealous man I have ever known. If Vera sat for half an hour at a party talking to a stranger there were shocking scenes, and his possessiveness extended to all the family. I caused an explosion by admitting that I never paid for my meals on the train; someone always offered to do so and I had thought this a natural arrangement. A Frenchman once shared my table in the dining-car and asked me to drink his wine with him, because, he said: "On voit que le monde vous amuse." In 1913 my arrival was particularly disastrous. An Italian officer, very small and neat with a huge unmanageable sword, made some excuse for conversation, put his arm round my waist, and kissed me as I stood looking at the view of the great valley where the train rushes down from Modane to Susa. Shocked and surprised I drew myself up and merely said severely: "I am English." "Ah, pardon, Mademoiselle, I thought French." I could not help laughing at the conciseness of this dialogue and we continued to chat amicably, though with propriety, until the unexpected sight of three relatives on the Turin platform to meet me caused the young officer to disappear. But I received as many picture cards as his garrison town supplied. They all began with a reference to eyes—bright, soft, sweet, unforgettable: they came with the factory mail in the morning and Mario evidently read them and handed them on in an offended way.

The long vacation in 1914 began with my mother in Venice. It was my first visit there, though Venice never loses that magic of appearing as if for the first time. We stayed in a cheap hotel, clean and friendly, where Italian bourgeois ate under a vine pergola in the shade, far from tourists. A sailor sat at the table next ours and amused us, as he was evidently just re-united to his family and inexpressibly bored by it, and I was too young and cruel to be touched by the wife's dim unattractive efforts to entertain him,—keeping the small boy from behaving like the little horror his papa evidently thought him. We spent a week or more sightseeing in the mornings and loitering with a gondola of our own through the afternoons. My mother painted in the galleries that run round the inside of St. Mark's and I spent the time dawdling about there, close to the great mosaic saints, looking on the Piazza from the terrace of the bronze horses, or hearing a Mass at the great altar below, so faint and far that it seemed as if the Christian Church were seen there in its distant setting of time framed in Byzantine gold. In the evening on the Piazza the municipal band played grand opera: the Venetian girls, 'wearing their dowries on their sleeves', promenaded heavily chaperoned in two slow opposite streams round and round while the young men looked them up and down from either side. One was carefully brought up before 1914: in Italy even Vera and I were not allowed out walking in a town without a maid a step or two behind us.

After a week or so in Venice my mother and I took the boat and reached Chioggia in a twilight that floated the houses in a mother of pearl sea. A porter took us up the long main street, whose centre is a waterway for ships with yellow sails, to *La Mano Amica*, a hotel so modest that the landlord was overcome by visitors of our quality and stuttered and stammered till we thought him drunk. Our room, quite clean, with dinner and breakfast, cost us less than 5/-.

I kept a diary with the stages of our journey and—to me at least—something of the neglected peace of that countryside and summer remains.

'We walked along fruit gardens and canals to Brondolo—a low white fort on an island with blue water of all gradations and long stretches of mud banks. The road runs along a canal, and boats move across the land with yellow, grey and tawny sails, sewn in stripes; they have an awning over the stern and touches of scarlet paint here and there. We were offered a lift by an old peasant whose gig took us at a trot to S. Anna—five houses off the road, on a sandy way bordered by acacias. I have never come on anything more peaceful and remote. Breakfast in the farmyard, with two small owls and a cuckoo, and a fox in a cage. Children came round and began to show off in a shy way, feeding their cuckoo from a little bag of flies. There is a train that runs four times a day along the grass-grown track buried in acacias; we waited for it and talked to the country people in the little waiting-room where the stationmaster (who was ticket collector and all as well) acted as host, and saw that the sunlight should not pour in to trouble us, and arranged the passengers' seats in a circle.

'We left the train at Cavanella d'Adige and walked through meadows and willows to the village; a broad canal flows through it to the Adige, which drifts there to the sea. A child in a red pinafore, with blue eyes and bare feet, got us lunch while her mother sat bewailing the absence of roast meat; the child was called Adalgisa Rizzio, and two years before a *capitano* and his wife had come, like us, and lunched in the woods and gone away in the evening: this was all her outside world, except the boats that passed her door on the canal.

'We took the little train again to Adria, modern and very hot, and on the next day, by sunset, to Rovigo, seated in gardens, with two square towers of brick along the walls—a very pleasant town, with tablets and inscriptions everywhere, and an illuminated manuscript of the fifteenth century, a translation of the Bible in the dialect of Padua. After two nights, on July 13th, we came on to Ferrara, where we reduced our luggage to two small baskets and sent our suit-case, which had become a curse, on separately by train.

'. . . Grass grows in the streets of Ferrara. The Via dei Pioppomi is dignified and splendid, mostly with terracotta cornices, sometimes a marble column and balcony. We reached the duomo last of all about sunset, when the rose of marble seemed to grow transparent. I have never before seen a church with an arcade of shops leaning up against it.

'14.7.14. Still Ferrara. We discovered Lucrezia Borgia's tomb in a convent behind the tiny baroque church of Corpus Domini; two black nuns, with veils over their heads so as to hide the eyes, let us in through a small door beside the chancel. The Este tombs—six or seven sculptured slabs—lie there in very quiet magnificence; Lucrezia is there with Alfonso and their two children. The nuns pray for them; but they are more interested in showing us the crucified Christ who spoke to St. Catherine. They are nuns of Sta Chiara, and once numbered over a hundred—now only twelve; but a new sister is entering to-morrow. Close by is Lucrezia's house, with herbs and flowers growing about the courtyard well, and a strange domestic unexpected charm; what is now convent was all garden and one cannot fancy a more delightful home.

'From Ferrara we made for Comacchio in the lagoons, famous for eels. We went by train and then changed into a tram, and were horrified to find all the velvet of the seats dotted with sleeping mosquitos. We had to clear a space to sit on, and this and the huge advertisements of malaria cures which began to appear everywhere, and the dampness of the twilight and heavy dew, gave us a sober and cautious feeling. The tram and road run alongside out into the swamps. First on one side only, then also on the other, the shallow waters lie; what land there is is dull, dark green and brown, and mud-caked and cracked along the shore. The waters reflect all the sky and hold wonderful lights; the landscape spreads endlessly, with a feeling of desolation.'

The diary ends here and does not describe Comacchio with its bridge and three flights of steps across a double stream; nor Pomposa Monastery, lost in the lagoons—the home of Aretino— whither we thought to sail in a fishing boat, and started gaily and early, and crawled with a dropped wind in a stench of rotting lagoon that grew intolerable as the strength of the sun sucked it up, till we reached the Monastery about 2 p.m., nearly asphyxiated; and I remember the frescoes only vaguely.

From here we followed the coast by Magnavacca, where Garibaldi landed on his retreat from Rome in '49 and stayed in a poor hut of that pestilential region, in danger of his life, till his wife Anita died; and we ended in Ravenna, and felt the splendour of Rome dying among barbarians in a way that I never felt again until I reached the ruins of the Levant. There the usual telegram from Mario arrived, and we took the train back to Dronero. My mother had been gay, loving, generous, the most charming companion, as she always was as soon as the Mario spell was removed. I ought to have been happy, but I was restless on this holiday and depressed by a craving for people of my own age, and I found myself being irritable without a cause.

At Dronero I now never arrived without being asked by my mother to take over the housekeeping from Vera. A dislike of housekeeping was, she thought, the cause of all Vera's un-happiness, and my holidays were uselessly immolated, for all Vera needed was to be left *alone* with her husband. She was still treated like a little girl; saw him only at meals and through the evening, when he and my mother sat together and the old factory shop went on uninterrupted. She was so miserable that she took no interest in the house or in anything else except her sculpture. The promise to live in separate households might never have been made. Vera wanted, she told me pathetically, to be young: she realized that she had lost that chance, and was so unhappy that I think she would have done anything to escape. That autumn, after I left, she wandered out by herself into the hills until a search was sent, and I think frightened Mario into some sort of feeling. She both felt and made life unbearable, and told me that she was so wretched that it pleased her to make everyone else so too. My father came back from Canada for a short spell just at this time. What he thought about it I never knew, as he never spoke of Mario; Vera told me that before her marriage he had seemed one day as if he meant to talk to her, but, after a long silence, he had come out with the advice to get up early in the morning, and had presented her with a scrubbing brush for her bath! This was the only preparation for matrimony she had, for my mother told neither of us anything, and Vera learned what it all meant accidentally a month or two before her wedding by reading a book called *L'Age Dangereux*! Luckily she liked Mario as a husband, though she never knew what it was to be in love. She was self-sufficing and became happy in a quiet way when alone, later on.

She loathed Dronero, and when we returned from our holiday begged to go to some seaside place for a change. Mario would have had to leave her there between week-ends with possible chances of dangerous meetings; he had all her money, already swallowed by the factory, and her prayers were disregarded. We were taken to a solitary little pub in the mountains instead: but mountains, Vera said, she already looked at all the year round. I loved them passionately and was so happy myself that I gave her much less sympathy than I might have done. The rift between her and my mother was now too deep for any impartial affection equally divided between them, and the time was coming when I should have to take one side or the other. The little mountain village wore even my cheerfulness away: it rained perpetually: my father joined us, gloomy over the news; Vera was unhappy, and the war broke out when we were there. The place has remained hateful to me.

In 1939, our second war came almost as a relief after years of anticipation; but 1914 was the sudden sinking of a world. Italy was neutral and her correspondents sent long eye-witness descriptions of the march of the Germans: a confusion of trampling armies used to agitate even my dreams. The papers in England at least gave the English side of the news: but we read day by day the forecasts—regretful forecasts—of German victory. It put a stop to our miserable holiday and we came back to Dronero. My father went to England to try to enlist: he tried for several months, but was too old, and returned sadly to Canada (he was fifty-nine). Italy was expected to come in, and I had no idea of going on with education: I decided to learn to nurse. We wrote to a friend of Mary Androutzos whose father was a well-known Italian doctor: and they arranged for me to be allowed into the clinic of St. Ursula in Bologna.

LETTERS FROM W. P. KER

95 *GOWER STREET,*
LONDON,
27 *Nov.,* 1913.

My dear Freya,

I send a print of the barbarous poem remembering the immortal summer.

A Madonna Freya
Sonetto barbaro
Settentrionale

Qual è colui che con lena affannata
Giunto alla cima fra le eterne nevi,
Lasciando riposar i piè non lievi,
Là ove vento amaro menò fiata,
Si stende sulla pietra riscaldata
Per ritrovar i soliti sollievi:
Pane, caffè bevuto in colpi brevi,
E lucida sardina delicata?
Cotal m'apparve un non so chè sognando
    dir sentii: Tu non sperasti mai
Poner sì tosto capo alla terzina.
Poi disse un'altra voce: Forse quando
Giù nelle strade lorde lento andrai,
Ricorderai la state grivolina.

W. P. K.

[144]

GOWER STREET,
6 *July*, 1914.

My dear Freya,

Only to say that I hope you are there in good weather, and that I wish I had been starting with you. It is very childish, but I have spent some time lately wanting this year to be last year over again. The Powers long ago settled that difficulty, and we have got to move on. I hope you saw the Leman Lake in a good light.

Do you know the poem as follows:

> "Either Lake Leman or Loch Lomond
> Would be convenient for a dromond;
> And so to travel, undismay'd,
> To Evian or Inversnaid."

I sometimes repeat this.

I hope you saw Martigny where the Great St. Bernard road begins to pass over to Aosta. There is much life about Aosta and a beautiful road up on the other side to Comboc and Mt. Emilius and so over to the Val Granson. But this is digressing.

I hope you saw Visp—Viége to the Balfinhorn (Balpin, Balfrin?), at the end of the valley, clear. The valley splits at Stalden—on the left you get the road to Saas which takes you to Mattmark and over the Monte Moro to Macugnaga in Italy. On the right hand is the road to St. Nicholas and Zermatt where there are walks. Not far above Stalden in the St. Nicholas valley there is a bridge—at Calpentras—there is a lime tree there, smelling sweet—I remembered it yesterday at Surbiton—there were lime trees there.

Now the remarkable thing is that I have been in these places more than once, and have found them quite real. Therefore the reasoning mind may infer that possibly it may be there again —in good company.

So send me a letter soon. And give my very kind regards to your mother, and if she could write to me I should be glad.

Always yours truly,

W. P. KER.

13

St. Ursula in Bologna. 1914-1916

THE Clinic of St. Ursula was a modern building, a fifteen minutes' walk or so beyond the San Vitale gate, near which, in a long street of porticos and palaces, a room for me had been found, small and low, on the *mezzanino*. This floor is interpolated between the lofty ground floor and even loftier *piano nobile* of an Italian palace, and is sought after because it is the only floor that is possible to keep warm in winter. Bologna has a bitter winter climate and I ran gladly through the postern in the immense hall door, past the statues in their perpetual twilight, and the huge stone balustrades, to my room whose sunny window looked out on the traceries of the cloister of the Servi just below. In the room adjoining lived Miss Smith who had taught English to several generations of the young female aristocracy of Bologna and could tell, with an air of impeccable refinement, the story of every love affair the town had known during the forty-odd years of her existence there. It was she who by her mere presence made my adventure possible and suffocated the breath of scandal, for no young woman of any family at all dreamed of nursing in Italy at that time.

My mother came with me, took me to the hospital, where a whole bevy of doctors and professors welcomed and showed us around, and next day I started work on my own with smelling salts in my pocket to keep myself from fainting. The two first mornings were the worst. I had nothing to do but stand and watch four operations in one morning; the room, kept as near the temperature of the human body as possible, was very hot and smelt of ether; the doctors told me later that my face became indistinguishable from the pale green of the wall behind me, and they felt sure I would never go on. I did not faint, though I was unable to eat when I got back, and my mother was so shocked by my looks that she wanted to take me away. This, of course, I refused to think of and she returned to Dronero. As soon as I had something to do in the hospital I was able to stand up to it better. The medical staff were all charming: the old professor walked his rounds with a hand on my shoulder, a convenient height below him, while he made a short oration about each recumbent figure to a train of students behind him. The doctors showed me everything, and in less than a month were allowing me to give the anaesthetics. I fainted once, after I had given an overdose of chloroform to a woman with a very weak heart: we had to bring her round again by artificial breathing, and when this was done I managed to hand over my instruments and reach the outside of the door where I fell in a heap on the mat. A young doctor, picking me up and reviving me at a window, remarked: "You must not get so agitated, Signorina; we have all killed somebody."

The giving of the anaesthetic was still in those days a very delicate thing to do, particularly in operations where only a bit of the patient's head was visible: the colour of the blood and movement of the eyes were the only things which allowed me to judge of the effect of the narcotic, which I dripped drop by drop on to a gauze mask held in my left hand. To give too little was bad, for if the sleep was not sound the shock to the nerves was greater. It used to fascinate me to watch the life of the patient in his eyes, the blind unconscious pupils dilating and contracting while he slept, and to realize the wonder of the heart, the fact that it *never stops* work, sleeping or waking, from birth to death, the only living thing that needs no rest. I had the run of the hospital. I was shown how slides were prepared for the microscope and was asked to help with the X-rays, and as I knew nothing of photography my first effort on the picture of someone's digestion turned quite black. He had to be given his revolting bismuth meal twice over, and the doctor told him that this was the regular routine.

There was no nursing to speak of: the nurses were as bad as the doctors were good, and the frequent excellence of Italian surgeons I take to be often due to the fact that they have to look after their cases from beginning to end themselves, and never trust to nurses: they did all the dressings and after the morning operations my chief work was to assist them. They had beautiful manners with me, neither flirtatious nor gruff, but gently chivalrous. I was the first 'lady' who came to work in a hospital in Bologna. The nurses were *all* women of the streets; only one was respectable, having been seduced by a doctor and stuck to him until he left her: she was called Norina, and was capable, pretty and embittered. The others carried on their two professions at once and it was so well-known, the doctors told me, that their evidence was never taken in a court of law. I had a strange and uncomfortable feeling with them long before I knew this; only Norina I liked. They hated me at sight, and were horrid out of jealousy: until at last I went up to them and asked what it was all about, and explained my feelings about the war (which, of course, had not yet touched Italy) and what it meant to us all, and they were kind to me ever after. I was sorry for one or two who looked sad and wistful; one especially who used to stop the others from making jokes when I was there, because—I once heard her say—"she isn't like *us*." Since knowing them, I have never felt that there is a real barrier between different sorts of women, only differences of the accidental sort that divide all human beings. My mother knew nothing of course and would have had a shock if she had learnt. She herself was quite innocent about such things and we were brought up in as complete ignorance as was possible in the Italy of that day, where a young woman alone was asking for importunate attentions from any passing stranger. I remember feeling neglected when I reached England, where one walked freely and no one tried even to peer under one's bonnet; so that there was a good deal of justification for all the *chaperonage*. Vera and I once escaped from the maid who walked behind us and took a boat to go out rowing on the river in Turin, and five boat-loads of young gallants instantly pursued.

Life outside the hospital was pleasant in Bologna. A few agreeable English married to Italians invited me whenever I was free and drove me about on Sundays into an Apennine landscape, soft as if its colours were run with milk. Twice a week they took me to their box at one or other of the two opera houses. We dressed for both, but in the grander of the two the decolleté was lower and ravishing small hats of feathers were worn sweeping to bare shoulders. The girls were placed in front well in view, and pretented not to notice the opera glasses of the young men who studied them from the pit. All the scandal of Bologna—the Marchesa M's new lover, the Contessa X's polychromatic past, were discussed in the twilight of the boxes. It was Mozart in real life. The operas were mostly dull—dreary Meyerbeer duets; and straight chorus rows lifting their hands together; Samson, a tiny man, on tiptoe to embrace a colossal Delilah; and no music more original than Puccini: the interest was all centred on the actual voice of the singers, and for this Bologna was held to be the most critical audience in Italy. I was still extremely pedantic and the free and easy life shocked me to the core, but I remember it pleasantly now. The people were rich—it is the richest part of Italy perhaps—very hospitable and gay. They lived in beautiful palaces, built round inner arcaded courtyards of their own, decorated with Renaissance delicacy and splendour.

The town itself, the square of San Petronio with its colour as if sunset were built into the walls, the many churches, the long arcaded streets, were a constant joy.

Under my windows at night the Church of the Servi rang the hours—only six, repeated four times a day: and at about 2 a.m. the people would come walking home from the opera, singing the arias over to themselves, with never a false note—for this is the most musical province in Italy.

On my way home to luncheon I would buy a paper for the

war news. One day, instead of the usual *Resto del Carlino* I was given the *Popolo d'Italia*, and so much admired the leading article that I stuck to the *Popolo* from then on. It was written by Benito Mussolini, of whom no one except the Socialists had heard at that time. I asked about him as I was so much impressed by the writing, and no one could tell me anything about him.

Miss Smith always joined me for luncheon in my room, very solid in black. She had disconcerting eyes because they squinted *outwards* so one never knew what she was looking at. She talked of the food, which bored me, and of the gossip which amused me, with the same unbending disapproval for both. Our landlady's son Aldo waited at table; it was all he did, I believe, except spend his mother's money. I got amusement out of his complete absence of any wish to have "nice feelings". He, also, would like to nurse, he said: he could bear any amount of pain *for other people*, "but if my own little finger hurts me, signorina, that I *cannot* stand." When I put on my black velvet dress he looked at it approvingly: "I also look well in black, signorina," he said.

The brother of the friend who sent us to Bologna was there, a bacteriologist called Guido Ruata. He was tall, with a short naval type of beard, distinguished to look at and very easy to talk to, and took much trouble to show us Bologna while my mother was there. He used to call on me, and send books and notes and flowers: at first he called once in a while, then once a week—by the time I went for Christmas to Dronero he was coming every day or two. We sat and talked while Miss Smith chaperoned comfortably from her bedroom through the partition, and I had very little idea of what was happening to me. When I went to Dronero, Mario—who travelled all over Italy for his factory—stopped at Bologna and asked Ruata his intentions: he naturally said he had none, and when this was told me I realized suddenly that I was very much in love (and furious with Mario for interfering).

A niece, little Leonarda, had been born. It was a happiness to go back to, and made Dronero much better. I spent Christmas

there. Vera, still in her bedroom, was the centre of attention, content to have that little dominion of her own. I stayed
a short while, sleeping, I remember, with Guido's photograph
under my pillow: was told to put him out of my mind: and
went back to Bologna thinking of nothing else. He hardly
came to see me, sending flowers now and then. But one evening
I was invited to Modena by a friend whose husband taught
there in the Military Academy. It is only a short train journey
from Modena to Bologna across the plain. Guido's brother
was staying with these people and Guido was of the party:
we went after dinner to hear *The Count of Luxembourg,* and
we took the last train back to Bologna (my friend said she
arranged it on purpose!). Very soon after he asked me to marry
him. He was full of doubts because of his age, which was
thirty-eight. I had no doubts at all, but that feeling of security
which comes with the reality of love. Most people luckily
have the short and perfect happiness of such a time in their
lives, when every moment shines as if in a halo of its own.
When I heard him walk up the stairs, as he now came every
evening, my heart felt as if it were being drawn out of its socket
—one could not tell whether it was pleasure or pain for a second.
It seems strange that one human being can do this to another.

I was busy now with an inundation of Italian ladies. Italy's
coming into war seemed to draw near and Red Cross classes
were started. Two volunteers had already joined me in hospital
some time before, and, as they belonged to the Upper Ten of
Bologna society, the respectability of nursing was established.
About thirty new ladies came pouring in and were divided into
batches to work in the hospital under us veterans, and our
troubles began in earnest. Marchesa M. arrived in a nursing
apron with her pearls and emerald clasp worn outside: there
were quarrels as to who went into the operating theatre first;
there were two English women who said that the Bologna
ladies were "not people I should like my daughters to mix with."
The doctors merely said, "Do what you like but keep them
away." I was quite incapable of coping with them, but I still

have somewhere an official card thanking me for the work done for the Red Cross in Bologna.

The two English women were unmarried, but they had collected a family of six orphans here and there: two from the Messina earthquake, two children of a Genoese washerwoman who went to the bad, and one—a tiny boy—had been brought to them one morning by one of the court chamberlains who said that they were known to be so good to the children and would they add this to the family? These little things were all brought up exactly alike, very religiously and lovingly, but the ones with the bad mother were already showing every sort of small vice, and the little court boy proved his origin with the greatest dignity in his tiny thin body: I have always believed in heredity after visiting that salad of a household. They were both charming women but they disapproved even of powdering one's face and were very difficult to mix with the Bologna ladies.

I left Bologna early in the year, perhaps March. I crept down my grand staircase in the cold and dark morning to Guido, who whistled 'God Save the King' under my window, so as not to disturb the sleeping Miss Smith. (Our talks used to go on so late that she would ring her alarum clock through the partition when she thought it was time for him to go!) We went together to Milan, where I had never been, and saw the cathedral and the Brera, and lunched in the Galleria Vittorio, and I have had a love for Milan ever since. Then he put me into the Turin train and joined me later in Dronero for a few days.

He and Mario already disliked each other and the atmosphere of Dronero was very different from romance in Bologna. By this time, brother-in-law or not, I detested Mario. In looking back I can only wonder at the slowness with which I became aware of it.

Guido's people lived in Perugia and we visited them in the spring. It was Easter time—the lovely spring of Umbria with red anemones under olive trees in the young corn. The family lived high up in a house on the great Etruscan wall. They were a bourgeois, intellectual household, with a long liberal tradition behind them of the sort that made the Risorgimento—a pathetic class in Italy, for it is always they who suffer in any war or revolution. They seemed sounder to me than the hidebound country noblesse of Piedmont, and indeed I thought them perfect, for they were a demonstrative family and welcomed me into an atmosphere of happiness and warmth. There was a fine grey-bearded patriarch of a father, who had been an innovator in the medicine of his day and a disciple of Lister; two sisters, handsome and gentle, who had taken doctor's degrees but carried them with Latin femininity that rubs the corners off emancipation; and there were the two children of one and the husband of the other sister, and such a genuine family affection that it seemed as if even the absent, the elder husband, the younger brother and his Russian wife, were present also, so often and kindly were they spoken of.

It was not proper for me to be in the same house as my fiancé so they took a room for me in the Hotel Brufani started by an Englishman with a comfortable Victorian insular taste in furnishing—carpeted bedrooms, brass fenders, cans of hot water —strange and amusing against the Umbrian landscape that lay below the windows. While Guido was with his father, the two sisters took me around and made me feel that they were fond of me: and then he would come and we would wander to Assisi, or about the churches of Perugia, or walk on the finely modelled hills. The grey landscape there is wistful, as if too much history had left it to its dreams. In the evening Guido took me to my hotel, and told me how much he loved me on the doorstep. How difficult it was to say good night and part, even for those few short dark and scented hours of the spring.

No one in Italy considered it possible at that time for a girl to go on nursing when she became engaged. As far as I remember I made no resistance for we expected to get married very soon. But in Dronero, by the early summer, I began to sicken with an obscure sort of illness, a pining away that nothing seemed to cure. I got thinner and thinner. My mother, like very many strong people, loathed sickness: when we had colds as children she used to say that we coughed on purpose, and we would almost suffocate under the bedclothes trying to suppress all noise: the result was that we never admitted to any illness and only let it be noticed when it was already serious. I think I was anxious too, and had perhaps had more of other people's troubles, over a long time, than I could take. Guido was expecting to go to the front as a military doctor, for Italy had come into the war in May. He had a huge depôt for the disinfecting and renovating of equipment collected on the battlefields. In summer I went to Viareggio to try to get well again and stopped three days in Bologna. It was all very different. My mother was with me and Guido disliked her, and she was so strangely unobservant that she never thought of leaving us. I asked her once to do so, and offended her. We had no evening talks—only one short interval when he took me over his new rooms. He was in uniform.

I shall never forget the sight of his great disinfecting station—a vast room piled almost to the ceiling with débris of the battlefields just as they arrived—uniforms, caps, boots, letters, knapsacks, puttees, torn and holed and blood-stained—empty clothes, more pitiful perhaps than the bodies of men themselves: it was my first sight of the world's sorrow, gathered together.

I spent two months in Viareggio trying to get strong and not enjoying it. I made friends with a Baroness Winspeare whose eyes were dark violet, the most strange and lovely eyes; and also with some Polish Jews from Warsaw (then under the Russians). The daughter could remember pogroms, herself being hurried by her nurse into a side path of the public gardens while Cossacks swept down the main avenue cutting down everyone they met, with their swords. No Pole, she said, would be seen talking to a Russian in the streets of Warsaw. Every day I wrote to Guido and he certainly wrote two or three times a week. I was back in Dronero for the autumn, and can remember little about it, and the next thing that happened was the death of my little niece Leonarda. She had colitis and neither Vera nor anyone else there had any notion of how to look after babies:

she got worse and in the late autumn we took her to Turin. There is something heartrending in nursing a baby too small to speak. Vera and I took it in turns to sit up with her: one night or more perhaps we had a nun in. There was very little hope left then, and I remember this nun because she had such wise and kind eyes, as if she had been through everything and knew it all, and looked at us with so much pity. Mario was broken-hearted as all hope faded away; he adored his children while they were small and entirely his own. And soon, while she was trying to settle the baby in the cot, Vera gave a pitiful little cry, and I came and saw Leonarda dead, just suddenly nothing. It was the first sight of death for us.

Leonarda had been named after Leonardo Bistolfi; a sculptor who lived in Turin and whom Mario so greatly admired that there was never any difficulty in our friendship with him. He and his wife came immediately and took Vera and me away, and she and I walked together next day in the hills behind Turin. I remember their splendour that day, crisp with snow, and the broken feeling of how small life is. It is still a happiness to think that I was with Vera then, for she bore many of her troubles alone and I was a comfort to her at that time.

The Bistolfis lived in a house attached to a studio where marble figures on all sides fluttered in an invisible wind. He was little and thin, with a long black beard he used to stroke, a great man in himself whatever his monuments may be judged to be. They were never as good as his clay sketches of them, because he left a lot of the work to his pupils, who ruined them. He was fond of me and would take us to see his statues and tell us what the marble was to express, with as much courtesy and interest as if we were art critics or kings. His voice was deep, beautiful and sure—a courageous voice; and he had great feeling for poetry and music as well as sculpture. His sketches were beautiful in a way of their own, like vivid Limoges enamel. In his house were all the values which we had lived among as children, and missed in the shadow of Mario, whose only god in this world was success: I think Bistolfi gauged this pretty accurately, and helped by giving us as much of the other things of life as he could on the rare occasions when we could go to him. He took me to *Die Meistersinger* one evening, and explained and interpreted it in the intervals in a way I have never forgotten. I met Toscanini at his house: he sat next me at table and told me how much he loved English poetry, particularly Keats and Shakespeare: but how the knowledge of them had been insufficient to enable him to reach his hotel in a London cab! He also told me that, of all the theatres in which he had conducted, the Metropolitan in New York was his favourite, because of the splendour of the fully-dressed audience: that glitter and luxury, he said, inspires a conductor. It was fascinating to watch these two—the fine aquiline faces, so sensitive, intelligent and powerful, and so happy together, for they were great friends. Bistolfi came from simple people in the Monferrat and his wife had remained a simple woman, entering little into his world and rather jealous of it: she was plump, with the remains of beauty in great heavy-lidded eyes: she had a charm which many people missed but which continued to hold him—she said her thoughts exactly as they came into her head. I cannot quite explain it but there seemed to be no forming process between the birth of her ideas and their expression: this gave a quality of unexpectedness to her talk. Most people took no notice of her at all, and she sat amiably aside while he went out into the world, neither helping nor hindering. The King of Italy used to call and take Bistolfi out for long drives, himself holding the wheel, and they were so busy talking one day that they noticed two punctured tyres only on their return: Bistolfi, who was very thin, had thought for a long time that the road was bumpy.

I was in Dronero that winter, feeling more and more ill. My mother was working far too hard and was as usual irritated by sickness. She thought it was imaginary and begged me to cure it by self-control (of which indeed I had a lot). At last a doctor came and said I had typhoid. Some masons were putting up a frieze in the room next door, and I lay in bed convinced that they were hammering King Charles I's scaffold, and we were so incompetent with illnesses that no one thought of asking the work to stop with a sick-room next door. The typhoid was supposed to be mild, and we relied on local doctors who did all the wrong things; it soon added to itself pleurisy and then pneumonia. My temperature went up to 107 degrees and still I was not really delirious; but I used to be haunted by a strange vague fear of certain colours—brown and grey: they had no shape, but they slowly gathered about me and left me paralysed with fright. My heart beat so that I could hardly bear it, and still the doctor said it was nothing very important and my mother begged me not to imagine things; but Mario became genuinely kind in sickness and arrived with a specialist from Turin, who discovered that I had been so dosed with drugs to bring down the fever that only a heart as unusually strong as mine could have stood it. He was a small neat man and danced about with fury when he heard what they had been doing, and my local doctor was had up before him: the only excuse he could find, they told me, for giving all these drugs was that "the chemist too must live." The specialist now came at intervals and I slowly turned that corner. A nun was brought to nurse me, a dreadful woman who looked upon the chief duty of nursing as a preparation for death. She stood over me and told me what I looked like—my thin arms and cheeks sunk to the bones, the eyes so dim, the peaked and sharpened nose, and fine pale lips: "how terrible is the coming of death," she said. Weak as I was I could not help laughing and it probably did me good. But she also tried to convert me, and I complained, and a kind nun came instead. It was during this illness that my mother became a Roman Catholic; we knew nothing of it till later. Guido came and I was well enough to see him for half an hour at a time. As soon as I could travel they put me into an ambulance for a nursing home in Turin: I felt then, and still feel now, how much better it is not to be looked after by one's family when ill. I am sure it is a job for experts. The typhoid, we discovered, had come down the mill-stream from an infected house above. I had been asking for over a year (when doing the housekeeping) that proper water should be laid on, but Mario laughed at this as English fussiness, and said "Why not drink wine?" and I have always resented this illness as a completely unnecessary one. But when eventually I recovered all traces of the long debility of the year before had vanished.

The great pleasure during convalescence in Turin was that Vera had a little flat there. Mario was doing work for the government: he was of an age to be conscripted and spent his time moving heaven and earth to avoid it, on the rather flimsy plea that a family man has no right to go to war. Vera used to listen in silence while my mother and Mario elaborated this theory, and complained to me, saying: "I wish they wouldn't make *me* responsible for his not going." So passive when it came to action, she never yielded to nonsense in her thoughts. One day, after a long monologue of her husband's on faithfulness in women (no one *could* be more faithful than Vera, she never had a chance to be otherwise), she told me she thought it a rather overrated virtue, "and why should women's honour be just in one physical locality?" We developed a War and Peace party in the house and I think it shocked my mother deeply not to find Vera on the side of her husband's efforts to stay. My mother never criticized Mario, even in her heart, yet she did all she could to make up for his deficiencies by working even harder than before. She kept the factory going on war work in his absence. It was made to saw timber instead of producing carpets, and my mother would go for long expeditions to look for suitable tree-trunks in the hills. She came back grey with fatigue and never rested, and tried to fulfil every other demand as well. She opened a little shop in the town, with a window of war pictures and magazines: they were given gratis at first, and no one ever asked for them: so she charged twopence each for the Red Cross and they sold out all the time. We also sheared our sheep to make winter socks for the troops (as it was autumn the sheep had to be fed in the stable all winter to keep them warm, so it was rather uneconomical). In spite of all this the war was remote in Piedmont. Verdun was being fought at the time of my illness and the horror of it kept wandering about in my semi-delirium.

Vera's happiest married year was spent in the little flat in Turin. She had made it gay and it was all her own. She looked matronly with another baby coming, and kept on forgetting her wedding-ring and walking about without it, to Mario's annoyance. He was always devoted to her and never looked at anyone else; and used to tell her how wonderful this was for hours together, and be a little chagrined at the way she took it for granted. She read Meredith's *Egoist* at that time and said to me: "Don't you think he is very like Mario?" I had thought so myself when I read Meredith five years before, but it seemed a strange discovery for a quite happily married young wife to make.

In the later spring, through all the difficulties of travel in war time, Viva came and took me to convalesce in Alassio. The casualties of the first war were worse than the second, but the dislocation of private living seems, on looking back, to have been far less. The Palace Hotel was open, though we had it almost to ourselves, and we spent long quiet days in the terraced gardens of an old Scottish baronet with whom nobody would have anything to do: he had walks of cypress with lavender hedges against the sea. The lovely feeling came of life returning, in spite of the war and in spite of anxiety of my own. My illness had, of course, put off my marriage: and Guido had then applied for a very good post as director of the 'cures' of Salsomaggiore and wished to wait till that was settled. He got it now, but was still anxious to wait. He was very busy and wrote less. I never admitted it, but I know now that I felt a dull fear. Our house was already chosen and my mother had made furniture in Dronero and painted it beautifully and had bought the rest in Florence: I think Guido disliked it, though he was polite about it; and I knew later that it would have been far better to buy less artistic things of our own, by ourselves. At the time I could not have believed that my mother could inspire anyone with dislike. Guido was very busy. I had not seen him for some months. One day, soon after the sinking of the *Lusitania*, a letter came. It broke off our engagement. It gave no reason. Viva was out, and when she returned saw by my face that something had happened. "We must go to Bologna," I said. She was quiet and good and understanding: we packed and took the next train. Luckily great pain or suffering brings a sort of narcotic with it, so one can remember little of it clearly.

We went to a hotel in Bologna. Guido did not wish even to see us, but Viva insisted and went alone to see him while I sat at my window and looked at an orange sky with swallows flying dark against it—and the sight of such a sky always brings back an ache of pain even now, though I do not often remember why. When Viva returned she said that he gave no reason. He came to dine and I saw him afterwards, and still he gave no reason beyond repeating many times that I was not the cause. I think Browning puts it in a poem—the bewilderment when all that pleased so short a while ago has become useless. I know that I offered, if marriage irked him, to remain with him un-married—all that seemed inessential. Very late I came away and we parted, and next day left Bologna. I remember nothing of how I got back to Dronero, except that dull feeling of walking about with a sort of corpse inside one. Later on I heard from my friend in Modena what had happened. He had lived for a long time with a musician, a well-known woman: she had left him and gone to America: when she heard about me and of his good appointment she came back and he married her a year or so later.

My mother took this matter in the worst possible way. She went to see the family in Perugia, who were all miserably distressed, but also offended by her violence. She wrote to Guido himself and went on asking for odds and ends of furniture, just as with the things at Ford Park years before. She lost on these occasions all control of reason. My prayers to drop it all were not even listened to. When, months later, I had gone to England, I received a letter from Guido himself asking me to stop my mother from corresponding: she was threatening proceedings to recover a sketch portrait of me which as a matter of fact he had sent back. I then wrote such a letter as did effectually stop it. It is most extraordinary how people think to comfort one by speaking ill of those who have been loved, when all that is left is to keep at least the memory clear and happy. My mother could not realize it and this bitter experience cut a deep division between us: it healed and the affection returned, but never the faith: my life was in my own hands from that day. When I returned to Dronero she wished to justify herself by telling me that she had recovered the little portrait; but Vera had already told me how it had been discovered accidentally, sent long before with the other things, and this attempt to throw one more onus on a man I had loved and who had already so much to answer for had an effect on me that I cannot describe. My mother never knew it. Her affection for me had made her anxious to remove the criticism in my letter and she had a very Continental attitude towards truth as such. In English this sounds a damaging thing to say—but it is only in England that truth is made a basis of morality, and my mother had been brought up in Italy and was Italian in her outlook. Charity and generosity are perhaps more important: she certainly thought so, and these she possessed. I think it was a fundamental cause of difference between her and Vera and myself, both of whom inherited my father's feeling for exactitude—not so much a moral quality as a fastidiousness, like the feeling for personal cleanliness: my mother thought it pedantry and managed to get on very well without it. Perhaps truthfulness towards others is not so vital, but nothing can be more important than to be honest with oneself, and it is very difficult to be one and not the other also.

The difference between our outlooks was shown by an incident with Vera a little later on. The head of the church in Dronero was an ascetic old priest supposed to look after Vera's soul: Vera took not the slightest interest in him or it—the affair of the baptism still rankled and she felt she had done enough for a religion in which she did not believe. My mother regretted the lack of courtesy and one day tried to cover it by sending some flowers to the church with a message as if from Vera: she thought to please the old man and this seemed good enough to her. Vera happened to meet him, and was thanked, and instantly explained that she had never sent the flowers: the whole difference between them lay in the little episode—and it would be hard to pronounce in favour of one or the other, except as a matter of personal predilection.

LETTERS FROM W. P. KER

95 *GOWER STREET,*
LONDON,

1915.
Eve of Lammas.

My dearest Freya,

What am I to be so happy with such a child? such a friend? Again I repeat "its of no consequence thank you" said Mr. Toots. But I go on wondering. Anyhow it is all taken out of my hands, do you see? It just comes so, like the Morning Star.

I fear I am not going to be able to travel this summer—I have taken on a job, and there is no sense in that unless you stick to it. It is a great disappointment—it is not yet certain, but I fear it is likely. I am pained and disabled. Now you must understand that I am not going to sit down and cry over it and you must also understand that I feel it very deeply all the more. It is just part of this inferior system—I am tired of thinking about the Nature of things.

I hope to see Mrs. Stark soon—Mrs. Jeyes tells me she may be coming. Mrs. Jeyes is working very hard but looking none the worse for it. I was at supper there last Sunday, and she came to tea one day since then—to talk about you.

Thank you for the edelweiss from the war.

With all my heart I am yours truly,

W. P. KER.

95 GOWER STREET
LONDON,
18 June, 1915.

Dearest Freya,

Thank you for letters—if I have not written yet I have been thinking. Words are poor. But we live in the real world and without words. I can say thank you—both to you and the Powers that sent you to talk to me and ask my good and highly respectable advice about the London Matric (short for matriculation examination). Sometimes I laugh—and then I see Freya coming running to meet me—me coming down from Tersiva or such, and I laugh and cry both together, and I know that my own life is not worth a windlestrae except for what has been put into it by other people. Do you know what a windlestrae is? It is rather like a piece of bent grass, and I would not have thought of it if I had not read it yesterday in a queer Scotch book. But this is irrelevant and unworthy of so severe and austere a critic as this here who writes to you—of me who write —who wish you well.

Yes I think of you often—affectionately as the saying is— but affection is a weak word, and love is strong.

I wish I could come to the wedding—I don't know yet—I will try. The Good Man will be a new friend of mine.

All good be with you, dear Freya, yours

W. P. KER.

FROM MY FATHER

CRESTON, B.C.
CANADA,
22 June, 1916.

Dear Freya,

I was glad to have another letter from Alassio. It means you are progressing and it's delightful to hear of your surroundings.

Now, as to coming over for the wedding, whenever that may be, I don't think it feasible for several reasons, though the thought of seeing you again sets me longing to do it, I can tell you. First of all there are the *spese*, because I should have to run back again and I should see little of you too. Another draw-back. And I cannot well leave the ranch to Tom's sole care; there is so much to do—takes both of us all the time to keep things going. It is to be thought well over however.

That's good news about Salsomaggiore. Congratulate Ruata for me. Fancy you installed there. I expect your estimate of the villa will prove about correct. I can see it too. It will be square, stuccoed, with ugly roof and horrid cornice. Too tall windows with *persiane* at regular intervals. A few balconies outside probably but not big enough to sit out on comfortably; approached by a depressing flight of steps; guarded on either side by statues (save the name) in cement; perfect samples of the *falso vero*. I won't continue.

One thing I am glad to be able to say that you won't have many Germans there for many years to come, for they will be so reduced in figure, especially the Fraus, that they won't have any rheumatics left either.

That poor antiquario. Surely you were born to be the undoing of all you meet. But brass plates. Don't for heaven's sake get any which are *carved*, only cast or moulded ones, like the Adam and Eve we had; the touch of a chisel spoils brass or copper.

We get a fair amount of news here from Italian papers published in New York, besides the English which I get pretty regularly, and the important items we have by telegram. I've been wondering how Herbert [Young] has been getting on, for, if not away from home, he will have been within sound of the guns of late. I know the country pretty well where they have been fighting. When I first came to Italy, I spent the summer up there. So complex are the valleys, that I lost my way for the first and only time in my life wandering about, so one can imagine what the fighting must have been.

Thank Mamma for her letter. I've got so many waiting to be answered that this one may do for you both for the time being perhaps. We are extra busy just now as haying commences next week. It's been a terrible summer or rather no summer at all as yet. One week of heat, and then just rain and cold; floods coming down from the mountains. Half the bridges gone out already; water in lake about 15 feet above normal and still rising, probably another 10 feet, before it's finished.

What is Mario doing and how is Vera?

All love to you

PIPS STARK.

The rush enclosed polishes metal; try it in a solder.

DRONERO,

1 *Sept.,* 1916.

My darling,

Your letters—two of them—the last from Dartmoor. It is a great joy to have you with those dear people.

I had decided not to send you Ruggi's certificate, for I don't want you to nurse. I think we have paid our Scot to the war— and though I want you to work for it—I don't want you to definitely ruin your health—or run risks to do so.

You are sad now—and have not much interest in your life, but it will blossom again—happily and richly—in spite of what you think and with or without Ruata—so do not throw it away recklessly. However, you are free, now as always and I will send you the letters.

Nothing can really alter the big things—for which God has given you a soul capable of understanding—nor does happi- ness—lasting—lie with this or that person. As long as you have a purpose and an anchor to your aspirations and sympathy and understanding for those who live beside you—you will be all right.

As to my epistolary talents—I agree with you! But you must remember the awful shock I was under; the deadly fear that it might be true, the need to supply you with plenty of money— to send you to Egypt or elsewhere, so that I could not be your companion but had to stay and work and so the necessity to draw on Pips's time. I knew it was not ideal, but he was the only possible person then.

No one will know what a dreadful time it was, and how less than nothing, anything, everything done to me appeared in comparison.

[165]

I am sorry I was not stronger, but this shock supervening on your illness of which distress I had not recovered morally in spite of Alassio's rest—was too much, my nerves had completely given way. Do you know that sometimes I never slept for three days and nights on end? And even sleep visits me but lightly.

However, I have an iron frame and there is no need to worry. I only mention this to explain many things.

B.

5 *Sept.,* 1916.

My dearest,

Time passes—rushes in one way and drags heavily in another. Pia has *not* a baby yet—I saw Nico yesterday, who sent his special saluti to you and bid me tell you he was going for a climb and did not you wish you were there too.

My dear!—schemes are already being made to find you a husband!

Eva brought in a young *Giovanardi* and *capitano* shortly to be, a nice boy, with 16 months war at his back, wounded, and then *congealed* feet—a good fellow. I could see what was in her mind quite well! He also brought news of Teresita; she is *not* a favourite with the family evidently. I think they must all be a little highflown and super-sensitive! Eva told me of tragic scenes with the "Bandiera" wound round the body of little Carluccio—and many other things. Of course it is hard for us to follow that sort of thing.

Clot dined with me and confided to me that she and her mother would like you to marry Gabriel de Bottini. It is really a great compliment. She assures me that her mother has long wished it when Gabriel should come home. So my dear— you have a choice. I sat and gasped and said I was très flattée! She also told me I had been wrong to leave you alone amongst "roturiers." But she still has a good word for Guido—she has seen so much of this nervous breakdown and it is so usual that she is still hopeful—tho' the only one perhaps here!

I have been a prey to neuralgia these days and am going to bed now to try to forget my troubles. Mme. Besio lent me

[166]

Les Paroles Secrētes par M. Reynès Monlaur. Get it! a real work of art, the experiences of a tiny innocent foolish man before the German advance and the burning of Rheims Cathedral. Really great art!

Good night my own darling, your

B.

14

The War in England. 1916–1917

I WENT to England in summer or early autumn, and for the
first time fully realized how truly I belonged there. There
was a gentleness and healing in every sight and line of the
land. I joined Mr. Bale at Rodborough, *The Bear Inn*, near
Stroud. It has an old bowling green. He used to go out
sketching and I would take walks, looking down the beech-wood
coombes and first getting to know the lovely grey of Cotswold
houses. Viva was right in thinking I needed to look after
someone: he was so dear, so gentle and sane and *decent*, and,
with the authority of his long life behind him, so helpful in
confidence and fortitude, that gradually I became able to face
the thought of my own life again. I was still too delicate from
the typhoid to nurse, but began to look for other work when
we returned to London, and did three weeks copying in the
British Museum for a woman who wrote about herb gardens.
Once or twice I went to help Viva at her canteen. This was in
Paddington station and she cut sandwiches and gave out coffee
and tea from midnight to 7 a.m. once a week. The trains
rumbled in at night, under the glass which no one feared then,
the troops came in with all their cocoon of equipment about
them: they shed it bit by bit and stood it up in a heap while
they drank their tea: sometimes they gathered in a little bunch,
and two old ladies who helped us were surprised because: "they
seem only to want a little hot water in their cups to drink."
Once a young officer handed us a huge and unattractive sandwich to get rid of for him: his mother had pressed it on him
and he had carried it all the way from Scotland, afraid to leave

it around and be fined for wasting bread. The Australians strode in looking like gods; when there were few at a time one could talk a little, hear about their leave and their families; then they shouldered their things and went on, sometimes a whole train-load, singing Tipperary, rumbling out into silence. The Battle of the Somme began that year: the casualties were appalling: I can still see the sheets of *The Times* printed closely over a whole page or more, column after column with the missing and the dead.

In late autumn two householders guaranteed me and I went on trial as a Censor. This consisted of three weeks' training during which the letters were re-censored by a supervisor. She was an embittered woman who spent her time in a long room full of desks telling us all what fools we were, but at the end of three weeks I was sent on into a building off the Strand, where I worked for thirty-five shillings a week. Once we were given a half holiday because the office was too cold to work in, though I do not think the rule for keeping windows open was relaxed. I kept a sporadic diary, positive and immature, but it describes the room we lived in:

'I suppose it holds about 300 people. The D.A. Censors sit at tables along the sides: they are all well-dressed and mostly good-looking, but whether this is cause or effect. . . .

'Occasionally the Major walks down between our (apparently) absorbed hard-working tables with an air of serene responsibility: we make quite a good background. . . .

'. . . all these . . . that move about, and frown over the bad writing and whisper to each other, and trouble to wrap themselves in different coloured clothes, when it suddenly comes to one that these are all living people with lives of their own, then I feel a kind of suffocation and long for a breath of solitude and a clear skyline and the coolness of wind that has come from spaces without a human voice.

'The people at my own table are seven besides myself and only one insufferable . . . wears little bits of glass and jewellery and lace and . . . persistent friendliness that nothing will subdue. Why does one get such a wish to be horrid to people? She has a thin mouth and long pointed jaw, and slits of eyes that have nothing behind them. . . .

'The person at my table who gets the most interesting letters is Miss Eldridge—half-Russian, daughter of a Consul in Syria. She looks too big for this place and walks about with an atmosphere of open air; big-boned and weather-beaten face, and amiable but very assured manner . . . hates the people and office work; says she wants to brush everyone out of her path as she goes along. She is the most interesting of the table, and I like to make her talk of brigands and Young Turks and the methods of the old Sultan, all of which she knows about.'

The letters I passed now went on my own responsibility: if I saw anything suspicious I sent it up with a form where the reasons for suspicion were given, and if the higher department thought the matter worth investigating the form was returned with a red star attached. I used to get from one to five stars a day, but a very stupid girl next me hardly got three a week, so I can't help thinking that a good many undesirable things slipped past her. I could read about 150 letters a day (German, French and Italian mail from or to Switzerland). They were mostly dull; no one would believe how often people say the same thing: we had a cold snap at the time, and 120 out of the 150 letters described bursting pipes. The suspicious letters were, of course, interesting: some one could make sure of—the morse code cut round stamp edges, the lining of envelopes, and the flourishes and underlinings used as guides to key words: but generally it was a sort of *instinct* which told me to look carefully, and I had some difficulty in finding words for my suspicions that I would write on the form: more often than not this vague feeling was right and a red star showed that the clue was being followed.

We had a big Who's Who black list and notices would often be sent round asking us to look out for particular things, mention of innocent words, like tea, or velvet, or they would tell us not to open certain letters which were sent to a special department and probably used to decoy more important information. I am sure that the training has been useful, particularly in my work during the next war: it developed that sort of sixth sense for what people are *really* meaning, which the whole of intelligence or propaganda work is built on. I was kept so hard at it that I had no time to think by day; only in the morning would wake with a blind sense of loss which comes after the anguish of sorrow. At the luncheon hour I often had time to spare, and would explore the law courts, hearing little snippets of cases; or sit in one or other of the churches nearby. At five in the evening one came out into darkness—dim-lighted buses like glow-worms, and searchlights and moonlight tangled and lovely over Trafalgar Square. The Strand was crowded with Colonial troops most anxious for company, and when I had a cold I discovered that any slight cough would bring two or three huge Australians looming out of the night like the hulls of ships, so that I had to hurry along, desperately sucking lozenges.

I heard *Figaro* and *Boris Goudounov* that summer, and listened to the crowds cheering a falling Zeppelin at night, and saw an air-raid of twenty-two *Taubes* in the sky.

At Christmas we went again to St. Margaret's Bay—so different from the time before. We walked on the downs, and were warned away from the fortified beaches, and found in the hotel desk a forgotten military report, which tried to explain with official dignity how the alarm and firing a night or two before had been caused by a sentry who mistook a donkey for a human being (a thing which happens to the best of us at times).

I became a censor only while waiting to get strong enough to nurse again, and remember feeling anxious at that time lest the war should end before I got into it somewhere. By early spring an offer came of six weeks training as V.A.D. in a cottage hospital in Highgate: no one, they said, would take me at the front on Italian training only. So I left the Censors, though they tempted me with the offer of a department and were very pleasant.

I bought the most unbecoming blue serge uniform imaginable and went to my cottage hospital, and arrived at the nurses' luncheon hour. About eight of us sat down to table with a Sister at one end and Matron at the head. When Matron offered me a second helping of suet pudding, I accepted: my plate was handed up in a silence of frozen reproof: one was always offered a second helping, but no one ever took it. When the Sister saw me trying to sweep a floor for the first time in my life and showed me how: "This is what they send us," her shoulders seemed to say as she went away. I had a ward with six beds, to be nursed and swept and dusted four times a day, and at first I thought it impossible to do it all in the time, but I soon grew quick, and was shown how beds could be made in two minutes and the sheet folded under the mattress in a neat triangle as one went along. As far as I remember we had a twelve-hour day and a holiday every third Sunday, or possibly every fortnight: and I was always hungry and tempted to take the patients' Ovaltine (because food was difficult in England then). The Matron was considerate; she had not forgotten her early days and showed me how to raise the foot of my bed to lessen the ache in my legs from so much standing. The patients mostly came from Highgate and I began to realize, with wonder, the ramifications of class feeling in England and all the shades which make it impossible for Mr. Smith to speak to Mr. Jones. Mine was a men's ward and presently they added to it a baby of which I got very fond, but it was more trouble than all the rest and everyone held me responsible when it cried. At the other end of the room a patient had delirium tremens and I was supposed to keep him quietly in bed: he was a rather engaging elderly man between his attacks, and a nurse at last showed me how to arrange the sheets so that he kept himself tucked in by his own weight; and this saved me a lot of wear and tear. I also learned to light the morning fire with paraffin when no one was looking. We had private rooms, too, to attend to, and meals to prepare for them on trays. I used to arrange them on the stairs, one below the other, and one day, when all was ready, the weight must have been badly distributed: I saw the top one slowly tilt outwards on to the next, which began to do likewise: the next, and the next, with increasing speed—four or six of them— landed in one smash round my ankles. The Matron, kind woman, rushing along, looked at my distressed face, and said nothing.

Highgate seemed a little village on its own, and London a city far away. On my Sundays I went to Viva and ate up her week's flour ration for her, so she said. When my six weeks were over I applied to join the Trevelyan Ambulance Unit in Italy, as it gave the only chance I could find of reaching the fighting. While waiting for an answer I went to Dartmoor. Dorothy had married her Maurice and he was down there, and used to ride with me on the moor and talk about all Dorothy's perfections. I had for a long time no wish for any happiness of this kind of my own, but I remember the surprise and comfort of realizing that it still existed in the world.

My stay was not half over before the summons came to London and I went to be interviewed by Mrs. George Trevelyan and Mrs. Spicer. I was too young, they said, but my knowledge of Italian and Italian hospitals carried weight, and eventually they chose me. I showed my ignorance of army ways by paying my own fare out so as to stop a week in Dronero on the way. The journey was a very easy one compared to the journey over, a year before. Then I had been a civilian: I was cross-questioned at Modane by three old suspicious Frenchmen, who said that someone with the same name as mine on her passport had been through a fortnight before: they asked my doings and dates in the past, and I realized how difficult it is to give an exact account of one's actions, and they eventually said "On vous pardonne cette fois, Mademoiselle," which annoyed me so much that I retorted that one could only be pardoned if one had done anything wrong, and left them looking with surprise after a turning worm. There had been hours of queues at Havre: a poor weeping woman from Madrid had lost the four days allotted for her journey in efforts to get through the formalities, and was being turned back because her visa had expired. In the queue at Havre a man in front of me was criticized for bringing parcels into the squash. "It isn't a parcel; it's my small boy," he said, pulling a submerged infant up into the air. I discovered as I went on board that I ought to have had the permit of the prefecture, but decided to risk it and got away with only a reprimand: and in the middle of the Channel our engines stopped: I woke from sleep and wondered, like the Duke of Wellington, whether to go with or without shoes on deck, and then we went on again. *This* time I belonged to the army and the outward journey was made as easy as possible: shepherds stood at every corner ready to help. An aunt and uncle were running the Y.M.C.A.s in Havre and I had a day or two with them; tea with a Chinese Labour battalion, whose tents were decorated with paper lanterns: their gay little figures circled round in the flicker of warmth, and have remained with me because of this fragility amid all the engines of war. I danced at a soldiers' dance and asked my partner, a sergeant, if there was to be a tango: "Nothing obscene here, miss," he said. They lost me my luggage at Modane, but the R.T.O. took the keys and sent it on: that line was now one of the main arteries of war, a constant stream of troops.

I can remember nothing of the few days in Dronero, except the arrival, late at night, with stars burning in their alpine brightness, and no one to meet me as I walked through the fields with that strange shrinking at my heart. Vera was there and her baby Angela was born: she had so many, the dates get mixed—one tiny boy only lived a week. Towards the end of August I went to Rome to report (far out of my way) and lived at Government expense at the hotel, being told by a gay young man of the Red Cross that no one could bother about me till some Ambassador had gone. Would I lunch? he said; but Viva had told me very strenuously that never under any pretext whatever did one visit young men in their flats, so I refused. What I really regret in my youth is the fact that for years I went on believing every one of the things I was told: so I drove about Rome all by myself, enjoying it greatly; and two days later travelled second-class (rank lieutenant for nurses) to Udine—the train getting more and more military as we went along. Carabiniers walked up and down asking for one's papers. We were rolling through all the rich Friuli country. Three officers got in on their way from leave and began to talk about how the women were behaving at home and what they felt about it: it made me feel so ashamed that I wept, tears rolling down my cheeks, and one of the officers looked at me curiously and I suppose thought someone belonging to me had died. At Udine we were at railhead, and a soldier helped me with my suit-case to a little canteen run by two English ladies. I was so excited. They just said: "Ah, you're the new arrival at Villa Trento. The lorry will be along soon," as if such things happened every day. They gave me eggs and bacon and a seat on a packing-case, and presently our lorry arrived and we collected letters and drove a few miles to where Villa Trento, with long wings and a classic pediment, stood a little back from the road, and a park of guns, on their way to the front, rested on the grass plot at the foot of the statues by the gates.

TO MY MOTHER

15 *KIDDERPORE AVENUE,*
HAMPSTEAD,
8 *Nov.,* 1916.

My own Biri,

There is such a lot to tell you of my doings!—I am here with the Edwards, and they are very kind—George is as charming as possible and I think Alice is getting quite fond of me!! She makes me *sew* blouses for her, in the misguided persuasion that I long for employment. I really do like her, only feel I am not quite *good enough.*

The week-end was splendid. Joan came to meet me and we

struggled up a steep path with my dressing bag to the tiny cottage. I have never seen any country more exquisite than those Sussex downs. Amberley lies in a broad shallow amphitheatre, with a ridge of white cliff over against you: the low ground is flooded, pale, pale blue in the sunlight with a swirl and foam at the edge where the Arun river makes a current. And the downs slope away on all sides, with scarlet, copper, and flame-like beechwoods creeping towards them; wonderful woods, of old trees, with smooth shiny roots. We walked under them that afternoon, and it was like long aisles of a temple, with gold leaves falling silently about one. And we came upon a round pool of dark water all covered with the brilliant leaves, and not a creature stirring there.

The party consisted of us two and a sister called Ursula, a fascinating girl with straw-gold hair and eyes that slant a little upwards at the corners. The Sunday came with the most terrific gale I have ever seen: the thatch roof lay mostly strewn about the lawn and when we put our heads out of doors the rain was like hail on our faces. Ursula said what a splendid thing to sail on the river! I backed her, Joan was torn between the excitement and the fear of the danger, and was unwillingly wrapped up for the expedition. We looked like a polar expedition when we sallied out. The wind was roaring like big guns: we had to run past the trees, as big branches were being hurled off. Unfortunately the boat was beached under some elms, so we had to haul it out in fear of our lives: Ursula and I did the work while Joan looked doubtful: we pulled the boat, a long narrow thing for sculling, to the edge of the flood and I was left to hold her while they went for the sail—and it was all I could do to keep her in shore against the wind. I really think it was the maddest thing I have ever done! Just as we started, we saw a train on the opposite shore going at full speed, and the wind was so strong that the smoke was blown along in front of the engine! So we thought we would be prudent and make for a sheltered bit of the river. We had a glorious time: the tide was racing along at such a pace that even the gale could not get us very fast up-stream and rather disgusted us. I held the mainsheet and learnt the mysteries of *gibing* and *close hauled*. It was very cold: our coats were no good against that downpour, and we sat in soaking garments thinking with joy of the horror of our absent families if they could have seen! And the pleasure was enhanced by the knowledge that we must certainly have drowned if we upset, as no-one could swim dressed as we were and with a tide of 6 miles an hour!

We came home wet through and famished and by the time I had got into some of their clothes, I found tea and a young man waiting. He was a nice young man, an admirer of Ursula's, whom we astonished with the history of the day. I discovered that he knew the Webbs, and the girls knew Elsie too; they had been in the party that went to Switzerland and to which I was invited—but went home instead. I remember feeling sad at giving it up, thinking it was all young people, with a young man each all round and great fun: but I heard a very different account from Joan. It seemed they were about 4 girls to every man and the Carrs made themselves popular by taking off three men at once, being the only girls who could ski:—and they also stayed away with them for two days, with the consequence that none of the *nice* people in the party will speak to them since.

A kiss to ma mia from her

FREYA

FROM MY MOTHER

DRONERO,
3 a.m.
15 *Nov.,* 1916.

My dearest,

Here I am doing my night shift during which I had hoped to find many quiet minutes in which to write you. Instead the men cannot be left a moment; there is always something wrong; either the ribbon saw must be sharpened, or it wobbles, or it breaks. As they are all peasants new to machinery, it requires the patience of Job to encourage them and keep them at it.

I do not at all dislike night work and I can see how essential it is with these people to always share their work and their discomforts, when one has authority. As one of them said—"sì: fa freddo verso le quattro, ma siamo tutti uomini assieme."

The worst of a saw mill is that one cannot shut it because of the big trunks going in and out all the time. But I have done my best with screens, etc., in front of each saw.

Oh, my dear—what naughty things you do, when your aged mother is not there! But what fun the river must have been; and you did not catch cold? Still! on the whole, I feel easier in my mind when you are with Viva!

I owe letters to everybody, but my life goes on in a continual accomplishing of immediate duties. As soon as I leave the works, I return to the home and must see to things there. Amongst not the least of which has been the wine-making.

The *second* wine turned out a terrible fiasco, because after giving all possible directions, and being very busy, I left it to Carlo to put in a big barrel, 700 litres of it. You should have tasted it! Cheap soap with a (perfume?) one seems to drink. Carlo in his enthusiasm had washed the cask first with soda.

Now I have been trying all sorts of things to get it remedied. I finally last evening put it all in the vat again, with more grapes, to let it boil again. This is the last hope—otherwise it must be thrown away.

Then there is Vera, who refuses to take a walk, unless I take her. Poor child, she is rather lonely, and sinks into a sort of lazy habit, unless one pulls her out. But it is not always easy to find time and energy to do it.

But the autumn tints have been wonderful this year and although we have had terrible rains, there have also been wonderful days, when the mountains were like jewels set in gold against the infinite blue.

General Ottavio has gone to Rome to serve on the 'Supreme Tribunale di Guerra.' He is already dreadfully harassed at the idea of having to sentence a fellow creature and has had headaches in consequence. No end!—Nico too is *likely* to have to join his ship, and everybody that ever was left is now going, even Cav: Marino!

My dear you must forgive a very interrupted letter!

I like your poem, dearest, you are improving—is it due to Karl W—s? and is he the W—s I used to know in Paris? If so, I have rather a bad conscience. He came to see me at Mrs. Bale's and they were nice to him as they always are; then he

became a *spasimante* of Viva's—as they all were, and Mrs. Bale
was exercised as to how best to stop him—as he was *not* desirable in those days. So he used to write me long letters, to
keep up a link, he thought, and I ended by not answering any
more. Poor W—!

An embrace to Viva

Your B.

PS. What *is* Sarrail doing at Salonica? The papers here
say he gives balls and dinner parties!

15

The War in Italy. 1917

VILLA TRENTO was a happy place. Everyone adored George Trevelyan and his chivalry and devotion went through everything—he gave a remarkable unity to our mixed company—doctors, nurses, drivers, mechanics—all were comrades. I think all were volunteers except possibly the mechanics. We ate together at a long table in the open, in front of the Villa, anyone sitting where they found room. The great painted saloon in the centre was a common room, and sometimes one could creep in and hear Geoffrey Young playing to himself on the piano. In my dormitory was another new arrival, an Irish girl called Ruth Trant, and Bessie Bosanquet, and I think one other. We washed in a little tin basin, dressed in ten minutes or so; made our beds (mattresses filled with straw); breakfasted at 7.30 and worked from 8, as far as I remember. There was a bath, and one put one's name down for it on a list, but someone from the out-stations nearly always came and pinched it. I think I only got one in two months. We had quite a number of out-stations where our wounded were collected (one I believe at Caporetto), and the ambulance side was perhaps the chief part of the work: George was always out there, trying to be as much under fire as he could. I was put to work under a Scottish sister in the Garibaldi ward, a long sort of attic over the wine cellars with thirty-five beds.

On my arrival the matron saw me, and asked if I could cook: after all those years of housekeeping I cooked rather well, but I saw a look in her eye which spelt 'kitchen' and hastily said I could nurse better: the people who were once seized for the kitchen never got out, I afterwards heard. My Sister was one of the kindest women: I can remember no single day when she spoke roughly to me. We worked ourselves to the bone for her merely because she worked so hard herself—if a convoy came in she would be there half an hour before her time and would greet me with surprise, not having even told me to be early. She would always try to send me away if she stayed late. I had an incorrigible habit of putting the little rubber pipes, used for draining wounds, to boil on the primus and then forgetting them, until reminded by a smell of burning rubber, but she never did more than shake her head; the ward soon took to reminding me and it became their morning joke. We did no sweeping, but had orderlies for the heavy work, usually convalescents who were only too glad to stay on: they washed the floor with carbolic, which went down through the chinks into the wine vats. My Sister told me I was a good nurse, and I loved the patients: who would not? No one can describe their resignation and gentleness and gratitude. We got to know the regiments: some had been two years at the front, for the management of the Italian army was rotten at that time—the inland towns of Italy crammed with shirkers (called *imboscati*) and the fighting soldier never given a rest: when they did go on leave it took them three months to recover their morale, an officer told me, so that Italy was divided into two halves, combatant and non-combatant. Hence Caporetto.

Ruth Trant was in the ward next to mine, under a far worse Sister, whose heart was better than her temper. "I'll knock spots out of you," she would go round saying, though no one paid much attention. Matron came round in the morning to inspect, and Ruth and I had to juggle with one kettle, which should have been two, and had to appear in both our kitchens. Ruth and I became rather notorious in our first fortnight, for she had met a Roman artillery major on the way out, who invited her and a friend to luncheon at their mess: this was strictly discouraged, but I suggested circumventing the regulations by inviting the head of our hospital to join us: we did this; he

accepted; no matronly disapproval could override the doctor—
we had a grand day. The Artillery H.Q. were at Cormons, a
little town well on the way to the battle area: the roads as we
drove there were screened with matting, and it was strange to pass
the little hills and see one side shimmering with life and business
like an ant hill and the other outwardly deserted. And when
we reached the artillery we sat one on each side of the colonel,
in his mess, and were given a sumptuous meal, and shown the
plans of the enemy gun positions; he finally offered a ride in an
observation balloon, and only the difficulty of climbing decently
in our narrow skirts in front of such an audience deterred us.
If we had been unpopular it would have taken us a long time to
live this down, but we were both liked; and in fact it was from
this year that I recovered a natural ease with my fellow creatures,
which our strange life in Dronero had crushed through the past
years. I liked human beings. At Villa Trento they were all
kind, and used to invite me to little parties when a parcel came
from home; and I remember being distressed because I never
had any parcels and could give nothing in return, until I persuaded the cook to make cakes if I procured the sugar.

Our work was less or more according to what was happening
at the front: when an offensive was on, our drivers took no rest
day or night; ambulances arrived; and we evacuated as soon as
we could to the base hospitals at Udine: otherwise we kept our
people, mostly wounded with shell splinters, and watched their
wounds closing, day by day, round the little rubber drain pipes.
I noticed that, on days when everything went well, I was far
less tired: when a patient was moaning or I was anxious, the
work seemed twice as hard. I also remembered my own illness
and noticed what a difference it made to one's nursing if one
remained serene *inside*, and I practised this discipline for the
sake of the patients. My Sister never hurried and never scolded
and her presence was soothing in itself, while the effect of 'sparks
flying' in the next ward reacted on all the men. I also discovered that I had a magnetic sort of hand and could soothe
pain by massaging gently, so that I never had any spare time at

all. One man we had who killed himself through fear: he had a very slight leg wound, and he was so terrified that it never got better and his leg finally was amputated, and then he said he would die and went on saying so until he did—no cause but fear. This was the first time I helped at an amputation; it is a strange and shocking thing to feel a limb become suddenly lifeless in one's hands. We saw the power of the mind every day, for the men in pain would beg for morphia, and we would give them an injection of water, and they would sleep peacefully. I think I saw why nurses are nearly always happy people: their life is constant drama, with no interval of boredom—people are always recovering or dying. With all the carnage that was going on, to be helping to save life was a comfort.

We were very near the fighting. From the little hills of the garden we could see it—the long ridge of the Carso where all the shells splintered on rock so that their danger was multiplied —to where the Isonzo flowed through Gorizia, hidden by low hills in front: to Monte Santo just taken, and Monte Gabriele where the trenches now ran, visible with slow clouds of gas by day, and shell-flickers by night; that high and evil line was never still. On the road in front, in the dust, the long processions plodded day by day, the big guns trailing branches. After two months we were expecting an offensive, and our wards were half-emptied in readiness for it—when we began to notice that traffic was heading the wrong way: the noise of the shelling came towards us instead of receding. It grew very loud, a huge gun dropped something near us every fifteen minutes or so: the windows rattled, the few men left in their beds hated it and some shivered like dogs or horses: it had a strangely tiring effect, though we knew too little of gunfire to be frightened. Our town of Cormons where the bread came from had been shelled, they said. I had my afternoon off that day, and was very anxious to see a shell hole for myself: I induced the girl who kept the linen store to come with me and we walked along the Cormons road: endless rows of troops were coming away. An officer stopped us and said we ought not to be there, but no one paid much attention. We reached Cormons, and found it had been evacuated of all civilians: I have never seen anything so dead as that town of empty houses, and streets littered with glass. The shelling had stopped an hour or so ago and began again at dusk. As we walked back we saw a civilian escorted by officers —an M.P. I was told—who raised his arms and said: "*Tutto e perduto*—all is lost." We could have got into trouble, no doubt, over this expedition, but the bad news was now pouring in: we were close to where the Caporetto road comes down from the hills to join the Udine road, and everyone arriving from our out-stations brought bad news. Our beds and a number of things were packed and sent off to start another hospital farther back; by this time our water supply had been cut. The enemy came on too fast for any ambulance to be driven ahead of them, but in the evening some walking cases arrived limping and miserable: we spread mattresses for them on the floor and sent them on to Udine next day.

As we were the only British unit, we were to have the honour of being the last hospital left to function. We sent away all the remaining heavily wounded to Udine base, and at about 5.p.m. one ambulance with about seven of the nurses was sent to the rear to start work, they hoped, at Pordenone. I was among them. I made a desperate effort to remain behind on the plea of my Italian, but Matron would not hear of it. As a matter of fact the other nurses started later but came much more quickly through the Third Army. We were involved in the retreating Second. We only reached Udine late at night in the chaos of the retreat: the streets were being looted by the Italians themselves and the railway station was so packed with refugees that going to get some bread at the buffet one had to force each foot between wedges of seated human beings: they waited there and never got away, I heard, and returned to find their villages burning. As we drove through the flat country a ring of these dumps and villages blazed all along the horizon of the east—the moon rose strangely out of it. I remember a river bed of white boulders and men asleep among them, dead tired, and the moon shining on them. We had seen a munition dump on fire some time before, but this was different—a mortal horror creeping up like paralysis. The great roads, running along raised dykes, were filled with lines of traffic three deep, and no control: on the second day we did one and a half miles in twelve hours: our driver never slept, every half-hour or so the column gave a jerk, a few yards would be gained. The infantry were all dispersed, marching weaponless across country, or plodding under strange loot—a goose, a 'cello, piles of clothing. The wounded trailed along with stained bandages, turned out from Udine. How glad I was our hospital had been empty, though I think we would have stayed by our wounded if any had remained. Meanwhile, constantly, we had to refuse help—people who asked for lifts which our heavily-loaded ambulance could not give. Two soldiers I remember, pathetic in the middle of the road, asking to be relieved of their regimental cash-box—which they tried, staggering, to carry between them. Our food was a little bread, some biscuits, sausages and plum-pudding, until our quartermaster in another ambulance overtook us and got a dish of polenta in a farm-house under pouring rain. We had half an hour or so to get tidy in a dingy room, whence Sister and I were recalled to a stable to dress a man wounded in the head. Now everything was slush, and more and more we looked like a rout. Only a small group of cavalry moved the other way, riding fully armed: they held up the enemy for a little and were all killed.

Rumours began to come that German detachments had been sent ahead with machine-guns: I believe this was true. They also said they were shelling with gas. The shells were following us in a desultory way, illuminating the night sky, and lighting the under-side of the clouds a faint opal-pink, lovely. Poor civilian carts with their furniture were now being tilted over into the ditches down the steep banks, to make way for the guns. The troops with mule transport had unharnessed and walked away their animals at the threat of gas, leaving the carts, so that all this had to be cleared before we could get on. And now we began to fear that we might not be across the Tagliamento before that vital bridge was blown up. Despatch riders on motor bicycles came asking us to hurry, and to abandon our lorry and walk. We consulted, but decided not to, as we felt that our ambulance was more precious than we were, and also it had its British origin printed on it in large letters, so that we did not wish it to go to the enemy.

In the middle of the second night we came to a cross-roads in a town (Codroipo) and there saw the Third Army, which under the Duke of Aosta was being sent to fight. He saved the situation by attacking at that time. The relief of seeing troops again, instead of rabble, is not to be described. We must have waited one hour or two, while column after column marched by, giving a password to a small group of officers standing in lantern light, while the shells lit the roofs of the houses and poplar trees and under-side of clouds. Early next morning a definite order came to leave the ambulance and hurry; we reached the bridge walking—it was a mile long with no parapets, and so deep in mud and so ground under the enormous weight of traffic that bits of it were flopping into the water which swirled in spate below. Our ambulance took all day to get across; but we were over in the early dawn, and into a stationary train on the Italian side, and sat there till evening. An aeroplane, which luckily had only two bombs left, dropped them towards the end of our long train—flying so low that I saw the features of the airman. We had nothing at all in the air: the bad weather saved us. The foolish soldiers, scattered on the grass, rushed *into* the train when the enemy came over. They discovered some closed trucks of meat and bread, wrenched them open and looted them; many ate the meat raw, some gathered in groups round fires. The rest of our party gradually collected here. The Matron had a hard cross-country journey with Geoffrey Young, on crutches owing to his amputated leg. They told us we had left Udine while the first Germans were reaching the opposite gate. We saw our lorries creeping over the long bridge, a jerk or two in the hour; but at sunset they were across. The bridge

crammed with people on all its length was blown up next day
or the day after. We went to Padova in rain and darkness,
stopping while carabiniers looked in for deserters, whom they
were handcuffing and sending, eventually, to France. Many of
the Italian officers were shot by their own men and nothing said.
We reached Padua late at night and got billets: Ruth and I
slept together in one bed and woke in darkness: we found we
had slept the clock right round.

*   *   *   *   *

I kept a diary during these months, and most of it is here
copied out crude as it is. It can be skipped without damage
to my story, and I include it only because it is a genuine document
of the 1914 war.

I had reached Villa Trento on the 3rd of September:

4th Sept. 1917.

Last night as I went to bed the heavy sound of the guns—as
if something were heaving with great vehemence through a
thick surface—came from the way of S. Gabriele. S. Gabriele
they say has fallen to-day: the spurs, Caterina and Daniele, still
to take.

Two of our men have been wounded: Sylvester—has had
shrapnel clean through his ankle—Sessions who already had
a medal has a fractured thigh and has not yet come: Geoffrey
Young is here also, wounded—all on the Gabriele.

The guns this morning came through a haze of sunlight, a
short sharp sound unlike last night; now (9.30 p.m.) a terrific
bombardment is going on again: Trant and I went up about
8.30 to see: there was still a sullen red glow of sunset over Italy,
but night already and pale stars to the east; the guns come in
short bursts, like far, reluctant thunder—an angry sound. Over
all the line the flashes come; ruddy and quick from the shells,
and the long pale star-shells hanging like new planets for some
seconds. Most come from the Hermada; a huge red flare
suddenly on Gabriele—one could almost see its shape—and from
our village Dolegnano a searchlight turns slowly round and

upward, inland towards us, in search of aircraft it seems; the church tower on the little hill (whence an *'austriacante'* priest was thrown down by the populace early in the war) is caught in the light and stands for a second like a beacon. In the growing darkness the battle seems to come nearer; one feels a part of the great pulse, a tremendous excitement and also a sense of awe at the grandeur of such a tragedy.

. . . to the S.W. . . . is Aquileia—the church tower just visible in the plain. Then the view is blocked by a nearer hill, Medea, which King Victor used as a kind of observatory whence to show his friends the battle. Then a dip, and on clear days we see the lagoons of Monfalcone; the Carso and its long body down there and one can follow it up, see Gradisca at its foot and Sagrado below the S. Michele; the S. Martino, the S. Michele, then a dip with the view of Hermada behind—to-day covered and wreathed with explosions; then, bending east, the Sei Busi, and long ridge of Faiti, with the Vipacco valley at its base. (N.B. The Italians never could understand why the British tommies insisted on bathing in the Vipacco, which was under fire.) The sunlight on Faiti lay just about as far as our men have reached—apparently half-way.

Gorizia, left of the Vipacco, is hidden by a little hill near here, and anyhow Podgora would hide it; one sees just the tip of the latter, behind nearer hills. Then comes the Gabriele, looking waste even from here, ten to twelve miles away . . . a reddish colour. Behind it stretches the plateau of Ternovo to a higher massif behind; we are already on the plateau, but the S. Daniele, to the right and hard to see, is still theirs and also the Sta Caterina. Next Gabriele is the Sabotino, with green scrub apparently climbing up it; its ridge is bare and, looking like a pathway, makes the whole seem a part of the Santo. But they are divided by the Isonzo. The Santo too is bare; the convent on its summit could be seen some days ago; is gone now, only a lighter colour on top shows the scattered stones: these three hills all have the reddish colour and one can see the seams of trenches up them. After Santo, a dip and the long back of the Vodice rises like some great animal; then Kuk; Plava is invisible behind a hill, but from the top here (behind our hospital among the vines) it comes just below the Kuk. Beyond all these hills is the higher barrier; one can only look and wonder and give praise.

An Italian officer joined us, coming to see the battle: he had got up five or six times during the night hearing the terrific bombardment; we gave him the news of S. Gabriele and he lent Dr. Brock and me his glasses to look through; told us that three large squadrons of aeroplanes had set out towards Hermada in the morning, and that the batteries (heavy) from Sabotino are being sent to the Trentino and some 149 *allungati* brought here instead; they have been passing in their lorries along our road. It seems there is to be an attack in the Trentino—not that that will stop us now! He spoke of the first days, when Monfalcone was taken and the Carso begun . . . with one heavy gun, and the wire had to be cut by hand with scissors! . . . Now there is no lack of guns; we have 65 English (6-inch howitzers) and the French 34—all down towards Hermada. Just in front of us, hiding Plava, is a hill with big 305 batteries which I mean to see if possible.

It seems that in April the hospital was still well in range; some shells passed over it and hit S. Giovanni di Manzano. No such excitement now, I fear. The Austrians seem to respect the Red Cross; beyond Ravna is a very exposed bit of road and one of our drivers goes along in broad day with a huge red cross like a sail in front of him and no hit yet.

I hear our gunners have been badly knocked about. As for the wounded drivers, Sessions has had his leg amputated in Gorizia; the bone was smashed through the knee. A terrible fear that Mr. Young will lose his leg also. The three casualties all happened on the same very dangerous stretch of road, which the Italians don't use; I am told Trevelyan was anxious for this reason that ours should stick to it—but the cost!

No patients have come to-day.

To-day has brought over 3,000 prisoners, lots of machine-guns and only one cannon, I hear.

I spent the afternoon lazily in the garden: there is a flat stretch behind the house with a few round beds where an enthusiastic Italian lieutenant arranged round white stones in patterns; these are few and far between; the rest is grass and varied tree—pine and acacia. Then there is a thicket of bamboos, and the sluggish moat . . . and a stretch of ground with a shed for convalescents and the orderlies' encampment of tents. The ground then rises, and the vines far apart on either side of the path make it into a kind of steep grassy avenue crowned by the farm and a clump of cypress and pine against the sky; and thence one looks widely and the battle lies before one, and northwards the sweep of the great hills, and westward low champaign hills sinking to Udine and the plain.

Trant and I walked here . . and found an old trench . . . with a piece of rusty wire in it. The acacias were already stretching across it; the edges have lost their hard contours; it is already sinking back into the earth.

5th Sept.

Monte Gabriele lost again. The men are coming in now, not in great numbers, but I heard Dr. Brock say that 20 or 30 daily are promised for the future.

I have been put in the Garibaldi ward—a long granary with only four patients this morning, but ten more have arrived to-day.

Sister is Scotch and most charming, with a pretty slow way of speaking and a gentle look and manner so that one loves her at once. Miss G., my senior V.A.D., is one of the cultured women (unmarried) with much intelligence . . . and little understanding . . . young eyes and rather mature wrinkles. I'm afraid she will be very trying to work with; I notice she always asks me to take temperatures when any dressing is to be done with sister. . . .

It is a comfort to speak Italian and be able to know what these poor boys are thinking and wanting; it is not the language so much as the point of view which is familiar to me and strange to the English nurses—so that they and the patients often seem to be moving in different worlds.

The ten people are:

1. Fractured both legs below the knee; came here in hysterics almost, and seemed quite recovered when I washed and changed him; but in great pain again now. . . .

2. A man from Reggio Calabria, wound in the leg.

3. Boy from the south; wound in the knee. Problem

because he refuses a bedpan and says he will rather die than use it, and he mustn't be moved, so there the matter rests at present.

4. A Turinese with cut head; so good and patient; he lights up when I speak to him in Piedmontese. He had a little tin locket which nurse seemed not to realize had value to him . . . so pleased when I brought it to him with a new silk ribbon.

5. A poor man shot through the neck and almost unable to swallow; have been coaxing him to take milk, but he is so weary and sorry for himself.

6. A boy shot in the thigh; not seen the wound.

The rest came when I was not there.

The work here seems chiefly dressings and not many operations.

. . . Enthralling to watch the traffic along the road, the chaos of lorries, cars, horses, every imaginable vehicle on all kinds of business, trooping to and fro from the front in the white dust between the dusty acacias. . . .

I came back late for matron, but she was later still. A very energetic, pleasant woman; something rather infantile and ingenuous in her manner—quick and blonde, pince-nez and nez retroussé, and very pretty I should think when young. She has been through Serbian campaign: name Miss Power.

The guns are terrific this evening.

6th Sept.

Work from 8 to 6.30; had the ward to myself in the afternoon. . . . Sister said I would do very well.

Miss G. much upset because a patient asked me for a newspaper to see the *encomio* of his regiment; she told me it was not allowed; then she came all the way down the long ward again and asked: "Were you in a very *small* hospital?" "I thought so." Talk of cats! . . .

All the men who came yesterday doing well. But a hand and leg are going badly of the earlier arrivals, there is fear the leg may be amputated. Also Geoffrey Young's I fear.

I saw Mr. Trevelyan to-night, though not to speak to . . . a Renaissance figure with slightly rounded back that makes it look stronger and throws the head forward with a look of much energy and keenness. He is very worried about Mr. Young, and could hardly sit quiet at table.

7th Sept.

Great influx of wounded during the night—all from S. Gabriele . . . poor men mostly asleep exhausted, temperature below normal; they all say they have not eaten for three or four days. Most wounded in the leg, some in the arms; one had eight wounds—little round holes where the lead has lodged. Sister extracted one piece as big as a hazel nut. They are very good and patient, not so stoic as our men but much more appreciative. My poor mouth case with a large hole at the back of his neck asked me if I didn't dislike feeding him! Then begged to be allowed to stay on here, but he is to go to a special hospital in Udine to-morrow.

It seems a hundred men arrived last night.

Geoffrey Young has had his leg cut off. One hoped to save it to the last.

Through the cloudy night, few round drops, and pale lightning now and then; the guns continue apparently over Gabriele; the Hermada seemed almost quiet from our hilltop.

8th Sept.

Another busy day. The man with the bad neck left before I came in the morning; one is always sorry to lose them. One constant rush till I came off duty at 6—hardly time to think and I feel so tired still; we just hurry through the meals knowing that whoever is left in the ward is waiting to be relieved. . . .

In the evening I went with Trant up the hill, all fragrant and moist with rain, and we sat and enjoyed the outline of the cypresses. One might have been in the depth of a country at peace. Trant is attractive and such a good sort—with red hair and a turn-up nose and mouth . . . she paints and has studied in Paris. Being both of us new to things here and sleeping in the same room, we have a feeling of comradeship. . . .

We still have no news of Caterina being taken, though now surrounded on three sides.

9th Sept.

We hear from the men from Gorizia that the offensive up here has come to an end, so no more influx of patients. Another 20 arrived to-day however, and one very bad case was brought in to Garibaldi; have been keeping him alive with injections and salines; doubtful if he will pull through. . . .

11th Sept.

I have had a half-day's holiday and spent the afternoon sleeping under a vine . . . in one of the long rows that stretch in a straight low avenue of tangled sun and shadow: the vintage is just over and the leaves begin to change colour.

Last night the bombardment was so loud the house shook and rattled with it. The night was hot and stuffy, a storm came up, and one could not tell if the almost continuous series of flashes were lightning or the reflection of the explosions on the western bank of clouds. The rain fell in torrents, and Struthers, who sleeps out, arrived for shelter about 2 a.m.

Three stretchers brought into my ward to-day, one fractured thigh, one with both hands, one arm, head and three body wounds. I had to feel his pulse at the temple. But he seemed quite strong, and horrified Sister Brechin by most voluble swearing.

The poor boy brought with fractured thigh on the 9th had to have the leg cut off and died early this morning. I got up to look at the flashes last night and heard him calling out wildly. He was a Ligurian, quite young, the poor boy.

Another death in next ward. It is horrible to do all one can and find it useless.

Mr. Trevelyan spoke to me yesterday . . . kind in his keen quick way; a most sensitive face, full of enthusiasm; we spoke of the mountains and poor Geoffrey Young: Mr. Trevelyan said that climbing was the one thing G. Y. really cared about.

Trant has had the devil of a time with her sister in the Aosta ward next door—so I wrote this limerick to console her:

> The sister who lives in Aosta
> Is a difficult person to foster;
> If you do a thing right
> You get chased from her sight
> And if wrong—she gets crosser and crosseder.

12th Sept.

To-day's rumour from the men at the out-stations is that the offensive is to go on a week still and then be given up if of no use.

A man wounded this morning says he left the Gabriele top in Austrian hands. . . .

I was taken in the staff car to Cormons with Dr. Brock and Sir Alexander Ogsten. Went by Blesivo where the roads are still hidden from the Austrians by tall screens of reeds. Rusty wire entanglements and old trenches all along the road and we passed endless streams of the steel-capped soldiers marching up to the line. The western sides of the hills are all one swarming camp, one sees the little round tents everywhere. We passed some huge siege guns on their high platforms looking very grim. One feels very near the war out on these roads, especially in a Red Cross car when all the officers salute. Cormons is still within range but not fired on, but Dr. Brock said a shell burst a few yards away from him while driving there.

On the way home we crossed the Judrio—the old Italian boundary—with a pub, *All'Italia,* on its banks.

13th Sept.

. . . The ward this evening seemed full of sighs and moans, most depressing. One of yesterday's patients had been a prisoner that same morning; the Austrian captain leading him to the rear was killed, and he just waited till the Italians came up again.

It's so amusing to read of the offensive in English papers; it seems so much more spectacular there than here, where we only know of it through personal impressions.

. . . Miss G. is most amiable to me now and has a kind of protective manner. I gave her a great shock by telling her how long I had given anaesthetics.

Quite cold to-day. Violent storm in the night and puddles all over Garibaldi. What it must be in winter!

14th Sept.

Rather a slack day, with intervals left for wondering what to polish next. . . . Went to the hill top for the sunset and drew a plan of the view. While there I saw an aeroplane fall down, somewhere between Carso and Hermada, first a cloud of smoke, small like a shell only more stationary, then a flash of the thing itself like a tiny gleaming silver fish, headlong through the still air.

. . . Met an Italian officer . . . with another soldier, both with rifles, and a party of workmen evidently stalking someone or something in the vines. . . . Austrian prisoner escaped? Or a deserter?

The Countess Gleichen with the ladies of her No. 4 Unit (by Cormons) came this afternoon and I met them coming along in very rigid khaki with red bands.

Sister Brechin went out this afternoon so I was alone till 4.30 in my ward and had an awful time with the poor boy who had both legs fractured and got his splint twisted. Instead of telling one where the pain is they lie and sob and cry 'Oh Dio, oh Dio.' . . .

The bombardment has stopped: for two nights all has been more or less quiet.

16th Sept.

. . . Two patients make a terrible noise and drive one distracted—one has both legs fractured and nothing can be done to ease him of the pain, and the other is mad—so Dr. Thompson says. I saw him operated upon to-day and he has now nearly all his leg slit up below the knee and a tube arranged to drip a disinfectant lotion constantly right along inside the wound; his temperature has sunk already, but pulse very bad.

The boy from Mondovi . . . was operated on but the shrapnel is too deep-seated—somewhere between the ribs and kidney, so that it is dangerous to get at, but I'm afraid one will have to come to that, he is always in such pain.

Oh, but one gets tired of telling people to buck up and talking for their good.

Cormons . . . is certainly not out of range as a shell burst there yesterday and injured six people.

. . . heard all day about entry into Gorizia last year, how (our ambulances) were only 3 hours after the attacking troops and how the bridge was destroyed when they got into Gorizia

so that they were shut up there for a time. . . . Also spoke of
the Italians and G. . . . told me the men had to be kept up to the
mark by the officers' revolvers and were not good fighters in cold
blood. I wonder how far this is true. [This proved to be
untrue]. He says the officers are good, and the Alpini and
Bersaglieri of course—but the rest only when excited.

Miss Ewebank and Sullivan have left to-day. Miss E. has
become engaged to a man here . . . and it is the first engagement
in the Unit.

17th Sept.

Lovely drive this morning in the staff car with Miss Gibson
. . . leaving (Gorizia road) where both sides are screened and a
screen is hung above our heads at intervals of about 30 yds.
One goes up a little hill outside Cormons, and I suppose it is this
which makes the precaution necessary; there is a Red Cross
hospital with huge red cross on it; our driver showed us some
limekilns which had been an advanced dressing station when
he came. The road we went along is new also—a most perfect
smooth road. On our way back we passed a French artillery
base with many cars and a heap of shell cases. . . .

I stayed out to watch the traffic in the night along the road,
and saw the endless line of lorries, some with light, some rattling
along in the darkness: most have only one light and blunder
clumsily along, like Polyphemus from his cave. . . .

18th Sept.

No. 72, our madman, has had to have his leg amputated. . . .
Heard to-day why we are only now getting the serious cases;
it seems the advance on the Gabriele was so quick that the
stretchers had to be carried a very long way and the men who
couldn't walk were only taken very gradually to the rear. One
waited 5 days before being taken to the first station, whither he
had to be carried 6 kilometres on a stretcher. Our . . . ward
was cleared at once of the light cases so that we were able to fill
up with the badly wounded whom we have now; but Aosta
kept their light-wounded and are therefore very slack at present.

. . . Went to S. Giovanni . . . to the Ospedale No. 022 . . . a
big hospital, and looks very full; an operation was going on in

a room with open window giving on to a narrow garden strip and S. Giovanni street beyond; not very hygienic, but one is not so careful here. . . . A charming way home through the fields. . . . The hills are quite small, and steep and sudden, like playthings. . . .

19th Sept.

I heard this morning that No. 72 died quite suddenly and early. One other patient left, so that we have 15 altogether, of which 7 fractured legs (compound, of course). They are all heavy dressings. One leg has 5 drainage tubes in it, being all riddled with shrapnel.

I was off at five to-day, too tired to do much, but I sat on the hill and enjoyed the late afternoon; the hills, even the Sabotino, were hidden behind a curtain of heavy cloud, and the guns came with a dull sound through the thick air. The feeling of autumn is everywhere, and the outline of the trees so beautiful.

We are just now discussing the weekly bath. Trant had her name down on the list . . . but found the door locked and someone splashing inside and is too delicate-minded to make remarks through the keyhole; it is believed to be one of the men just come from an out-station, so that one can't be severe with him.

I had a visit in my ward from one of our English patients who had been throwing cigarettes to my two fractured thigh cases, they can't move out of the ward and smoking isn't allowed, so I have left them the problem to solve and not mentioned the cigarettes to sister.

20th Sept.

Very sad day. Little 94, who has already lost his right arm, had to have the leg taken off at 9 this morning. I was there and held it during the amputation; he was so thin it was not a long business. And now one wonders if he will live through the night, his pulse is so flickery.

It has been a hard day . . . I got only one hour off, so that I have been working hard for 11 hours to-day, and feel tired. Haven't seen the new V.A.D. but Trant tells me she is aggressively British and doesn't like coffee for breakfast; we believe that she would disapprove of people who powder their faces (like us) but that she will do so herself by the time she is 45. . . .

21st Sept.

Comparatively lazy day. No. 94 is better; pulse stronger; he is an unsatisfactory patient, most dissatisfied and unwilling to take courage, but we hope to pull him through now. . . .

. . . Went up the hill with Mr. Glazebrook. From his out-station at Ravna one can sit on the balcony and watch the exposed bit of road, and see the ambulances coming along among the shells, wondering if they will escape, and knowing that one has to run the gauntlet in a while; all the cross-roads are constantly sprinkled with shells—the small brass ones, 'Carabinieri ticklers'; the bit of road where our three drivers were wounded, 'the rock', is out of sight of the Austrians, but they have the position and it is the only way up Gabriele so they shell it constantly. On the visible bits they seem to try to avoid the red cross. It seems that the Austrian side has very bad roads, just mule tracks, so that their lorries have to stop a long way behind the front, and it must cause great difficulties to their transport: such a contrast to the Italian side.

Went up the hill with Trant after dinner . . . could not see the bursting shells themselves, they were hidden in the mist, but all the district behind the lines was visible, the signals from the near hills, the traffic moving and twinkling along the roads, a constant flash of artillery signals in the valley below us, and the lights of an Austrian prisoners' camp behind us in the plain: one felt surrounded by an intense active life everywhere, feeling its way in the night. Suddenly on our left a pink glow, like the rising moon . . . over the crest of the hill; it rose, and glowed, and sank, and rose again . . . more like a picture by Blake than anything else; it suddenly towered right up into the sky, there was a column of white smoke clouds, the under part red with a streak of flame; after a few seconds, a terrific rolling noise; the light sank; then all was repeated two or three times. We decided it was an ammunition dump on fire, and one shed after another exploding, and two men who presently came up told us it was Caporetto way . . . is still going on; while writing this in bed it has thrice rattled at my door and shaken the camp-bed, and the guns are going on without a pause.

The two drivers who joined us out there say that Oct. 1st is the date of the next offensive, so we must be ready for more wounded.

22nd Sept.

... Last night's explosion a French munition store ... went on exploding till about five o'clock this morning. Dr. Thompson and Mr. Ashby were driving there by chance when a sentry told them to go no further because it was so dangerous; Mrs. Thompson is at Dolegno canteen, so Dr. Tommy made the car go all the faster and met the canteen people trooping out like refugees. They came to spend the night at S. Giovanni, as their own house was so near it rocked up and down with the shocks.

Everything going well in the ward to-day. 94 much better; he is very spoilt—Dr. Thompson calls him a 'little devil', and hates being told he is better, or eating well, or sleeping well; after sighing and groaning all day, Miss Gordon started a game of tombola in the ward and all his troubles were instantly forgotten; he won too, by general consent I suspect—which shows how nice the people are to each other.

Capitano Varaldi came round with 6 bottles of champagne and there was great excitement in the ward. One was presented to us and we drank it after 9 p.m. Matron arrived just as the cork was coming off so that it had to be hidden under difficulties. It didn't taste quite like champagne out of a china bowl, but it was a great event all the same.

To-night the bombardment seems to have stopped but there is an endless stream of lorries up the road. Perhaps also one gets used to the guns and notices them less after a time.

24th Sept.

Last night we had a service, taken by Dr. Thompson, who made a good sincere sermon. The men from Gorizia south (The Haymarket) brought a looted Austrian harmonium to accompany the hymns, and afterwards, in the evening, we had music, Mr. Henderson on the harmonium, Mr. Mayer on hi violin, and Miss G— singing: it was better without her, as she has the drawing-room voice, as if she had a hot potato in her mouth. The lounge is a most uncomfortable place on Sunday evening when a crowd of men collect there and all the V.A.Ds suddenly melt away and one is left alone. I stayed some time under these conditions till Miss G. came up and looked . . . annoyed at finding me . . . talking to the performers, whom she seemed to consider her own special property. Everyone asks me how I like her, which is . . . trying—but I find they all share my opinion! We had to stop the music because of a patient downstairs, and the harmonium was loaded up again for Gorizia.

To-night I spent first running a race with Gibson to the gate, then talking to Mr. Glazebrook who was waiting for her to finish some odd jobs and walk up the hill—this is the usual evening diversion. The young Belgian then came up and told me that a whole lot of Italian aeroplanes had just passed over our heads with lights on them to raid the Austrian lines; the lights are presumably put out when they get close . . . Trant says they were not flying together, but far apart, one after another.

Last night they were practising artillery signals on the road just outside our gates, lovely yellow and green rockets like fireworks. To-day the road has been most animated; Austrian prisoners being led back, a troupe of theatrical ladies going to the *teatro del soldato* near here, and breaking down opposite us; and lorry after lorry of men racing to the front, waving and shouting and firing up into the air—a sad sight for us who see how they return.

25th Sept.

Finished my map to-day and put in the three hills—Santo, Sabotino, Gabriele—Mr. Glazebrook this evening tells me the village below is Quisca. He took me up the hill in a most wonderful moonlight, all the plain lying under swathes of mist, the air quite warm. The bombardment was going on in a constant series of flashes; a searchlight came full upon us from the Carso—the Austrian side—lighting up every blade of grass; Mr. Glazebrook told me these lights are the most useful way they have of seeing how to drive—but rather terrifying at first.

He tells me that the feeling of waiting to load wounded under fire, with no cover, is merely a sickening fear, so that one must just grip one's nerves and pull through with it. During the offensives the drivers get scarcely any sleep; four hours after 20 of driving! He came home so tired that he could not remember passing Cormons at all, and fell asleep every few seconds. The lorry that went over the bridge parapet just before I came was sent there by the driver's being asleep. Beyond S. Lorenzo they all drive in the dark, and the strain on the eyes is so severe that several people have injured their sight quite seriously; there is too little light to wear goggles, and the dust is awful.

Coming home we saw another fire with flames shooting up and explosions north of Udine. And high in the sky, Gradisca way, a series of yellow sparkles, like broken slivers of mirror, which was shrapnel from anti-aircraft guns. There is always something going on.

. . . The new V.A.D. is a trial; she always talks about herself and what she is accustomed to—and Trant and I would like to hand her over to Miss G. and let them fight it out together.

27th Sept.

. . . A whole day off yesterday; started 7.30 for Udine with Bonnie . . . a good deal of shopping; the place is full of military, very lively and bustling, but with far more than here the feeling of a place behind the lines. Lovely piazza, with loggia and arcades.

To-day was quite hard work. Found two new patients . . . One Sicilian very disgusted because we don't give him bread or meat and only *roba da bambini*. We hope to move back to Garibaldi to-morrow and have spent the day cleaning out cupboards.

Sister appears to be looking forward to next week when G— has gone and we shall have the ward to ourselves.

The guns are more insistent than ever. The offensive is rumoured for the 1st or 20th of next month, but I think the latter more likely.

I saw Capt. Dunstan at tea yesterday and I think Dr. Brock was rather shocked at our shaking hands.

We had an irruption of ladies this afternoon in wonderful clothes—a lot of artistes going to the *teatro del soldato*—looking remarkably second rate too. Their car had been smashed by one of the 4th Unit's, and they borrowed a lorry and came here to be patched up; no serious hurts. The ladies stood about in the front smoking, in front of the astonished Sessions and Sylvester, who were sitting out under the trees in pink and blue pyjamas.

The hills are too misty to see what happens; one clearer day I tried my field glasses and the Santo seemed right in front of me. It is exciting to use them for aeroplanes ... the people at Gorizia north were watching an Austrian one day (not through glasses) and saw him bend over his machine and drop the bomb; they got indoors pretty quick, and the thing exploded in the next door garden. It seems that one doesn't hear a shell which makes straight for one; only those that go sideways towards you or are going overhead; sometimes there is a horrid feeling, when you hear the explosion at the gun, the whizz of the shell, then the bang close by you, all one upon the other; that was the kind of shell that did hit the Gorizia station where Hamish Allen was wounded. Sylvester showed me a snapshot of the place where he and Mr. Young were hit. Mr. Glazebrook has only had rocks falling on the bonnet of his car when running along the 'rock'; it is overhung by a ledge of precipice over which the fragments roll when a shell bursts on the top.

28th Sept.

Busy day getting our people back to Garibaldi ... left all straight by 9 o'clock. It is nice to be back in our own ward; all the patients seem pleased, and we look wonderfully clean and whitewashed, though our floor is more uneven than before.

I am now allowed to put on fomentations by myself; hope to be promoted to dressings soon.

There is a rumour that all the English artillery here is being withdrawn owing to friction with the French, who are taking over the whole line.

...The new V.A.D. went walking up the hill last night with one of our least polished members—so we don't hope for very much from her.

An ambulance just arrived in the moonlight, with some stretchers.

29th Sept.

Five new patients to-day, wounded this morning on Gabriele —enfilade from the San Marco. Haven't seen the dressings— two legs, one shoulder, two hands; the hands seem bad.

We have the Aosta patients in our ward, as theirs is now being whitewashed, so I spent the afternoon putting up 10 beds in isolation ward to be ready for a rush.

Latest rumour about the artillery is that the French are leaving and we take the whole line. Another version says that both are leaving!

Huge fire to-night between here and Isonzo. Could almost see the flames, and the clouds were lit brilliant red as by sunset; a column of smoke rising into the sky, terrible to watch. No explosions, but a hill intervened and may have deadened the noise. Gibby, Murray and I watched it from the hill-top with the full moon shining above in a pale sky and felt rather like Neros; somebody met us . . . and said 'what a glorious fire', and struck one as particularly horrible.

Seabrook home from leave near Turin; says the discontent still seems to be fermenting there, and our uniform most unpopular.

30th Sept.

. . . Service to-night taken by Dr. Thompson; Mrs. Thompson singing with the most beautiful clear voice. There was a great deal of music; Mr. Percival sang—he was an opera singer, then lost his voice; then Elliott Seabrooke, an artist; then Miss G—, not a success after Mrs. Thompson. . . .

1st Oct.

. . . Four patients left this morning (the Sicilian painter, another Sicilian, the Bergamese carabiniere and a Neapolitan *malato*). Three more arrived this evening, wounded in an assault on a fortified gallery of the Gabriele; the major had killed two Austrian officers but the men had not surrendered when our two were wounded. Before coming to the ward they are bathed downstairs under Captain Varaldi's directions, and very badly too as they reach us with their dressings wet through and through.

. . . I hear that the lights we see on the aeroplanes at night are from the exhausts. We thought we saw one to-night— Trant and I on the hill-side—but it turned out to be a real star, the last thing one looks for in the eastern sky nowadays. The pharmacy *tenente* came and escorted us home though we did not want him. . . .

2nd Oct.

Busy day. One new patient early this morning. 23 altogether. We did 14 dressings in the morning, average 15 minutes each. . . .

5th Oct.

Garibaldi is now full again—35 beds. Most of the new arrivals are light cases, arrived to-day. One English driver from 3 Unit, needs a rest chiefly . . .

Yesterday General Capello sent an A.D.C. to enquire after No. 94. Matron got me to interpret and I found him standing forlornly in the hall: I followed up the ward and was able to translate sister to him and put in a few additions. Most exciting to translate so as to make things suitable for Italians.

A lot of troops are passing towards the front on motors— the *Arditi*, all young, single men, who get 26 c/m extra pay and are chosen for the assault. They cheer and sing as they go along, and one hates the sound.

6th Oct.

. . . Englishman gets on well, finds the ward very noisy! I believe it is far and away the cheerfulest in hospital.

Geoffrey Young and Sessions were presented with the silver medal for valour to-day, by Col. Santucci, head of the *Sanità*, of the 2nd Army; he made a speech in the quaintest imaginable English before the Unit men, Sanità men, and V.A.Ds, all drawn up at attention in the hall. We were drilled just beforehand, but the only thing our instructor impressed upon us was "don't talk", and that had no effect. Mr. Young and Sessions looked very depressed through the ceremony; Dr. Brock made an excellent speech of thanks. We had tea beforehand in the hall, and there were nurses from Versa, English artillery officers, canteen people, and the Italians. I saw and spoke to Capt. Dunstan, who invited me to lunch in Udine; he also made a very good straight speech, blushing very much. . . .

7th Oct.

Ward still full. Had Struthers there . . . she has one side and I the other. All the patients doing well now, and dreadfully noisy, so that Sister Carr next door congratulated her V.A.D.—Trant—on the quietness of her ward. She is not very popular with the patients: an orderly came in to-day with a message from 'Sister Carr' and we heard an astonished voice from No. 101: "*Cara? si chiama cara, quella li?*" [Darling? is that one called darling?]

Spent my off time in a long walk with Struthers to the empty house on the hill-top; gorgeous view of hills all round, Faiti with three shells bursting there, Monte Nero white with first snow, and snow behind Ternovo and all along the Dolomites. The wind was icy, it has been cold all day; we picked some tiny shrivelled pomegranates, looked through the empty rooms filled with soldiers' clothes—it is now used as a kind of laundry—and then came away. In one of the rooms where a lovely stucco ceiling is slowly falling to pieces, a notice is put up: "position reserved for the 7th battery", but the war has gone far ahead now.

The latest news is that both the French and English artillery are leaving: huge French guns, long noses, painted over for camouflage, passed through Udine yesterday. . . .

Mr. Talbot, the English artillery's chaplain, came to take the service to-night. I think something must be the matter with me, I weep so easily now . . . when there are prayers about the war: one feels that so much more out here.

This evening the V.A.Ds invited some of the Unit men to their table, but I was on duty and missed the fun. We had music afterwards. Mr. Henderson played, and sang too; he played Beethoven, Chopin, and beautifully, all by ear.

Mr. Newsome has promised me an Austrian helmet tomorrow.

[205]

One of the drivers to-day was blown right off his seat by a shell, and not hurt a bit.

8th Oct.

Holy Communion this morning. Usual sort of day. Sister Brechin is really pleased with my work, now that S. has come and is slower than me. . . .

I found two cigarettes this afternoon, one was actually being smoked by No. 101—and was thrown out of window determinedly. The little kitten, Gabriele, came into the ward and was handed to each patient to play with in turn, unbeknown to sister.

Sessions is walking about on crutches now, and to-day—going upstairs—took a step on the leg that isn't there and fell: fortunately no harm was done.

11th Oct.

Fifteen will leave to-morrow morning. I believe it means a new offensive; the whole hospital is being cleared.

I went out last night with Edinger who was telling me that the real reason for the English guns leaving has been a quarrel—and the French too. It seems we put on some very unnecessary airs of superiority—a pity. But the offensive is to go on just the same.

There has been a great noise of guns . . . Carso way lately. . . . Last night was wonderful, hot and dark, with a blinding lightning flash now and then and the searchlights sweeping round like huge fans; a constant flicker of shells, and now and then the far outlines showed against a glare made by the liquid fire. Eringer was describing more wonderful views from their Gorizia station, with . . . Sabotino above, rising dark from an ocean of mists into which the shells and shooting star-shells plunged and were lost . . . all seen with a foreground of black ruins and the deep Isonzo running between, lit up now and then by a red glare of the guns. All the men I have spoken to loathe the war with an intensity of hate; the sordidness and grime of it all. Eringer told me that what has impressed him most was an early beautiful dawn, with the sun just lifted above the Gabriele crest and looking down on the ruined piazza of Salcano; an absolute solitude and stillness, and in the quiet clear morning in the middle of the way, a mule and a soldier, dead, with the early shadows chasing over them.

12th Oct.

15 patients left this morning; two hand cases are still uncertain, and one is sorry to lose them before knowing, though they all say they will write ... Strenuous morning sweeping the ward, polishing the furniture and bed-making. In the afternoon Sister and S. went to the English hospital at Versa and I was left in charge and spent my time painting soap boxes (made out of half a sterilized milk tin) with a scarlet G for Garibaldi ward, on a white ground.

Three khaki men from Gradisca came to see my English patient, and I noticed how much worse their manners were than those of the common soldiers here; much annoyed with them for sitting on sister's table dangling their legs and making themselves quite at home!

13th Oct.

New case in this morning; simple fracture of thigh, probable internal haemorrhage, delirious; pulse 140 this evening, temp. 101. Big, heavy carabinier—very doubtful case.

... Delightful day with Trant and Dr. Brock ... to Cormons to call on her friend Major Fausto di Tondo, who looks after the grey sausages that we look at through our glasses every afternoon. We couldn't find the place, and went a few kilometres down towards the Carso to the home of the Neuport aeroplanes first, by mistake: the Carso hills rise up enormously when you get nearer to them. Major Di Tondo has a lovely villa with palms in Cormons; showed us maps, photographs taken from balloon and aeroplane, and a plan of all the enemy guns they have been able to locate, which is constantly kept up to date, so that we could see the alterations and erasures. We then went in a grey hooded car to Vipulzano, left it on our right with cypresses round it on a ridge, and came to a sequestered little valley where one of the balloons lives. It was got out for our inspection; the parachute—looking like a crumpled silk ball dress—was unfolded, and a *tenente* got into the tiny square padded basket, put on the parachute, and went up a little way to let us see how it was all done . . . a huge thing, sailing slowly up: is spoken of as a ship, with three squads of men to look after bows, stern and centre. It is let up and brought down by strong cable let out from a motor engine, and which serves for telephone messages; the answering message is phoned wirelessly in the Italian (not in the French and English). Last few days saw two of the monsters burnt, but the officers saved by their parachutes; the storms too are very dangerous.

We lunched with the mess of the Umberto cavalry—risotto, salmon, beefsteak and potato, a wonderful soufflé, fruit, white wine and coffee—and a tablecloth and napkins! They were all very polite: we had to shake hands all round and be introduced to everyone. . . .

16th Oct.

. . . Air raids to-day, the first for a long while. I counted 6 Austrian machines right overhead: the sound of their guns is very short and sharp, different from the heavy thud of the real bombardment. One did not realize how near the enemy planes were till a machine-gun, just down the road, started firing its quick rattle. The orderly assured me that a shellcase had fallen just behind the house, so I sent him to look for it as a souvenir—but it was not found. . . .

Walked with Trant to Corno without brassards—and of course met Matron out driving with Mr. Young, but I don't think she noticed. Corno is a pretty straggling village with a river, and mules and tents camped all round it. We came back by Cividale–Cormons road; one has to look out as there is no speed limit and the huge lorries rush by, leaving less than a handbreadth space.

So cold now that we go to bed after dinner for warmth, and write and sew there.

17th Oct.

. . . Heavy bombardment all last night. We hear there is a big Austrian attack on, but have no wounded as yet.

.   .   .   .   .

19th Oct.

No further news of the Austrian offensive.

Carabinier slightly better; has made me black and blue with his fist on my chest.

Busy getting Monday's picnic ready. Gilda at the farm is going to provide hay to sit on, and a fire and saucepan for the punch. Nino in the kitchen will produce the cake if we provide sugar, so we collect what we can from every meal, clearing all the sugar basins—hope soon to have a half kilo.

A's car was smashed the other day, while he was out of it for a few minutes. . . .

20th Oct.

The Austrian offensive, foretold for to-day, must have started; the guns are sounding, all day and all night.

We have had 6 new 'medicals', and 10 in the next ward. English patient . . . has left this morning.

21st Oct.

No new arrivals.

Feeling very tired . . . Mayer, Henderson and Mrs. Thompson were playing and singing, and the evening was very pleasant; Dr. Brock sat with us too.

The bombardment continues heavily. One could see little, but one huge mine exploded while I was on the hill, just on Faiti ridge, and about two-thirds as high as Carso from here; it spread out slowly in a fan of thick smoke and hung there in the heavy air. . . .

22nd Oct.

We hear that the Austrian offensive has begun all along the line from Trentino to the sea. All yesterday, through the night and all to-day at intervals, they have been shelling our neighbourhood with their heavy long-range guns. Cormons has been hit (two people killed that we know of) and the pharmacist *tenente* was coming through Brazzano quite near here when a shell dropped. They say they are trying to get at some munition dumps between us and Cormons. The shots come one at a time, at long intervals, like something very heavy falling from the dazzling blue sky; the walls shake, and everything rattles; last night I thought someone was trying to get in at my door and shaking it! It is quite possible that we may get a shell ourselves.

The day was lovely, but not clear enough to see anything ... the vines are just turning colour and the fine sunny days are gorgeous.

S. has left on leave with her brother and Hamish Allen, who is to be operated for his stiff knee. They all went this morning, the last sight being Bosy rushing after the ... lorry with S's hot-water bottle carefully filled.

... My poem on Dr. Tommy ... read out on Sunday night, and passed round with joy especially to his wife.

24th Oct.

Since midday the bombardment has continued without a break, one constant indescribable roar. In any room with the windows open it is like being on board ship, with the throb in one's ears and all the woodwork creaking and rattling, and now and then a louder buffet, like a big wave slapping against the side. The attack is chiefly south over the Carso, but a few lights in our sector too and one or two fires nearer to us. It has been pouring with steady rain all day; the troops march by at a weary plod, with their hoods well drawn over their faces.

The bombardment of our neighbourhood continues regularly, and I believe some of the shells were nearer than yesterday; they come with a sudden crash that makes one jump, and the whole house sways and one can feel it quaking for a second or two; then a second, very slight shock seems to follow, rattling our doors and windows gently. The loudest report of all came a few minutes ago, and there is now a strange stillness, just a cart creaking along the road. ...

"Nous ne sommes hommes, et ne nous tenons les uns aux autres, que par la parole" (Montaigne, Ch. IX. 1. 1.).

"Mens immota manet, lachrymae volvuntur inanes" (Aeneid L. IV, v. 449).

25th Oct.

Half-day's holiday ... lovely weather ... With Gibby ... walked to Brazzano to see the two shell holes; they are about

20 minutes walk from here, but fell in a motor deposit, so we could not go and look. We heard there that Cormons was in ruins; walked on, past long trains of big guns drawn by tractors, past whole families plodding away with their belongings: one poor woman, with her two copper buckets and a blanket, was trailing along sobbing in the middle of the road. Cormons itself was a desert, and most dreary; soldiers in the streets; the *carabinieri* at the street corners had their steel helmets on; all the visible glass in the windows was broken, but most shutters were closed, many nailed down; the piazza was quite bare, every window shuttered, and the desolation indescribable. People stood talking despondently at their back doors, and the soldiers were taking last provisions from the shops. We did not understand what it all meant, and only learnt later that the order had been given to evacuate; we wandered about, asking for biscuits and chocolate, quite surprised to find the place suddenly cleared of its stores. We only saw one house really smashed, a huge hole letting the sky in from above . . . rafters across the street kept the walls from falling—but we crunched over broken glass and saw little bits chipped off the church, etc. . . . The bombardment had stopped about an hour before we arrived; has started again now, by the sound; they send over very heavy stuff; Daddy Dyne was spattered . . . yesterday at a hundred yards distance from the shell.

On our way home we had an Austrian plane sailing just over us, quite low so that we could see the colours painted on it and the engine; but it must have been observing, as no bomb fell. An Italian car with two officers in front and an old gentleman stopped and asked us about the bombardment and seemed quite annoyed when Gibby tactlessly told him it was safe now. His face was familiar; I think he must be something in the government.

We came back though a . . . red sunset . . . heavy guns with their long nozzles covered with leaves, and short double-barrelled howitzers, all trudging on against the orange sky. The traffic lulled . . . then started again in the dusk. Staff cars, motor cycles . . . intense excitement everywhere but no disorder. On our way we stopped at a dump and got a shell-case each, but I think it was rather wrong of us. Getting here, we are told that no woman is to go to Cormons at all ... civilians being cleared out as fast as possible; we are not even to get our bread there as hitherto, but will have soldiers' rations. The ladies from the 4th Unit are here too now, having been turned out of Cormons. The wonder is that we were allowed to go unquestioned.

The news that spreads about is rather disquieting. Caporetto they say was taken by the enemy who broke through our first line this morning; but has since been retaken by us. The 2nd Unit have that station and three of their cars have been smashed and one driver wounded, they sent a message asking for a loan of cars from us last night, and we are sending this evening 5 cars and about 6 men, to be lent to the 26th Army Corps with a station probably near Lovjsce. The latest rumour is that our own station—the most advanced we have, of Ravna— has been taken. The trenches round here, a few hundred yards away, are being got in order and filling with men: altogether we have a feeling of disquietude; the attack is going to be a very big thing. There are Germans, Bulgarians, Turks against us as well as the Austrians: a German aeroplane was brought down yesterday.

Our English batteries that were to leave have not yet gone I am told, and are shooting as hard as they can down Carso way; but at present the chief danger seems to the north of us ... Our army corps as yet seems hardly engaged ... and no orders to clear the hospital.

Just heard about the two ladies from the 4th Unit who are sleeping here. They have been bombed constantly for the last 5 days, and now the men of the radiograph section have decided to sleep downstairs for greater safety and to send their two girls here to us ... Their place ... about 4 or 5 kilometres from here.

26th Oct.

This has been a very long eventful day. We were told at breakfast to have a suit-case ready with all our indispensable property so as to be able to leave at a moment's notice. In the morning an order came to clear the hospital of all patients; we had a great rush to get our fractures into uniforms while ambulance after ambulance drove up to carry them all away.

The guns were pounding at slow intervals, nearer than yesterday it seemed; we were too busy to listen, but I once heard the shell most plainly, the report of its departure, a shrieking whistle in the air, and the heavy report of where it struck. Poor little Celeste with his amputated leg and arm sat and shivered with nervousness.

We got all our beds stripped, the pillows, sheets, and covers tied in a bundle on each bed. About 2 p.m. Braithwaite came to tell us to dismount 25 beds that were to go at once to the rear with some V.A.Ds; our stretcher cases were not yet all cleared off. By tea-time they had all gone however and our beds dismounted and carried down, and our dressings, etc., packed— the ward looking like a desert.

The rumours meanwhile were most various. Ravna it seems is really lost; the paper to-day admits losses on the Bainsizza plateau; Caporetto went and the Austrians reached the Isonzo at Canale. A poor little *Alpino*, limping along with a shot in his leg, came to us and told us this, and also that we are leaving the guns in the enemy's hands, they come up so quickly with their machine-guns. The road in front here was a sad sight all day—one long dejected stream, soldiers, guns, endless Red Cross ambulances, women and children, carts with household goods, and always more guns and more soldiers—all going towards the rear.

Well, at tea we were told that the order to evacuate had come; we were to take as little as possible—only luggage we could carry ourselves, and leave the rest in the hope of retrieving it later. I did my whole business in 3/4 hour, left my bedding piled in a bundle with my name, and went back to finish packing the ward. Then comes the new order—we must stay here and are to prepare for wounded at once. All the beds to make again. We leave the 25 that are dismounted in case of another order, which is quite probable, and lay mattresses along the empty space. A lot of our old patients return; they had wandered from S. Giovanni along the packed roads in all the confusion and instead of getting to Udine arrived here very pleased with themselves. We got them some soup and pudding, all that could be scraped together, as no one expected to have another meal at Villa Trento. Our ward now has 3 bad cases in beds and 20 on the mattresses along the floor; they look very uncomfortable, but we have done all that is possible and they have plenty of covers and a clean pillow—but none are allowed to undress as we may have to leave suddenly. We got them to take their boots off and wash hands and faces; as an aggravation of difficulties the water supply has given up; it comes from near Cividale and a shell must have damaged the aqueduct; so all we have in the house is to be for drinking purposes only.

The news to-night is still bad. Gorizia expected to fall to-morrow; G. came to see us at supper before going back to clear the last things from our station there; expects to be all night at the job on account of the crowded roads. Our cars have been carrying refugees to-day—streams of them, and now Udine is in panic too and people leaving as fast as they can.

One comforting thing is that our new out-station, which had to be given up this morning, is to be re-started to-night; and they say we are going to have a big counter attack.

Am now going to sleep without sheet or pillow-case, with the chance of being called any time in the night to leave, and the Austrians about 9 miles away.

27th Oct. Afternoon.

Were not roused in the night after all, and Bosy's precaution sleeping with her hair done up turned out unnecessary; after all, one may as well be captured in one's nightgown as in one's corsets, so I undressed completely and got what sleep was possible with the horrible stream of retreating men tramping below the windows. A few shells came now and then—one notices them much less though I believe they are fairly near; the guns are not much heard, the fighting being up to the north, behind a hill that shuts off the noise—but the bombardment has been the heaviest since the war began, lasting five days. There seems always to be a lull in the traffic at dawn; such a sad ominous silence this morning, in the grey light.

To-day we live in the same uncertainty as to our future. But we are to be the last hospital to move, which is satisfactory so far. Meanwhile a place is found at Conegliano, 80 kilometres west, and our 25 beds are just being loaded and sent on

there with all requisites for a start. I hope not to be one of the
V.A.Ds sent there to open the place. We remain here to
collect what wounded there are, but most must have been taken
prisoner, we only get stragglers. Cormons hospital is deserted
—no one there but a corporal who had not even a drop of iodine
to dress a wound which came on to us this morning; Abbazia
on the hill behind us I hear is also closed.

Aosta and Garibaldi are the only two wards kept open, and
Garibaldi looks a desert with all the mattresses on the floor.
We have had all the work there is there; about half a dozen
limping soldiers, soiled, ragged, walking with no stockings in
their boots—one with a pair of boots picked up by the roadside. We dress the wounds, lay them on the mattresses and
find what little food we can get, and the next ambulance takes
them along to the rear. Did all the dressings this morning
with my own forceps as the ward ones were packed; none of the
men are undressed; we just take the boots off to rest the poor
feet.

Trevvy is back; had one glimpse of him down a corridor
before he went to Capriva. Nearly all our men are here;
Plava, Ravna are untenable; some of the 2nd Unit had actually
to run to escape the Austrians. G. and a few are in Gorizia still
and we are anxious about them.

This morning's news was that the enemy tried to surround
Gorizia and failed. Now Dr. Tommy says Santo, Kuk,
Gabriele, all is lost to the Isonzo. The train of soldiers coming to
the rear is endless, and now there are guns, long lines of them,
chiefly field guns: and civilians still with bundles; the roads
are almost impracticable—they say everyone seems to have
lost his head. We have only our own cars to rely on and they
can only crawl along. One of the men this morning had walked
to Plava with a contused foot, and then by lorry here and the
drive took twelve hours.

Now all the cases are cleared off and we have nothing to do.
The weather continues lovely—a golden autumn day.

28th Oct. In car No. 88, near Codroipo.

About 3 o'clock yesterday Matron told Sister Brechin, Trant,
Gibby, Murray, Hurley, Bosy and me to be ready at once to

start for Conegliano to prepare the new hospital. We had our hand-bags waiting outside the front door in about 15 minutes, and our boxes—which we shall probably never see again—in the hall . . . We had tea, and the whistle called us to start on the retreat. . . .

We left at 5.15 a wonderful evening. The hospital quite empty, except for two stragglers who had just limped in. Ambler was driving us; Cobby Wood with motor stores followed; Miss Kemball with a new and inexperienced driver left separately and we have seen nothing of her yet.

Through the twilight till the moon came up, a few shells sounding behind us; the road packed with traffic three deep, *carabinieri* all along to keep order; all talking, shouting, or very tired. One got more and more to feel it as the retreat. Behind us flares went up along the skyline where our men were exploding the stores and munition dumps before the Austrians got them. We got stuck for half-hours at a time, the whole road lined with tired figures, sleeping anywhere, in heaps on the banks; some limping along without their regiments; all so tired. Bivouacs in the fields; big guns with caterpillar tractors; the moon and white villages and cypress hills formed a wonderful background. Very near S. Giovanni a despatch rider stopped by us in the crush and asked if we were from Villa Trento; I took his message, to hunt up an English captain at the Hotel Europa in Conegliano—we are still on the way now. We saw two lorries overturned—one dead horse lying in the road; and near Udine, where we cross the broad river-bed, the tired men were scattered sleeping on the white stones, and made one realize a battlefield with its dead.

Reached Udine at 9—20 kilometres—and as Miss Kemball foolishly had all the rations, went into the station to find some food; so packed with refugees one had to hew a way through them—most pitiful; we got some bread and cheese at last, just a small allowance.

Everyone was turning out of Udine. The flare of the explosions was visible all along the sky; turned to a dull red sunset blaze and it started to rain—with all those poor tired sleepers in the open. The lines of traffic continued three deep. We have now been travelling $20\frac{1}{2}$ hours and are only 16 kilometres from Udine. For one stretch the two columns were distinct, one for horses, the other for motors, but then comes a jumble, and we just wait till the thing ahead moves a few yards.

We had sandwich of potted sausage between two sweet biscuits and cold plum pudding at about 2 a.m., all squashed into the ambulance with rain and wind buffetting outside. The men and refugees all come to look in at us and want to have a lift, and we are already overweighted.

Wood caught us up last night and has kept close behind us ever since.

We saw a good deal of fresh cavalry coming out during the night. Pouring rain and wind: strange black sky, plain intensely black, and lurid pale strip in Gorizia direction.

In the morning we saw Braithwaite; had left his car and hurried up to us walking. The retreat looks like a panic; Udine evacuated; wounded trudge in the rain with the hospital blanket over their shoulders. I saw one man drop it and not have the energy to pick it up. We stayed ages at this village before Codroipo, and found some boiled polenta and made cocoa in a house crammed with soldiers; bread not to be had. We dressed man wounded in the head and resting in a stable. . . . We have two women and children in our car; Wood has a few wounded; both heavily overloaded—and petrol threatens to run short. But Braithwaite has gone on to find quarters at Pordenone where there is a dump and we shall stay for a night anyway.

Our orderlies just arrived from Villa Trento, walking from Udine. They had the order to evacuate as soon as we left yesterday, and the Austrians were in Cividale this morning. It seems the Tagliamento is to make the next stand; the rendezvous is a hill just behind—and we are in the thick of the crush; no one can possibly realise what this means.

29th Oct. Cross the Tagliamento at 5.30 a.m.

The retreat has a rudiment of organization; some aero planes have been flying over the road to set the congestion right; and the soldiers all seem to have been given some hard rations like dog biscuits to eat.

We passed one fallen aeroplane close by the road last night, glimmering with new paint through the rain.

I believe there are plenty of men still, but most of our artillery was lost on the Bainsizza and higher up the river.

Poor Braithwaite is white as a sheet and so sad; and the men coming down to-day seem quite cheerful, glad to think that the fighting is over on the heights—only the officers look unhappy about the war—so that we wonder if it is only our own hearts that feel broken. The horror, horror of it.

30*th Oct.* 10 a.m. Hotel Savoia, Padua.

About dusk on the 28th, Johnson, a new man, came up to us walking. Had been outside Udine when the alarm of the German arrival was given . . . a panic spread, all the horses were taken out of their carts and the lorries abandoned, so that it became impossible to get any motors along the road; a lieutenant came up to tell them to leave everything and hurry along on foot if they wished to escape, and the Austrians were now reported 5 or 6 miles from us. We were going at a snail's pace just then, the block ahead being quite impossible: in fact we reached a record by progressing only 2 kilometres in 12 hours on the morning of the 28th. The question was put to us by the men whether we would rather walk on and get across the bridge before they might have to blow it up, or stick to the car and trust to luck; we decided to stay as we were, not having any contrary orders, and also because we thought these were the only two cars that had a chance of escaping so that it was important to save them. Decided to turn down a side road if the Austrians came. (NB. So as not to be enfiladed.) Anyway the probabilities were only of a temporary imprisonment. Having so decided we dug out H's plum cake, tackled our *fiasco* of wine, put on our brassards conspicuously, and waited for the block ahead to clear away. It was a slow business: in the growing darkness the traffic was being arranged in three columns—motors, carts, and men who were sent by a different side road altogether; the evening cleared and the stars shone; then there was a fire in Udine direction, and shells began landing in the country behind; we saw nothing except the long crowded road throbbing with the impatient motors, but the explosions seemed to come nearer, on either side of the road, in an irregular tentative sort of way. A cheerful artillery man told us that they might be peppering the *retrovie* with gas shells: but a new bridge was being got ready over the river nearby to hurry us up a bit. At last we crossed the little stream and the pace got better. The first signs of a stand began to show—cavalry, encamped by the road in fields, and a gun emplacement.

We reached Codroipo about 9 p.m. There the Udine and Gradisca roads across the Tagliamento meet, and the congestion was one solid mass, which a bevy of officers were disentangling. We waited for quite an hour while troops filed by with all their kit, just silhouettes and sudden flashes of light from matches and lanterns; there was a pleasant feeling of order and hurry—one felt they were very anxious to get us along quickly. The shells continued to fall somewhere in the neighbourhood; the whole sky flushed a delicate pink with all its little clouds, and seemed infinitely high above the houses. An officer came and and asked who we were and hoped that the soldiers treated us well along the road—a very kind thought in the midst of all that hurry

About 10 p.m. who should come along but all the V.A.Ds with a Colonel Hailey from the Gradisca artillery. They had taken a southern road and come faster than we, but had left their cars about 5 in the afternoon by Hailey's advice, and were walking to get across the bridge. We gave Hay and Willie a lift, but the others went on, and we didn't like to offer to change places as the ambulance was the more dangerous—but hoped to catch them up later.

We left Codroipo in a deluge of wind and rain again; dead horses on the way, in the desolate shuttered streets with the endless caterpillar of lorries snuffling along them. Wood's car broke down, but he looted an exchange piece from an over-turned lorry in the ditch, and rejoined us to our great relief. Percy also overtook us, with Nino the cook, and Luigia, all tired out. He had been one of the last in Udine, when flaming depots were all round and the Italian soldiery was looting the place—wounded men in the streets crying helplessly to be taken; deserted waggons cramming up the road; the officers trying to keep order with their revolvers, and the shots increasing the panic with the thought of the enemy. Percy and his people tried to get some of the machines out of the way, but it was a hopeless business and they left the car and trudged on foot: he also was quite exhausted.

The slowness of our pace increased, it seemed. The river retreated further and further; the country became uneven again, very bare and rather marshy, good defensible ground with well arranged ditches and little ridges: I saw a few shadowy silhouettes move in these trenches, but the sensation was one of desolation and solitude—and a slight mist over all, and the moon behind clouds.

The hours wore on, and yet the pace was as slow as ever— about 20 yards, then a stop of half an hour or more. Towards 4. a.m. I could see that our men were getting anxious, and even I knew enough to expect the bridge to be shelled as soon as daylight came. At about 5 Percy said we must get out and walk and wait for the ambulance on the other bank if it could get through. We started at a breathless pace, single file, anxiously kept together by Percy in front and Haston (who turned up in the night, also car-less) in the rear: they guided splendidly, in and out of the big wheels, under the noses of the mules, threading the tired files of troops, and all in great haste and well over our ankles in soft mud. We must have gone so about one and a half miles; it is confused like a nightmare. At 5.30 the horizon opened; the great width of the Tagliamento spread in front of us, with the long bridge curving across without a parapet, all cold and grey in the first dawn.

The country on either side is flat; on our right were the hills, quite near apparently. The terrible rain of the last days has made the river rise, so it will be difficult for the Austrians to get across. [This was inaccurate, for the river sank again before they reached it.] There was a half-finished bridge alongside ours, half-broken through by floods I believe; our own was giving way in places under the strain of traffic. Got over about 6 a.m., but Percy still hurried us on through the mud. and I was loaded with coat, overcoat, mackintosh and knap-sack. At last we reached Casarsa; found a house, all crammed with soldiers where they gave us water to wash and drink; the woman there was very good and quite brave, though expecting to have to leave; she refused any money.

At Casarsa we came upon the others and luckily got a train and two carriages reserved for us to Treviso; no sooner had we crawled out a little way than a German aeroplane flew over the place dropping bombs. I don't know how near to us but the train was rather in a panic, everyone rushing back to the shelter of the carriages, so I didn't like to increase the confusion by getting out to see. The enemy plane came along and passed us, flying very low and looking most immaculate black and white, like an ill-omened magpie, just above the trees it seemed. It was disgusting not to see any of ours out after it, or a single gun to make it keep at least a respectful distance.

Our meals showed a distinct improvement after this. Colonel Hailey I think produced the tinned salmon. Then someone saw a loaf of bread fall from a van; the soldiers realized that provisions were there, got at the vans, and looted them clean, scrambling up in disorder, some carrying away 5 or 6 loaves, some getting nothing at all; all one could see was a mass of grey-green and hands outstretched for bread. A lieutenant got us some too (the officers could do nothing to stop the business) and gave us a tin of butter to go with it—and then someone arrived from Pordenone with wine.

Penman now joined us, having had to leave the car and come along on foot with his two kit-bags from three miles behind Codroipo. We had news of Geoffrey Young and Matron by this time; he had had to leave the car and hobbled on crutches till Phil Noel Baker took him into a smaller car; Penman told us they were on the road but not yet near the bridge; so we were still anxious. Miss Kemball was also seen by Sister Brechin coming along in a car ahead of ours.

The train was actually slower than our cars! We watched the road and its traffic going along parallel to us with some trees and meadows between, and the things seemed to be moving quite briskly at last. As for us, we stopped, crawled on, and stopped again; the people got out and sat on the grass, and scrambled up when the train went on; the soldiers were trooping across the open country everywhere, thinking of nothing except to enjoy the sunshine and the looted food: they got at some frozen meat vans, and were cutting the beef up into great chunks, some eating it raw and some cooking over little stick fires: but for the uniforms we might have been watching a lot of happy picnic parties.

About 6 p.m. we got out of the train and found some of our cars that had got over the bridge waiting in the road: we had sent word to them by G. on foot—the quickest way of getting along. Things were moving better now along the road . . . and we were in Pordenone before 7, and found a whole lot of the Unit there, including—to our great relief—Mr. Young and matron . . . and Trevvy himself. We heard that all except three were safely through, with or without their cars.

Our hopes of a night at Pordenone were soon done away with; the place was getting too crowded for anything, and they wanted us to move back before a crush came; so we had a drink of water . . . a basket of rations, and off we went for Conegliano, all packed the same old way in two ambulances. Most of my party changed into Wood's car, to give the more comfortable one to those who had had to walk the ten miles to Casarsa.

Conegliano we saw by moonlight only. We stopped there for food, but were not to spend the night even here. Padua was to be the goal. So we got some reluctant waiters to fork out soup, a fried egg each and some bread—more difficult to get than anything else.

Trevvy was with us, and we also had an Italian nurse from Sta Lucia, right under Gabriele, who had stopped a night in Udine and was now making her way to Treviso; she told us of a Polish nurse who remained in Udine with about 56 wounded who could not be moved. On the way a soldier came up and begged us to take a lady as far as Conegliano; we were able to take her, as Gibby, Murray and Trant were in Dr. Tommy's car; her sick husband had got out of his bed ill with pleurisy, and they had sent their two children separately in a cart from Codroipo and didn't know what had become of them nor whether they were yet over the bridge. We left them at Conegliano and the other three got in again, and we went on in pouring rain.

The army was being reorganized between Pordenone and Conegliano; no soldier allowed to pass, the *carabinieri* collected and arrested all the deserters as they came along; they asked us if we had any Italians with us and gave a look into the car. Murray tells me she saw quite a riot between soldiers and *carabinieri*.

After Conegliano I fell asleep and woke to find all asleep around me, the car standing still in a by-road and the rain still swishing down; a most alarming feeling to have nothing at all moving after the days of tumult. But it turned out to be only a halt for the sake of our poor drivers who had been at it with no rest from 5.15 p.m. on the 27th—about 56 hours; so they had three and a half hours sleep. We could now run along at a fine pace; the roads were clear. We got to Padova towards 9 this morning and are here at the Savoia. The cars are all being ranged up in the station. We have been 64 hours on the way, and shall be glad of rest.

1st Nov. Milan.

We left all the cars ranged in the station yard and made for the Hotel Savoia where Braithwaite had provided a room. Here we got a decent wash. The men used Ambler's car as a dressing-room, rather disturbed by the large crowd which had collected round to look.

So strange to be in an ordinary town with real clothes and shops about; the last days were all unreal like a dream. No one here knew much of what goes on. The communiqués say nothing at all, and the town looks very gay and extraordinarily careless. The officers do seem very preoccupied. One of the Unit men told me that they really were behaving splendidly.

We found quite a lot of our men here . . . they kept on arriving all through the day. We spent most of the morning tidying, and met them all at lunch at the Fanti. Sessions also had come along from Udine having found it impossible to leave the place by train; he seemed as cheerful and calm as ever; all the men have been too splendid for words, but some look tired to death—one is quite anxious for poor Cobby Wood, I have never seen anyone look so exhausted.

Dunstan is in Padua too. Gave us better news yesterday; the Italian cavalry charged the Austrians four times and sent them back. They had not yet got into Udine except perhaps with some Uhlan patrols, and we had already sent 5 train-loads of French and English; then came also the rumour that we have retaken Cividale.

To-day, however, the news is very bad; the Tagliamento bridge is blown up, but the Austrians were already across and there is no other decent line of defence. No one knows what this may mean. We would all so gladly have given our lives— everything, to avoid this horror.

We heard yesterday that the hospital was to be finished as all our equipment is lost. I offered myself at once to Dr. Brock to work in an Italian place for the rush that is bound to come, and some of the others did the same later; the matter was laid before the Comando Supremo by Lord Monson, but an order came saying all English nurses were to be got away, so they will all go home except Barty and Jameson who returned from leave a few days ago, were blocked at Treviso, and found our old pharmacist in a hospital there very glad to accept their help.

We all met again at supper; it was a real assembly of the dear old Villa, Giovanni served us in his same old benevolent style, and we even kept our one fork and knife. A boy called Heathcote was by me, from Gorizia. Told me of the panic there . . . the French and Italians both trying to get away, and when the French saw that no way was being made for them they just drew their heavy guns together in a mass and came riding along steadily regardless of anything in the way: a friend of Heathcote's happened to be in the way and saw that the thing was going to turn out unpleasant, and he drove his car straight at the horses and through them, overturning a few and killing one man it is thought. [This proved to be untrue.] This sort of thing happened along the road: Heathcote and several others were threatened with revolvers by men who wanted to get into the car; they just sat stolidly, till the men changed their minds!

We hear that the 3rd Unit, down along the Carso, has all been taken prisoner except three men.

Bonnie and I were billeted at the Aquila Nera; went to bed early—the delight of it! Am quite well however, except that my legs and arms have all swollen up.

The Unit is leaving . . . for Mantua to reconstitute—about

a fortnight or so I suppose. Miss Kemball is to go as house-keeper with two of us—she chose Bonnie and me, but it seems they thought me too young and beautiful (!) and also I am useful to have nearby in case I am wanted—so I go home for the time being and Bosy is with Bonnie instead. . . .

Said good-bye to all. Trevvy said we V.A.Ds had done well in the retreat: I told him we would go to whichever end of the world he sent us, and so we would.

. . . Page turned up and we saw him in the evening; he stuck for three days and nights to his old car and got it through; says he rested in Udine for an hour and a half while the Austrians occupied the town.

. . . Gibby has her cat Gabriele safe in a basket from Villa Trento; I have my hold-all and some have the whole of their luggage.

Captain Pinsett, of No. 4 Unit, organized us at the station in the crowd of refugees. We waited over an hour in the Red Cross *posto di soccorso*; some bad cases were brought in; only one nurse about, the rest were orderlies. When the train was due we were arranged in groups of three at intervals with our luggage—one of the men to each group to get us settled. Dr. Tommy got my group in splendidly; there was a great scrimmage for the rest however. . . .

At Milan we found the canteen people. . . .

We passed a number of French troops going up.

The English are most unpopular in Milan and Turin just now; we are advised to make ourselves as little conspicuous as possible, not to wear brassards, or go about in large groups.

This is the end of the retreat for me, I hope; we have come to the end of refugees, the trains actually go instead of crawling —and the last week is like a confused dream. We have come out extremely well considering, though all the kit and stores worth speaking of have gone and we have lost 20 cars out of 35; but all the men have come through safely. . . . Heard that Celeste and the other patients we cleared out on the 26th went no further than Udine and are probably there now in Austrian hands. Some Italian nurses on the train came from Aquileia where they had to leave one of their number dying and too ill to be moved.

2nd Nov. Train to Dronero.

Gorgeous sleep last night . . . Spent all day shopping; it is so amazing to be near pretty clothes again. I had to buy a chiffon blouse.

. . . Depressing news: Treviso heavily bombarded. No certainty yet of the Tagliamento being crossed, but one has not much hope now—Milan, Venice, both expected to go: these Turin people who have never done anything, just stand in the streets and talk. How one hates them. . . .

We find no trace of our unpopularity: the people all seem very friendly . . . much relieved at knowing the English are going up, though the Lord knows what they are going to do there. The R.T.O. says any amount of troops are through, but the guns not yet—and what can be done without guns?

The papers give no information; shall never believe them again after seeing the difference between what they say and the state of things really. . . .

MAY, 1917

PLAVA

Sing a song of the Plava run,
Of the cars that go down by night,
Down from Verhovlje
Down in the dusk
Mid the sombre trees,
And a scent of musk
And pine borne by on the evening breeze;
While up on high in the midnight sky
The Pleiades burn
And the Planets turn;
And down in the valley, a faint dim gleam—
Plava! white, in a misty dream,
Folded about by Isonzo stream.

Plava lies low in the river's bow
Where it bends away to the South,
With lights that twinkle
And move and mingle;
Or lights that burn
Like a corpse-light urn;
And over the bridge with push and rush
Men and mules and wounded crush;—
Plava that lures and captivates,
Where horror with beauty alternates—
Lures and repels and fascinates.

Sing a song of the Plava run,
Of the cars that go down in the dark,
Climbing from Visnjevik up to the crest
Where the column gathers; while up in the West
Verhovlje church, a dark silhouette
Against the light of the late sunset
Lingers deep purple and deeper yet.
Down in the dusk to the distant gleam,
To the gloomy valley and silver stream—
Under the Quota where Plava lies,
Plava that burns with a thousand eyes—
Then up by the new road climbing high
Steadily mounting and winding by
Up to S. Gendra against the sky.

GEOFFREY YOUNG.

16

End of Dronero. 1917-1919

I HOPED to remain in a resuscitated hospital in the Euganean hills, but only two nurses were kept, and they said I was too young to be one of them. I then tried to reach Asolo, but that was all military: Herbert had been forced to go to Rome and the house was requisitioned. So I returned by Milan and Turin to Dronero, taking with me our doctor's wife who needed a rest—and the first thing we did on our way was to buy ourselves things in chiffon, as unlike uniform as we could. For a fortnight we felt more tired every day, and then recovered; except that for some months I hated to see the moon rise, for the picture of her round white face over the rim of smouldering villages was still in my mind.

Dronero was little changed: my mother tired and absorbed, drugging herself with work, blind to the deadness around her; Mario still chanting endlessly, like a cock on a dunghill, the continuous saga of himself; and Vera withdrawn as in childhood, into her own world, now filled with babies. It was not long before they sent me to Turin, to a hospital presented by Sir Walter Becker. He was a self-made man, with a little beard and a sombrero, born, they said, on board a British ship off Patagonia and not British in any other way, but kind with a benevolence that moved uneasily amid his riches. His hospital was off the main line and, when I reached it, had a staff of ninety people to look after five patients; a young sailor, alone in bed in a big ward, said: "Good Lord, not *another* nurse?" when he saw me. We had nothing to do but polish and dust. The Italian hospitals were terribly overworked; and I heard that they would welcome help, and got the Matron to ask if some of us could not be 'lent', but this was far beyond the initiative of authority. So we spent our days polishing empty rooms.

I wrote an account of our retreat and sent it to George Trevelyan who thanked me in a letter that I value; and when I had time to spare, I went to see friends in Turin, which was quite a long way away. Once, when already very late on the way home, my tram was delayed by an argument between the conductor and a fierce tiny man beside him who stood with feet planted apart on the little open platform: neither would stop and they went at it hammer and tongs while the tram stood still; the crowded benches sat and listened with their Mediterranean patience, and at last I asked some tall Yorkshire tommies who happened to be there if they could not carry the little man out. "Certainly, miss, if you says it," they answered, quite delighted. They lifted him up in the middle of a sentence and deposited him over the tram platform on the road, and the tram rang its bell and went on, leaving him astonished and still talking!

We had one or two of the Yorkshire men as orderlies and loved them. One of them had made his way on foot from near Udine where he had been hiding through the Austrian occupation like Athos in a cellar, and drinking beer for days on end; he remembered it with enjoyment. He had got into trouble after heaving a brick at an officer. "But why," I asked, "did you heave a brick at an officer?" "Well, miss, he was aggravating"—that was all I ever heard.

Some friends in Turin came closely into my life at this time. They belonged to an ancient noble family, Barons De Bottini de Ste Agnès, and owned a sunless *palazzo* tucked among back streets in Dronero, with a few treasures of furniture and pictures, and family trophies from Lepanto, among chairs upholstered in red damask, hard as tennis balls, antimacassars, woolwork footstools, cushions with sporting dogs embroidered on them, and royal photographs with flourishing signatures in crowned silver frames. There was an old mother called Honorine, two brothers both in the army, and an elder sister, Clot (for Clotilde) who was plump, plain, short-sighted, a torrential talker and eccentric. It was a real old Piedmontese family untouched by any outside influence at all, something belonging to an age before 1789; they talked French and not Italian. Clot conceived an affection for me, embarrassingly demonstrative, but so genuine that I soon came to be very fond of her. She had made up her mind that I was to marry the elder brother; I guessed this and eventually she spoke of it quite openly. I was extremely anxious to marry at that time—chiefly, I realize now on looking back, to get away from the nightmare of Dronero: of course I was brought up to think a 'mariage de convenance' very natural, and my attempt to depart from it had been a failure.

I met Gabriel, the elder brother, that year and liked him: with the usual perversity of things, Achille, the young one, a very dashing young cavalry man, liked me. While these plots were hatching in Clot's mind, I loved to go to her stuffy Turin house when I had a night off duty, and to have breakfast brought me on a tray loaded with ancient silver and the family arms while a chorus of protest greeted the discovery that I slept with the double windows open. Turin was and still is the most feudal and provincial of Italian towns: no one of the old-fashioned noblesse ever invited strange young girls, only Clot's known eccentricity made it possible. The two brothers were charming to me, and when I went to stay, one or the other would renounce his evening walk after dinner under the arcades of Piazza Castello. I spent my Christmas with them all, and had to get back to hospital by midnight, so that we walked out at about eleven to look for a cab: at last through the deserted streets, an ancient fiacre came clip-clopping, stopped, saw the three uniforms beside me, whipped up its horses and was for trotting off with some insulting words: the Italian army was extremely un-popular in Turin at that time. Achille sprang and seized one of the horses by the nostrils, while Gabriel remained beside me and a hostile crowd gathered in the twinkling of an eye. It saw that we meant business and dispersed; and I noticed for the first time how the menace of a crowd comes from the back, when people can either push forward with impunity or slink away unobserved. These slunk away, and we jogged behind the cabby, now quite friendly, through suburbs over the moonlit snow. My friends explained that the war had become so unpopular in Turin that it was always better for an officer to go about in mufti if he did not wish to be molested.

I think I left the hospital from sheer want of work and it closed down soon after. It was too small to make it worth anyone's while to send special train-loads of wounded, and there were no other British hospitals in Turin. One would have thought they could have taken over a few Italians, but that was beyond the red tape of either nation.

Clot was a nurse too, and a fully-trained one, and annexed me to help organize the Dronero civil hospital on a military basis for the casualties expected in the summer campaign of 1918. She was soon sent away to run a hospital train, and I was left to do the best I could with the local authorities and to extract things like beds and operating theatre out of reluctant municipal pockets. The result was very primitive, but the essentials for a hospital were collected; various young Dronero girls were enlisted, and the devastating business of getting work out of volunteers was undertaken: we cleaned and scrubbed, and were eventually inspected and ready: but the great Austrian offensive of June petered out and the hospitals remained mercifully empty.

During this time my father came over, delighted to cross the Atlantic at the height of the submarine war because he said they treated every meal as if it were the last and made it good. He travelled with Colonel Fay, secretary chaplain to the Cardinal of Baltimore, a charming man, stupendously fat, whom he brought to Dronero. It was years, said Colonel Fay, since he had seen his own feet, and my father had to lace his shoes for him. We gave him a party to meet the local ecclesiastics, thinking they could talk Latin, but the two Latins turned out to be mutually unintelligible and it was a very sticky party. Colonel Fay was on a Red Cross commission charged with distributing all sorts of things, and my hospital received bales of bandages

[231]

and all luxuries. Mario, busy with local politics, tried to use him and his gifts in the way he annexed everything, but my father—so passive on his own account—reacted strongly and took the colonel away. It was the time when President Wilson was the most popular figure in Italy and every town had a street named after him, to be whitewashed out very soon afterwards when the crisis over Fiume became acute.

My hospital had been organized, and two carabiniers had come one morning with an illuminated testimonial of thanks from the Municipality, when the epidemic of influenza that ravaged Europe reached Dronero. It was in autumn; I cannot remember the month exactly. It was like a plague of the Middle Ages. It carried away hundreds of people; the schools were closed: the bells were forbidden to toll. Sextons and grave-diggers all died, till it became a problem how to bury the dead, and funerals in churches were forbidden. We had some hundreds of refugees at the time from Friuli and Venetia—the provinces occupied by Austria. When they first came, a collection had been made; I drove round with an ox-cart to farms and villages and got stores of corn, fruit and potatoes, and found that half the peasants did not even know that the war was being fought in Italy. The refugees were packed in overcrowded houses and no one did much for them. Clot had taken them in her stride with the innumerable people she was always attending to and handed them over to me when she left. The epidemic came, and I went about doing what little I could, but I was up against the fact that the municipal doctor took no interest in patients who did not pay. Four people lay in a room, one dead, one terribly sick, the child in the same bed, and a wife beside them in a miasma of stench and flies. The man was sinking and speechless and a soporific had been prescribed. I felt sure that the only thing that could do any good was a stimulant, and hurried to find the doctor to make him revise his prescription. He was furious with me, furious that I should see the way in which these people were left to die: I went from him, in a cold anger, and hunted round for some superior authority. I cannot now recall what happened, but I got another prescription and hurried to that miserable room, and found the man dead. One's efforts seemed like twigs beating an iron door. A few days later I fell ill myself and remember the relief of being able to go to bed and forsake those impotent visits where one could only see the misery and do nothing to relieve it.

On November the 4th, when the epidemic had worn itself out, the Italian war ended. The Austrian armies surrendered en masse, embarrassing their captors by their numbers. The general armistice followed. On a wet morning we went across our cobble-stones to hear a *Te Deum* for victory: very few people were there, old men and women, and the grey-green uniform of soldiers—poor peasants giving thanks for the lifting of a cloud come from so far and so little known. The war had worked itself into the very texture of our lives: it was like a cancer being taken away—I wondered how much of us would remain when it had gone.

My father was soon to return to Canada again. For the first year out there he had lived in a tent and then in a hut, till his little wooden house was built and his land planted. He was happy, leading the sort of life he loved. Before he left Dronero he asked me what I meant to do now that the war was over, and I told him how impossible it was to go on living as we were. There was no chance of a happy life for Vera unless my mother were somehow got away: the separate houses had proved unattainable again and again, and Vera had now wrapped herself in an ice-cold indifference and talked to my mother as if she were a stranger: my mother, with an almost unbelievable capacity for self-deception, put it down to "undemonstrativeness". There were two babies now—Angela and little Paolo, who was wheeled up and down in his perambulator in the winter sun; and Vera was contented with them and had no great wish to discover more of the world than lay within her reach. All that was necessary was to free her from my mother, so that she might enjoy a life and a home of her own; my father decided to buy me a little cottage somewhere on the Riviera, near enough for

Vera and the children to come to in summer. In a painful strenuous talk with my mother, I said that I was leaving and that she could choose whether to come with me or remain. To Mario we spoke of a summer cottage, which he welcomed. He and my mother both thought of it as of little importance: we had so often attempted independence and failed. But Vera was desperate and resolute now, and I saw things clearly at last and had no doubts at all. The factory had grown and grown; the more it grew, the more substance it seemed to require, and the less it gave out: it had swallowed my father's money and Mario's fortunes, inherited from his mother and his aunt; it had swallowed Vera's two thousand pounds of which she never handled a penny, and my mother's salary which she never saw: it gave Mario prestige and helped him in local politics, but though I knew nothing of its finances, I knew enough of Mario's character to be quite sure that it would never succeed while he ran it. My mother was a bundle of nerves and tempests after the terrific exertion of her work there in the war: unintrospective as she was, even she must have felt vaguely that a family life was there ready to develop happily without her. She shut her eyes desperately. But she came with my father and me on a walking tour to Ventimiglia and along the coast to look at houses. It was a difficult expedition: my parents walked always about fifty yards apart, and I had to be a shuttle-cock between them: they were friendly in a rather studied way, but there was nothing left for them to say to each other. With the long strain of our growing years in mind, I have been passionately in favour of divorce, especially for the children's sake.

The Riviera was deserted. Confiscated German houses were scattered like derelicts about it. We saw many and liked none: either they were near the sea and crowdedly suburban, or, if old and pleasant, perched high and inaccessible in narrow valleys of olive terraces and vines. We happened to stop at a little inn just inside the Italian border at Grimaldi, and there explained our wishes to the landlady, a person of great charm and no reputation, called Claudina. I liked her: she told us

[234]

that, having once inherited a small sum of money, instead of investing it in a useful way, she spent it on a carriage drive of three days all by herself from Sospel to the Col di Tenda and back again by Ventimiglia. We told her we wanted something very inexpensive, but it must be by the sea, and she took us to a four-roomed cottage in a vineyard, on a little bay adjoining the Hanbury gardens at La Mortola. The trains ran between it and the sea, as they do in most places along this coast, but the beach was beyond, and was reached by a little tunnel under the railway from the vineyard. There were in all about two and a half acres of land and they belonged to five people: we told her to buy if she could: all had to be bought simultaneously, and indeed it was almost as hard to negotiate as an alliance in the Balkans. She took an artistic interest in the affair and by the early summer had bought it—only one of the owners, who had no share in the house, held out and I had to pay much more for his land later. We had some rough furniture made by the Dronero carpenter to begin with, and went into residence at once. The old name of the land was L'Arma; and we liked it and kept it.

It was a poor little place, but it seemed Paradise to me. That awful constriction of Dronero was lifted and one could lead a sort of life of one's own. My mother was happy too: she meant to settle me and go back to Dronero and had told Mario so, but I knew nothing of that at the time. My father left us, and we spent some months down there and worked like slaves painting and arranging. The four rooms made little bedrooms, and a front hall, quite tiny, was our only salon till we could add two large rooms to complete the whole. We went out down a slope of the vineyard to kitchen and dining-room. I designed wardrobes to reach the ceiling with a shelf-cupboard on top for stores, and my mother painted them—one room to represent each of the four seasons. The land was all neglected, and one of the chief expenses was a windmill to draw water from the well: water is scarce on that coast, and they store it in round tanks of cement like oil reservoirs, dotted all over the hills and costly to build. We could not yet afford one, and relied on the wind and our deep well, and I suffered for my little plants through the hot days when the water-wheel stood motionless against a blue sky. The villagers were easy-going, pleasant, and liked us: they saw us working and were far nicer than they ever were to the rich people about them; they would come and help in their free time in the evening, and tell me what to do about vines and orange trees and manures. On holidays they danced under their olive trees, on platforms of hard terraced earth; the band sat on high stools, each man with a bottle of wine beside him, to help his breath with the trombone.

The place itself had an atmosphere of happiness—the Mediterranean happiness kneaded with air and sun; even the shadows on the olive terraces seemed to be suffused with light, and a thin sea breeze threaded the heat of noon; in the vine rows strong sticky leaves opened and spread and shaded the flowering bunches that are almost invisible and smell so sweet. From a promontory close by—rocks and pines—the French coast appeared, a theatrical outline of cliffs and bays with towns below and villages above. On our horizon, on the eastern side, the sunset reddened the chapel of St. Ampeglio at Bordighera on the last tongue of land, and a wide gentle sweep of inhabited country sloped illuminated, terraced and cared for wherever the steepness allowed. A ruin called Castel d'Appio crowned the highest hill and the fort and old town of Ventimiglia were on a slope, hiding the modern ugliness of the bay beyond them. Fine square villas of the Genoese, and white martello towers here and there now turned to houses, gave a comfortable human feeling to the view. Every evening I looked out at it across the sea when it was gathering its shadows, and filled myself with an ecstasy of peace; and every morning as I dressed, I looked out to my own vines terraced up the hill, to olive trees overhanging, and the colour-washed little tower of Mortola church rising among them, against a sky of such deep blue that it made one dizzy to look into, as if it were an abyss.

11 *GROVE END ROAD*,
ST. JOHN'S WOOD,
13 *Nov.*, 1918.

Dearest Freya,

I wanted to write to you and your mother when Italy had her great successes—then Papa wrote and I waited—now we may rejoice in the greater victory—it could hardly be more complete though the navy is very sick that they have had no chance to get at the German fleet—and the army equally disappointed when they were so near German soil. However, they will have plenty to do in occupying the Rhine provinces and I am told our canteen may be wanted *for several years*. I shall die at my cocoa urn and you can put on my tablet: "She never let it burn." To tell you a little of what has been happening these days—(How much I wish you had been here to enjoy the sights)—On Monday I was in Baker Street when the maroons went off at 11 o'clock—everyone in the streets—and flags all out in a few moments—crowds everywhere—taxicabs filled with people waving flags—buses covered with shouting young men and women—streets filled with processions—such fun! but it made one almost weep—specially at little pathetic figures in widow's weeds. In the afternoon I took Papa and a Canadian Padre, a cousin of Agnes Scott, to the Coliseum for the Russian ballet. The audience was immense and filled it from floor to roof. They sang 'Land of Hope and Glory'; also 'God Save the King.' We got back safely though the crowds of course were great. Papa none the worse for his outing. That night at the Canteen, I served 1,000 men—such a night! but I never ran short. All the men sober except three young officers and a major—they were polite but insisted on pouring something into their cups of tea—after *many* cups of tea they got very silly and presently I requested them to leave—

which they did. It was such a pity before the men; otherwise they were quite harmless.

Last night I went again to the Ballet and afterwards walked about Trafalgar Square for nearly an hour. Such a wonderful sight—under the clear moonlit sky—the dense masses of people surged this way and that filling all the roadway—dancing and singing—but no hooliganism of any kind. They did start bonfires at the base of Nelson's Column and the light from the flames shone on their faces—soldier, sailor, gentlemen and rag-pickers, girls of every description and old women and children. Meanwhile from the fires the sparks flew everywhere and they sang: 'Keep the Home Fires Burning.' They shouted with laughter when some boys got hold of some slats from the omni-buses and threw on the fire—then poles from the roadway and blocks of tarred wood—it was a grand sight.

To-day the King and Queen are to drive through the East End, and by the end of the week all will be quiet and the people will realize that much has yet to be done before Peace is signed. But let us be optimistic—'*ce malheureux globe ou La Nature a mêlé un peu de bien avec beaucoup de mal*' as Candide says, we must make the best of it.

Very much love from

VIVA

FROM MY MOTHER

28 *May*, 1919.

Dearest,

Vera, Mario, Angelo and Maria are off to-day to L'Arma and will stay there five or six days and then I go down to take their place, and protect the house. Did I tell you that I made an arrangement with Sciacca to sleep there during my absence, in the downstairs bedroom at a franc a night.

Beppa was up before seven this morning—so excited at the thought of going. Mario will see to the water question and if possible come to some arrangement with Maurizio too. Your dress will, I am sorry to say, not be ready till *next* Monday, when I hope it will be sent without fail.

There are several things I wanted to write to you about, but my brain is like an empty box this morning, *resoundingly hollow*.

There is a growing feeling that Orlando has been making Italy make a Cattiva figura—and that even Giolitti would have been better. Imagine Coriolano's horror on hearing that Orlando wept in piena Conferenza about Fiume—Così imparano a mander dei meridionali and (I thought to myself) not gentlemen! Democracy however is bound to pass through these experiences before it is worth anything.

Cila tells of how strong the feeling is against Wilson in Florence. Large multitudes assembled in Piazza Signoria before the Palazzo Vecchio and clamoured that the paper conferring him their citizenship should be publicly torn—Ma uno straccio di carta è rispettato in Italia and so the Florentine consoles himself by buying American bacon cheap and asking for 'un etto di Wilson' instead of *Ventresca*. I can imagine the joy of the Fiorentino at indirectly so calling him pig!

Don Richard is back in the office and, though he smells of incense mixed with goodness knows what, it is an ineffable rest to have someone one can be sure will do his work exactly as one tells him—and I keep the window open for the rest.

Not that I am much in the office. My books are ready for the tax man and I use the time for starting the coloured carpets again.

Dronero Ente [government office for the collection and sale of corn] declares 22,500 profit on a sum of 780,000 francs of business and most of our stuff had to be bought through the Cuneo Ente, resold at the same price as they did, and bought from them at a considerably superior price than they paid—a most unfair Government decree—Moral: the profit is owing chiefly to the economy and control of Flora Stark, no thefts, no bureaucracy, and no large staff. Dronero and the valley are fully satisfied too. Cuneo and Dronero are the only two Enti that declare a dividend—most have failed for heavy sums—Mondovi, Alessandria, etc., for sums varying between 500,000 and a million which the towns must cover—as they were guaranteed, and so public money is wasted.

This has been *my* war work after all and it has cost me a lot, not the least the secret rebellion and disapproval of my family—is it not so? *Basta*—we cannot all go to the Red Cross or do Government work. I hope at least half the profit will here go to a fund for new schools. The old ones are shocking. But there is much ill feeling over here and England is the reverse of popular—not because of France so much as because of the commercial conventions. Giolitti is considered to have much better understood the true interests of Italy—and this by quite serious people. According to these, the silk question has been shamefully used to Italy's loss. She cannot send herself to Germany, and England and France are her only buyers (because Creditors) and have put in a claim to the whole output to sell to Germany at an immense profit—instead of allowing Italy to sell direct and taking the payments. This is of course legal, but does seem a trifle sharp practice. Then there are various other points (not all justified by facts) and they consider they have given proof enough to deserve to be trusted. Altogether we are in the minority here. France also has not been fair about the coal, sending very bad quality and not recognizing any claim. All the rubbish was sent to Italy at top prices and no discussion allowed. We ourselves saw what very poor stuff used to pass, and better could have been had, or at least a reduction been made.

Why can't we go to sleep for ten years—even at the cost of waking up ten years older!

It is not at all warm yet but the hay is waiting to be cut— only there is a thunderstorm every other day.

I have not had any letter since your two first, because I expected to go down—and the Benbows have not forwarded. Vera will send them on and then I will have a feast.

My love to Viva, your

B.

17

Return to the Alps. 1919

ALL through the war I lost the mountains except for a few short escapes from Dronero, which I remember small and brilliant as Memling pictures with sharp detail of rock and weather: a walk of three days with my mother, across the upper valleys that branch from Val Maira, beside swift glassy curves of streams: a night high above Valdieri in a *grangia*—with shepherds from Arles—their bed filled the inner half of the hut and room was made for me, the mother of the family sleeping between me and her husband and son, while the men of our party managed to rest as they could on the floor. One long day with my father, from the highlands of Maira to those of Casteldelfino, into whose country the folds of Monte Viso descend; here we were caught by mist on the pass where snow lay six feet deep and more, and lost our way, and my father taught me to listen to the tiny voice of water dripping far under the ice towards the valley, and we made our way down by the sound. He walked me afterwards in my heavy boots along the main road for hours, so that I reached home with eight blisters on my feet and fainted at table. We were so well trained in endurance, that I had never even thought to complain. I went up with Mario and Vera to the remotest pastures beyond Acceglio, in the summer when the people of the *grangia* set out at three o'clock in moonlight to cut their hay, and return after dark: and I left the party and went with an old smuggler who was famous in the hills, to climb a small needle called the Rocca Provenzale, which no woman had climbed before. This was not because of its difficulty but because these Alps were—and still are—scarcely known, with poor hotels. My smuggler guide had been shot and was stiff in one leg, and could not negotiate the twist of the outer edge without a rope: he sent me on to lead, and I must have been frightened without knowing it, for my foot shook so that it was hard to keep it steady on the tiny jut of rock from which I started; it was a short corner— but for a minute or so one had to wriggle along a ledge under an overhang, with no foothold behind and no handhold in front and the far drop of the valley below, and I felt waves of panic threatening me, and faced them, and looked right down to the miniature villages and fields, and thought that the worst that could happen would be to fall and die; this steadied me; I twisted myself out over the ledge and caught the rough rocks beyond, and fastened the rope for the old smuggler, who was enchanted, and took me up another mountain unclimbed by woman, and far more dangerous; but it was possible for him to lead all the way, so that I had a rope to rely on and missed the sight of danger, and therefore felt no fear.

In all these years I longed to climb Monte Viso, and have not done so yet: we made an expedition when the war was over—my mother and the elder of the De Bottini brothers and I—but we were kept back by weather, and returned to find Dronero scandalized to its roots by the impropriety of even so chaperoned an outing, and Mario assured me that my good name was gone for ever.

That was the end of my Dronero mountaineering, but the great Alps drew me year by year. In 1919 my mother and I travelled from L'Arma and met W. P. Ker in Aosta, and drove next day four and a half hours, in an open carriage with two horses, to Courmayeur. W. P. had done this with his father long before, and had always wished to do it again. I remember the delight and wonder of finding the noblest of valleys still the same after six years of war.

I was not the same, the magic had gone a little—that first fine rapture had gone, and other things had come. But the mountains continued to give more and more, and so did the friendship of

W. P.; both perhaps had the same quality of steadfastness, rooted out of sight in things that do not change. One afternoon lives most vividly, as we came down from the Glacier du Brouillard, with high black needles of rock overhead, and walked under the pines on the soft turf, and stopped to drink milk at a châlet, at peace with all the world. My mother was sketching that afternoon, and W. P. and I were happy to be together and perfectly content. On another afternoon, we walked along the grassy trough of Val Ferret and looked at the Grandes Jorasses, the greatest wall that I had ever seen. And he and I climbed to the hut on the Col des Géants: he was ill there suddenly—it must have been a slight symptom of the heart weakness which killed him four years later—but he recovered, and I gave it no thought—in fact felt a shock of disappointment at the prospect of having to return; my unselfish impulses come second and are not as instinctive as they might be. While we stayed up there we saw a thunderstorm in Italy below, with soft whorls of cloud and lightning boiling at our feet.

Courmayeur was fashionable that year. Crowds of profiteers were spending their money as fast as they could. Only a few hundred yards of road ran between the hotel and the hills, but they went up and down it in expensive Lancias all day long. Their small doll-like children had to change from one starched frock to another every few hours. Their table manners were uncertain and it amused us to see that when in doubt they turned to look into our modest corner—the only non-dressed one— where we enjoyed doing the wrong things to lead them astray. This crop from the industrial cities, which had got rich by selling bad boots, bad cloth, bad shells to the men fighting, all vanished in a year or two. But they made us leave Courmayeur. We decided to walk round Monte Rosa, starting under the Matterhorn at Breuil. There W. P. and I climbed the Breithorn, a long snow-plod on that side, across a high saucer of snowfields where the rivers are stored: as we walked hour after hour upon it I could understand why the flow of the rivers never ceases. We walked fifteen and a half hours that day; in the soft snow, I

thought every footstep was going to be the last I could do: our
guide, who had said he was in training, swayed as if drunk and
W. P. jerked him fiercely back into position with the rope:
when he came to be paid next day he held out his hand, for it
is always etiquette to shake hands with your guide when you
part, but W. P. put his own hands behind his back and said
firmly: "Je ne donne pas ma main à un menteur." I admired
this, but could not help feeling sorry for the poor little worm
creeping out.

We had two Arcadian walks across the passes of Cimes
Blanches and Bettafurca, that separate the valleys of Monte Rosa,
—Monte Rosa, voluminous and delicately coloured, a queen
among mountains, always in sight as we came to the high places.
When we reached the inns at the heads of the valleys we found
everyone of them crammed with profiteers who never walked
and might just as well be somewhere else. Nothing is more
melancholy than to arrive tired at the end of a day and find no
room at the inn. We slept in a bathroom at Fiery. At Gres-
soney we gave it up and took a motor-bus down to Ivrea, which
is the gate of the plain and a place where no one stays. It was
a quiet comfortable little town with a castle on the River Dora
and an inn only too pleased to attend to us; the waiter said
"subitissimo" if we gave an order, and the landlord has not yet,
I believe, recovered from the shock of hearing W. P. say that
the bill was incorrect and then learning—as he bridled—that he
had omitted to put in two teas.

W. P. was the only person I ever saw my mother shy with:
they might not have been friends spontaneously, but they grew
to like each other during the mountain days. The only thing
that made W. P. wince, though he never said anything, was my
mother, happily unaware and bad at it, ordering the wine. W. P.
was a connoisseur, and when we were alone used to study the list
with great deliberation, and ask if I would "share a bottle", of
which I took a small glass while he consumed the rest. When
he dined with Dorothy Waller and Maurice, who had no taste for
wine, he would lift the glass, sniff it, and put it down untouched.

We spent a few days in Ivrea, and then W. P. offered to drive us round the hills by Lake Orta to Macugnaga, where our walking tour was to have ended. It was a long pleasant day through the vine-growing lands of Gattinara, little hills; we lunched at Omegna on Orta, which is the friendliest and smallest of the lakes I know. In the evening, driving up Val Anzasca, we came to Macugnaga, which later we knew so well, and saw Monte Rosa break like a wave of perpendicular glacier above the open valley: a little church, grey with lichen, stands against that background; a lime tree is beside it and old graves—one to "Pierre—Bon Guide et honnête homme." The houses are châlets carved with a fretwork of hearts, crosses and other devices, with geraniums hanging from their balconies in long festoons. The meadow-space has clumps of roses, and is filled with sweet smells of mountain hay. I read Virgil in the shade, and climbed with W. P. the Pizzo Bianco, a small sentinel of Monte Rosa. The mountain itself is here most difficult and no woman had been up it. W. P. had a strong prejudice against women climbers, and I chafed and longed to try. He said that we allow stones to roll down on other people's heads. "Many have wished to scale Monte Rosa from here," he said, and stopped, and added incisively: "They are there in the cemetery." As a matter of fact the three who first tried from this side were carried away by an avalanche down what has been named after them the Marinelli couloir.

We all ran out of our money at Macugnaga, and left W. P. with a stray volume of *Lothair* he had discovered, in pawn at the hotel until we could send him a cheque from Turin. Such a thing had never happened to him before and it amused him; he rejoined us at L'Arma. His visits became a yearly habit till his death. We trained him to treat a sea bathe not as a discipline of the dawn, but as a civilized social affair over which one spent the morning. Our unfinished house was still bare and primitive, but it had a palm tree near the door where we lunched and sat in the shade, and a fig tree over the stairway to the beach, where we gathered a hatful of figs as we went down. When provisions got scarce, W. P. and I walked to Menton with what he called a "ridicule", and filled and carried it home. The wine, which I made myself, was excellent, and W. P. was happy in this simple life. He never thought of small things as unimportant, and remembered everything beautiful or gay or good. Once a fortnight or so until his death his letters came, written in fine Renaissance hand, nearly always remembering some incident that we had seen or been in together, with often a sheaf of bad little snapshots of picnics in the hills.

FROM VIVA JEYES

> 11 *GROVE END ROAD,*
> *ST. JOHN'S WOOD*
> 18 *July*, 1921.

Dearest Freya,

The Professor came last eve and stayed talking with me in the garden till nearly midnight. It was cool and presently the moon rose, and we talked of *you* and of your coming. He tells me that he is going out to the mountain this week—that he has written to ask you to meet him (over your side) for some climbing. *Do go;* it will do you good—and you have had no change for so long.

He wants to go to L'Arma in September and I said that as long as you came to me by the 20th all would be well. So he suggested that you should return with him. Is not this a good plan?

I imagine that your visit to Dartmoor is a movable one—anyway, I was careful not to let it interfere with your having him at L'Arma in Sept. if you wish. You would probably enjoy the moor just as much later on in the autumn? This is scribbled in great haste while waiting for Papa to come downstairs after his bath. There is more air to-day, thank heaven. Yesterday was 82 again and very sultry. We had about three drips of rain and then no more.

I do hope you will not feel that you must give up this little holiday in the mountain. Truly, I believe it is better to take hold of one's chance of a little joy. Write to him you will join him. I will take all your lace for you if that will help you! He really wants you to go, and it will do you so much good. Try hard to arrange it. Of course I write in total ignorance of your difficulties, but I know (*we* know) that one *can* manage to fit things in if one really wants to. I feel like saying: "let Vigna go to——". Anyway, you must get someone to look after it for a little while.

Love from your VIVA.

18

Housebuilding at L'Arma. 1919-1922

THE troubles at L'Arma were chiefly financial. My income was ninety pounds a year and my mother should have had enough of her own to live on. A third of the factory was hers (on paper) apart from my father's sixteen hundred pounds—now worth a great deal more with its accumulated interest. But it was impossible ever to get any of it. More and more letters were required to extract it from Mario, and less and less was sent. This side of life was a nightmare and nearly wrecked my relations with my mother for good. Time after time she promised to make it clear to Mario that she was leaving Dronero, only to try again to please all parties by telling each a different story—a fatal thing to do: and until he realized that he could not coerce her, there was no hope of making him pay what he owed. There was very little hope anyway. My mother's ordeal was the leaving of a life that had made her happiness: and my poor job was to make her do this, and to keep ourselves alive while the transition was accomplished. I now know that I might have shown more sympathy than I did; a waspish exasperation shows in my letters during these years and many years to come. Yet the fact remains that she never honestly tried to break away, though Vera's whole life depended upon it; nor made a spontaneous effort to get her own money: every letter had to be urged and forced out of her until the thought of it gave me a cold and clammy feeling of nausea. Meanwhile, after the first few instalments had trickled out and dried, we had somehow or other to keep everything going on ninety pounds a year including the building of our house.

The thought of money became a horror. I used to lie awake at night and wonder how the next week's food could be supplied, and ponder over cheap and filling things like beans and potatoes. Butter and sugar became luxuries we could rarely afford. My mother worked assiduously at the painting and arranging; when it came to the drab task of economizing, she left it to me. And I had little help. The peasant's wife came for an hour or two in the morning to cook and clean and I worked in the vineyard as well, and hoped to make it pay. But the vineyard alone was already too much for me; I carried heavy cans of water up and down the uneven stone stairways for three or four or five hours every day, and in a year or two began to realize that I was failing. I felt an immense bitterness towards my mother, a bitterness which happily melted away long ago. I felt that she was making great weather over the loss of her own life and caring very little for the waste of mine; and it was at this time that I decided, if ever I could reach an income sufficient for us both (and I thought of three hundred pounds a year), that I would go away and never, if I could help it, worry over financial things again.

We still had friends to stay, and with natural optimism put a creditable face on our difficulties. I believe no one guessed how poor we were. Some dear people in Bordighera who had clothes to give away used to make me presents of them: I never had new dresses any longer. On Fridays, we gave luncheon to anyone who liked to come, a plate of rice or vegetables, and they brought their own sandwiches from Bordighera or Menton. Those years showed how little our friendships depended on money. Yet our poverty deprived me of time, and much of that time might have been spent with W. P. In the autumn, with great difficulty, we collected enough for a fortnight or three weeks in the hills, when he paid all the guides, and then, when we were at the end of our financial tether, we made some excuse to go away, and incidentally rather hurt his feelings. He wanted us to stay as his guests, and I know now that it would have been far better to accept; the sight of one's friends is more than money, even if it is their money and not ours. And when he came down to L'Arma, the visit was always a little spoiled by constant anxiety as to how to pay even for his food. In 1921, when I had the building to pay for, he asked if something was on my mind, and I admitted that I had a debt of three hundred pounds: he told me that he made a yearly allowance to all his godchildren and asked to lend it. I finally accepted, after refusing for some time, and he presently came with the cheque in his hand, looking at me fiercely, and said: "This is *not* to be returned. It's taken from my Will!" This was the only help I had in these years, and it paid for part of the house and a bit of land just two yards from our bedroom windows which we were obliged to buy.

Viva and Mr. Bale camped with us for a fortnight before the additions to the house were built, and my mother's mother came for the winter. She was over ninety, and her feelings had been hurt by the air lines—still in their infancy—who had not accepted her as a passenger on her way out from England. She sat under the trees while two masons hammered at the house, and she taught me Spanish in my small intervals of leisure. A friend at this time found me cooking—so she says—with a ladle in one hand and Virgil in the other, and indeed the Georgics came to me in these years with a strong enchantment, enhanced by my daily labour amid the vines—"*Mitis in apricis coquitur vindemia saxis*": the words seem to hold the sun and magic of the Ligurian hills.

I began to try to learn about horticulture, of which I knew nothing. Once when I was quite small I heard my mother say that peasants are lazy because they always rest one foot on their spade whenever they can: I now realized that my mother knew nothing about digging, for who would not take any excuse to stop doing it for a minute or two? It was too hard for me, and a man from Dronero dug most of the two acres, and planted them with vines, and roses for marketing. Little peach trees too, but they all went yellow and died: and broad beans, and they got a disease and went *black*. Virgil certainly glosses over the wickedness of the insects a farmer has to meet. We grew vegetables, and made wine, and sold flowers, and the vineyard on the whole paid for itself and gave us food. I bought a goat for milk: an old man brought it but no milk came and I sent for him, and he told me it must be lonely, for it had always lived in the company of human beings. So we hired a little girl to sit near it while it grazed, and the milk came. I discovered what a business it is to get milk all the year round: one has to attend incessantly to the animals' private life, and even then all sorts of caprices intervene. When we wanted goats' meat to eat we sent word to another old man, who came round with a live kid on his shoulder and the neighbours chose what parts they liked: when it was all partitioned, he went off and killed it and brought to each his piece.

There was no road to L'Arma, but a twisting breakneck path with a drop on one side, down which our furniture was carried bit by bit. I grew so accustomed to it that I could scramble down easily in the dark, lit by the far lights of Ventimiglia across the bay, and in day-time would run down the zigzags from the village and the main road in one and a half minutes (I did it once for a bet), and dive, as if it were a bath, into our sea atmosphere of sun and lavender and pines. We had the Hanbury gardens beside us; the old Aurelian way cut across them between two walls. It no longer connected either with Ventimiglia or Menton, but was broken off by landslides at either side; and I used to walk along the railway line till I picked it up beyond the break. This meant going through tunnels, of which the eastern one was short and all in daylight; but the western turned a corner, and fifty yards were in darkness; I walked trailing a stick along the wall, on a narrow pavement with niches which I tried to find if a train came, though there was just room on the pavement also. The train belched fire in the dark, making a noise like an earthquake. I was accustomed to it, but it gave a shock to visitors whom I brought that way to save a détour of several miles from Menton. I was nearly caught once in the eastern tunnel, when I thought I had time to cross the line, and wedged my heel in the rail; I pulled my foot out as the engine hissed like a huge bull, and when it had passed with all its clattering carriages behind it I was so frightened that my knees would not hold and I leaned against the wall. It was forbidden to walk along the rails, but after a while the officials pretended not to see. I pointed out that all our neighbours allowed us to cross their land and why not the railway company? "At least not in a red dress," said the inspector, "it worries the engine drivers." The guards too, on the frontier, grew accustomed to the illegality and knew me as "the signorina who walks so well along the rails." The guards liked us; they could flirt with our maid and rest on our bench under the trees.

The Hanbury gardens had been rearranged pretentiously, but they had a lower promontory they could not close to the public, which was left wild and beautiful. The Aurelian way led across it to a headland scattered with yellow coronella under pines. Flat rocks kneaded out of conglomerated fossil shells pushed into the sea and the barrel of a gun dropped by Napoleon's armies was visible on quiet days under the water. Here you could look out to Menton across the bay, and Cap Martin and Monte Carlo, and the heights of Turbie where Augustus built his arch to awe the Ligurian tribes: it was a far more theatrical view than that on our side facing Bordighera, and I thought of it as of a classic profile which is always the same, compared to a more ordinary one, whose expression varies and is unexpected and full of surprises, and perhaps more satisfactory for every day. From this point of land you could walk up through pine woods to the road, or round the outer wall of the Hanbury vineyard to our beach by a little path among the rocks. I fell off it once in the twilight and landed on my cheek on a ledge about six feet below, and discovered what a lot of thoughts one thinks even in so short a fall, though they register in one's mind more slowly after arrival. I often took this sunset walk.

In the spring, we began to add to the house—two big rooms and a loggia on top. I made the design and had two masons and a boy, and struggled over the problems of architecture and the fitting in of stairs. I had to buy all materials, and the men would come suddenly and say: "There is no sand, or bricks, or lime, for to-morrow." I would go by train for miles down the coast to various places to find all these things. The people liked me, because I was poor and did the work myself, and I got no end of help from plumbers, and merchants, and the neighbouring owners of vineyards. If it had not been for the constant difficulty of keeping alive, I could not have been happier: and even as it was, it was far happier than Dronero. After four years of war, there was comfort in doing anything so useful as growing food for human beings: I thought of this as I spent long days pruning, or picking the vine leaves to let the sun reach the unobtrusive greenish bunches of blossom, scented with a sweet delicate scent. The watering had to be done twice a day for things like carnation cuttings, which I now started, and baby tomatoes; it meant carrying over a hundred heavy buckets. The summer was agonizing; day after day the windmill would not turn and the water in the little cistern grew lower and lower, and my plants drooped: and it was three or four years before we could afford a proper cistern and eventually get the whole neighbourhood to collaborate in bringing its water from Ventimiglia. Our man came only for the first winter and had to leave, and I then got a Tuscan with his family. A little house had to be built for them: I cannot imagine now how it was all done. He was a red-haired, long-headed, big-boned man and hard working, with a little vixen thief of a wife whose face I once slapped in a moment of exasperation—a thing I have not done to anyone since, except to a small coolie boy in Baghdad. I often had to scold the Tuscan and hated doing so, and he would help me out by saying: "I know, signorina, you wish to tell me that I have forgotten to water the roses"—or whatever the crime might be. It made everything much easier for us both.

The new rooms, built in 1921, were pleasant. My mother painted the lower one with a landscape of gold and blue, and designed a whitewash frieze on grey for the drawing-room above. She found a beautiful baroque cupboard of deal and painted it white with bunches of flowers: and we had many things from

[253]

Ford Park to make the house look our own. When the trains rushed by, the house shook, and no one talked until they had passed; we could tell our friends' nationality by the remarks they then made: the English all said what a snag it was, the Italians "how gay to have the railway so near!" When people we knew came or went we waved to them and tried to throw flowers into their window as they passed.

Very soon after I reached L'Arma someone told me that you could always win money at Monte Carlo by the simple method of doubling your stakes. This advice I greeted hopefully in my difficulties, walked in to Menton, sat in the dreary little tram for an hour, and spent days gambling, not with any pleasure, but in the hope of paying for the bricks or the timber or the vines. I gave it up when I saw the failure of the doubling, but for years I still thought there might be something in it and one day, finding twenty gold pieces forgotten from a journey in Arabia, I went with Jock Murray and tried out the system while he sat surprised and a little troubled and watched me lose them all. I have no real liking for this sort of gambling and have never tried it again.

Clot De Bottini delighted in it. She came to stay with us and we went together, and I soon had to restrain her, for she would have played her last jewel, and had to be dragged away. We amused the dreary days of the croupiers who offered us chocolates. Clot had a locket with a silver St. Antony who she said, brought luck: she always put him on the table beside her. One day, the luck turned suddenly and completely against her, and she looked, and St. Antony was no longer there; he had fallen face down by the leg of the table. Clot was furious with him and left him where he was through our luncheon: "parce qu'il savait bien que je ne l'avais pas fait tomber exprès"; and he was found by the man who pokes about under the tables with a lantern, later on. She always spoke loudly, quite careless of what she said, with her hat very much on one side over her round, short-sighted face. We came back elated or dejected as the case might be and walked down in the dark through the

Hanbury gardens, filled with the scents of night-flowering trees, and told our luck to my mother and grandmother, who were both full of optimism about gambling, as indeed their whole life went to show. The chaplain of Monte Carlo later told me that he could never appoint a hymn number below thirty-six, as his congregation went immediately to play it at roulette: and Clot capped the story by telling me that the local gamblers leave their counters on the high altar of the cathedral a night before playing them, for luck.

L'Arma is one of the few places in the world where the climate is lovely all the year round. I liked the summer even better than the winter. Very still days would come in May, the water like glass; the maze of currents, "lulled by the coil of his crystalline streams," was visible from above, and there was a circle differently shaded where a deep sweet spring welled up far out at sea. People had made many efforts to tap it on its way down underground from the hills, but with no success. At night the fishing boats set out into this quiet sea with strong lanterns at their prow to fish for anchovies and later sardines, which both made an annual progress eastward from Gibraltar round all the Mediterranean coasts. Word of their coming would go round before them. Each lighted boat had a dark sister ship that laid a net around it, enclosing the crowd of flickering fish that danced in the green water below the lighted prow. Gradually the two ships neared each other, the circular net drew in, and the catch was lifted up between them. I always thought of these two ships, the light and dark, as life and death, working together.

The whole coast, on summer nights, was full of vitality and business. The boats with their lights at sea, the stars almost tangled among them, the fishermen wading with lanterns after octopus among the seaweed and rocks, the fireflies that, with a luminous mist, filled the Aurelian way, all made a sort of orchestra so that you could not tell where land or sea or sky began. In boats near the coast, carrying a headlight, fishermen speared the illuminated water; the half-naked figures, lit from below, looked like moving bronzes as they flung their spears.

[255]

The day seemed quieter than the liveliness of the night. After the long morning's work in my vineyard, I went down to bathe and swam out in the tranquillity of noon. As I lay on my back in the sea, I saw the village and its church on the steep slope billowing with olives, and read the time on the face of the church-tower clock under the belfry, and felt the clean joy of the sun, of the Mediterranean, of the oldest civilized life of human kind.

TO MY FATHER IN CANADA

L'ARMA,
LA MORTOLA,
2 *Nov.,* 1920.

Dearest Pips,

I believe I haven't written to you for ages, since the *vendem-mia* last month; it has all been a rush ever since. There was a lovely long letter of yours of Aug. 3, and now I have just got the one of Sept. 22. I wish I had been with you for the camping! those mountains seem to be just the right sort of thing—I should love to be out with you looking for bears and climbing. It would be a splendid plan; as soon as this place can be left to itself a little I might go out in spring and come back together in autumn? What do you say? I am just hungry for a sight of you, and a talk now and then—and I shall be quite experienced 'on the land' soon—only I suppose there are no vines for me to show off on? I am meanwhile sending you a newspaper cutting that might give a hope of your coming *next* year; it seems a more reasonable route——

I have such a lot of news I don't know where to begin: so first for your questions—— About the bit of Wetherall land, I am hoping to get to the moor sometime next year, autumn perhaps, and could then find out what things are like, and sell if there is any really good chance. The plan is to let this house for a month or two when nothing is doing in the vigna and go to England on the proceeds! *Vedremo——*

As to tools which you ask about, I do want them *very* badly; especially a cultivator and any *digger* if there is such a thing: the vines need to be dug and dug, one can't do it too often. I was looking at the hills on the way to Lyons, where every vine is worth its weight in gold almost, and they are a wonderful sight, the earth all soft and crumbly round and not a weed showing. Not like my poor vigna now, which is a wilderness.

I sold the grapes for 2,500 francs clear and have about 1,000 worth of wine now fermenting in the *cantina*: there is white (bianco secco) and red—the pale pink you liked—and a few bottles of raisin wine, specially good, which will be kept for when you come. I am writing your name on the bottles. It is great fun making it, and deciding how long it is to ferment and choosing which person's advice to take out of seven or eight all equally competent. I am so relieved when at last it is safely got into bottles.

Altogether I am quite pleased with the first year of this little place. It has given 4 % on what it has cost altogether, land, building and all. Don't you think that is quite good? Of course the *vigna* hasn't paid all the expenses that were put into it, but that couldn't be expected the first year. The grapes were the best in the neighbourhood, huge yellow bunches, a joy to behold, looking as if the sun lived inside them. Now I have a small bit of strawberries and a lot of peas and some artichokes to attend to, and am planting lots of potatoes to sell about Easter time. And I have A MAN! He is quite young, just married, and wants to settle in life: has been a *bersagliere* and comes from Dolceacqua. I thought of what you said about the 'mezzadria,' so I have taken him for one year as a labourer, with the promise of giving him an extra share of whatever profits there may be: and by the end of that time one will know how things develop over here. I will not have to slave away like last year I hope, but will do some of the work, also so as not to be in any danger of dispossession by Bolshevists.

They have been pretty bad here and in the big towns things are more or less at a standstill: in Turin the workers (so-called) took hold of the factories, filled them with machine-guns, and there were killed and wounded every day. And prices are getting higher and higher: I sometimes don't know what to do for housekeeping: it is a blessing to have vegetables and milk of one's own. We are all going back to the old patriarchal ways of living more and more and it is not a bad way either.

The building isn't yet done: there seems to be no end, and the various saints whose festas have to be kept are endless. The loggia is done, and the top room: next month I hope we shall see the end of it and have a quiet life. It looks very well: as soon as there is a fine day I will send you a snapshot, but we have had over a month of rain, torrents and hurricanes, with huge waves over the promontory, and mud to wade in whenever one goes out. Prof. Ker came in September, and now Viva and Mr. Bale, and it is very disgusting to give them this sort of weather. But they like the place and the house very much and we got a few good walks—a fine one round Cap Martin in a wood of old pines and olives, and one or two good scrambles in the hills.

I expect you will be interested to hear of Alfred Gilbert [Sir Alfred Gilbert, R.A., Sculptor]. He was your friend wasn't he? He has turned up again after having disappeared all through the war: he was all the time in Belgium, and has now come back to England with a Belgian wife (a widow with a large family of her own) and is doing splendid work again. A rich admirer of his bequeathed a large sum to be spent in buying any work he might do, and he is also working for the Fine Arts Society—and apparently is as quarrelsome as ever.

The *Literary Times* come at intervals and are very welcome; they are the only way I keep a little in touch with what goes on in literature. I have been reading Borrow—Romany Rye, and Lavengro and enjoying every word: that is the way to talk of travels! He and Jane Austen have been my two authors lately—both very pleasant in bed in the evening when snuggling down under an eiderdown: that is Riviera temperature at present.

Have you got enough warm things to get through the winter? I hope you will keep a sharp look-out for that pneumonia and not let it come again; it is so easy after you have once had it. I should feel much happier if you invested at once in a few boxes of "Thermogene wool" (at any chemist's)—and if you get any cold on the chest you sprinkle it with a little alcohol and wrap it round you, and keep it day and night till the cold is over: that and a few hot grogs (weak) ought to keep you well rid of the microbes.—Do be careful dear old Pips.—It's so horrid to have you ill so far away; I should like to know you take all precautions.

Must stop this long letter and hope not to delay so much before the next. Send me the snapshots you speak of: I should like one of the ranch too if there are any going.—

Lots and lots of love dearest Pips, from your

FREYA.

TO W. P. KER

L'ARMA,
18 *Feb.,* 1921.

Dearest Professor,

I have been very bad lately—only meaning to write and not doing so—because there was no time, or at least only in small pieces which mean hasty scribbles and not letters to you. But it is a joy always to see your handwriting, even with a bad conscience.

We like your friends very much and would like to see much more of them. It was a good day at Castellar—omelette and dry white wine overlooking the sea and many loops of the coast and hills with villages and olives. We have been trying for Villatella since, but the rain (one day) and battles of flowers have been getting in the way and now mama has left for Dronero for some weeks: but perhaps I will try to conduct them and hope to find those little paths in the long grass. Do you remember Stefano's description of the way when we met him in the woods? I hope September will come again soon, with you.

There is spring here, in the air and covering the hills with mistiness. There are almond blossoms against the sea. I am going to plant a little wood of blossoms in the front of the house, to submerge the railway lines, and marguerites and such things under them. We have a new goat and lots of baby rabbits, and I am picking and selling peas and planting lots of things. The house also is getting to have a comparatively finished look and possessing a real genuine bath and terrifying geyser: isn't it uninterestingly civilized? We shall still be painting doors and banisters for months however.

I remember the Trinity MS. I can still see the pages quite plainly. How I should like to be thinking of Samson Agonistes and those good things. I still read Horace in the evening, going through the books the second time, with greater enjoyment after the grammar has been unravelled so as not to interrupt all the time. I have also been reading Maynard Keynes' *Economic Peace*, with the portraits of the Peace Conference and thought it a fine book although it seems to have the effect of helping German propaganda in Italy. There are too many Boches already on this Riviera—*tedeschi e pescicani*—the old 1913 world had pleasanter people on its highways.

I came from Ventimiglia to-day, bicycling in the early moon-light without lamps, like a bat in dusk that is already like summer: and all the hills are covered with mimosa blossom so that the scent hangs everywhere. It is lovely to go through a country-side where everything is awakening: in Dronero the snow is on the ground, lying long after spring has come and the buds are on the trees—it robs one of the best of the time. What a happy invention to have the *Mañanas de avril y mayo* all over again every year.

I would like to see Arran in April—or London too. That will be for the autumn, with luck we will let L'Arma, and not think of *vignas* or housekeeping for some months, and the Professor will take us to Prince's Restaurant where they give one little paper fans and one walks back along Regent Street with moonlight over the house-tops.

I was looking over *Colonel Bramble* the other day and the verses. Do you remember "Margot . . . vaut bien la Sévigné—Pourvu qu'elle se taise?" I thought of your quotation of Lord Morley to Mrs. Asquith !

I am all alone here till mama comes back—possibly a Scotch friend—a Miss Murray from Edinburgh—will come for a day.

But I do not really mind the solitude, there are a lot of things to think about.

We will write to you from Villatella if we get so far—if not from Sant Antonio—and think of you always dearest Professor with all loving thoughts.

Your FREYA.

19

Neighbours. 1919-1922

A FEW Italian neighbours lived in villas and orange groves, strung along the coast towards Ventimiglia. The sea was encroaching upon them and they spent their fortunes throwing huge blocks of cement for the waves to eat every year—a sort of Andromache story with no Perseus. Their gardens had nearly all gone and already the great square Genoese painted houses stood almost at the water's edge. Our closest friends were two brothers, who lived in a house painted yellow ochre, with imitations of windows and shutters where the symmetry required it, a high square saloon that took two storeys' space, and a baroque, twisted staircase outside. Their father had been President of the Council of Ministers in those days when Florence was the Italian capital. Their mother then was so beautiful that the audience in Florence stood up in a body to look at her as she came into the opera; and now she was still dignified and fine, with a lovely voice—and both her sons adored her. I used to visit her often, and always found her sitting placidly, with hands at rest, in a porch under the great curve of the stair balustrade, and she told me that as a young woman she had learnt to sit happily doing nothing, and that, of all her accomplishments, this was the one most valuable to her in old age. Her eldest son, the colonel, left the artillery to devote himself to his mother and his lands; he had the most charming gentle personality, like a huge St. Bernard, very tall and burly: and used to come wandering along to see us painting at the tops of ladders, or working in the vineyard. He became attached to us, and would dine once a week or so, saying that he liked the English way of being asked whether there was anything to eat or not. He once asked me what I would most like to be and I said, without thinking, "a widow"—and distressed my mother, who thought of him kindly as a possible son-in-law. His brother came less, as he was a diplomat in Rome and had handed the Italian declaration of war to the Austrian ambassador in 1914. He was called Gustino, and became a faithful friend; and so did his half Russian wife, Lolette, who is now the only one left of them all, alone in the tall house with her two sons.

Beyond them lived the Marchesi Orengo, more countrified, and helpful with advice on agriculture, old naval people with a son who looked like one of those ancestral pictures full of character and out of drawing. They lived in a square tower once built as a refuge from Saracen raiders, with whitewashed walls nine feet thick, and rooms renovated with parquet floors, and windows. The old marchese remembered when there was no entrance except by way of a ladder to the upper storey and described their journeys to Rome fifty years or so before, when they drove in their own carriage and waited, sometimes three days, for streams swollen by sudden storms to subside. I smuggled an early Sienese picture into France for them. We had been two years or so at L'Arma when a French connoisseur, Bernard d'Hendecourt, came to stay, and saw the picture and offered a thousand pounds for it and a hundred pounds to me if I could get it across the border. I would have done a great deal for a hundred pounds just then, and I thought the picture small: when it came off its high wall, it appeared as a solid block painted and carved in one with its gilt frame, and five feet by three. I placed it face downwards in a cart and on top settled a Scottish friend with all her little bags who was just leaving. We drove through the four frontier posts, chatting to the guard. He leaned with his elbow on the back of our Madonna, who would have been confiscated if she had been found.

I needed the hundred pounds, but enjoyed smuggling for its own sake. Our shopping was done in Menton and I brought back what I needed. Smuggling came naturally: the shepherds

in the Alps above Dronero made an art of it and in the last years
of the war took Italian deserters across in batches of forty, under
the windows of the guards, and deposited them at Barcelonnette
where the French had faked passports waiting with only the
name to fill in. My father once took us to see an old man in
those hills who had run away as a boy to join in the siege of
Sebastapol: when he came home again, the guards caught him
one day with a bag of salt on his shoulders on a mountain slope.
They handcuffed him and made him walk with his bag before
them: but he gained a short start, and began to run: he knew his
ground and outdistanced his captors: when they reached his
house the bag had disappeared and the handcuffs were used ever
after as a chain to bolt his door at night—he showed them to us.

My smuggling at L'Arma was not so exciting, and I got to
know the guards. One of them, one day, took hold of my hand-
bag and felt the coffee berries inside it (at that time the chief
item of illicit traffic). "What is here?" he asked. "You had
better not look," I said, and he let them through. My father,
like most men, disapproved of this particularly feminine amusement. I would slip parcels of coffee into his pocket without his
knowledge and watch him pass the barriers with a conscious innocence that no one could query. The whole of our district seemed
to live by smuggling and still continues to do so—I was there in
1946 and learned that a regular tariff of a thousand lire was then
being paid to the police every time a smuggler went across. Any
traveller who wished to be conveyed without a passport paid
fifteen thousand lire. Apart from the Orengos' primitive picture, I only carried small household stores as I needed them, and
the guards knew me; one very hot day, a young recruit held me
up for a packet of sugar while he called his chief from his siesta:
the man came along crossly and apologized: "One must forgive
him, signorina; he is new here, and still attached to the regulations: he will learn."

The buyer of the picture, Bernard d'Hendecourt, was a tall
silent and modest Frenchman, fond of us, perhaps because we
lived a life so different from his own. He gambled away two

fortunes before he was twenty-three, and then pulled himself together and started to trade in works of art, with so sure a taste that Durlachers, the Bond Street dealers, adopted him without capital as a partner. He now made as much money as he liked and filled with treasures the mews off Grosvenor Street in which he lived. He was a simple man in himself; and liked to come to L'Arma to sit and do nothing and walk about our little house in a panther-skin dressing-gown. He bought a yacht one year and landed in our bay, and the coastguard made him open out his suit-case on the shingle, with all his very elegant ties on top; the coastguard with round eyes asked him if he 'travelled in cravats.' He had everything he could wish for—good looks, good family, talent and wealth—and a few years later fell ill of cancer; I made a journey to Evian to see him, and left him dying among those low green hills.

There were no English nearby when first we went to L'Arma, except for Cecil Hanbury and his family, sister, gardener and guests. All were kind to us except Mrs. Hanbury, who resented out little Naboth's vineyard on her doorstep; I have a small collection of notes from her husband apologizing, in patient and apparently accustomed language, for her impetuosity in warning our friends off the public beach. I never met her, but used to pull up little trees in the Via Aurelia, with which she tried to plant out the Roman right of way. Her villa was very commonplace; but in it, when the Geoffrey Youngs were staying there, I met Norman Douglas—his eyes dancing with mischief, his talk sparkling like a fountain in the sun—the Youngs were uncertain of my reactions but he was the first person to make me consciously decide that I would like or dislike people for themselves and not for their reputations.

There were no other English at this time nearer than Bordighera, where there was a bevy of old ladies. Mrs. Robertson, born a German, had been Bismarck's favourite niece. She was in his house when he sent the Ems telegram, and told me how she gave him breakfast—his own family were all late risers and very casual—while he walked up and down in a dressing-gown

stopping for a sip of coffee now and then, with the Ems correspondence and a blue pencil in his hand. She was the most dear
and stimulating old lady I have known, and her daughter was
like her. There were many others; anyone aged only seventy
was young in Bordighera. Mrs. Miller had known my grandmother before I was born, and was blind; she still took me for
long days walking in the hills, and would ask me to turn her
round for the view, and would describe it. Mr. Berry too came
walking, looking like an aged, ageless faun, and knew the history
of the countryside.

We got to know the neighbourhood of L'Arma chiefly
through expeditions with visitors. We went to Monte Carlo
with Clot, or the sisters from Thornworthy, with whom I tried
to find a palace built there by a Persian and called the Palace of
Wisdom: we looked and looked, and at last asked a policeman,
who said that "the only palace of wisdom in Monte Carlo is the
police station." I took W. P. to Monte Carlo and we began
rather badly by being turned aside from the Casino doors to
have his dusty shoes polished: he had never seen roulette before,
looked at it sadly, and turned away saying: "It is too difficult,"
and we then walked up the steep causeway track to La Turbie,
where we had omelette and wine and looked down at the world
below. Every afternoon, when he stayed with us, we walked
about the hills and saw the sea from a different shoulder, so
that the scents of thyme and lavender, cystus, broom, pine and
sun, along the steep rocky paths, make me think of him now.
He sent us the Leonard Whibleys, to walk with; and they spent
a night or two at L'Arma. Leonard wrote a Horatian ode in
Latin for me, and came down to breakfast declaring he had been
kept awake by the fear of a false quantity—so strange an idea
to me that I thought it a joke—I had not yet met the Arabs and
their passion for linguistic form.

Our house was not finished in 1921, because we could only
go on when I had enough money to pay my two men and the
boy, but it was very nearly done. My two and a half acres were
all planted with sheets of stocks and carnations, and I thought

of the day when a comfortable income could be made from them: meanwhile they paid for most of what we lived on, and we were slowly adding to the house, with great events now and then, like the buying of a bath and geyser, or the building of a seat under the olive trees and palm, where we lived all summer. Our guests picnicked with us and took us as they found us.

An old friend of my parents, Herbert Olivier, the painter, came with his daughter Mary, just grown up. They were so enchanted by the place that they asked my mother to buy them the next property above, if she could get it for two thousand pounds. She did so, and Herbert grew more and more involved in this place, which he adored, and wanted to make, he said, like a small Versailles. It was a square box on a narrow terraced ledge, as little like Versailles as could be, but he built hanging gardens in terraces around it and spent huge sums, and it came to look much more imposing though never beautiful. He was happy, and we loved him, though we had all his troubles to deal with as well as our own. When it rained, always a deluge, most of the new walls collapsed, and I once teased him by saying that I should have to consider his land mine if it fell on to my property below, an idea which exasperated him in a manner only possible to the male sex, whose heart-roots are buried in the soil.

The chief of our difficulties, after money, was always water. With infinite trouble, and with another outlay that seemed almost superhumanly unmanageable, I at last got pipes laid from Castel d'Appio for a number of contributors: when it was all done, the people who had *not* paid their share attached themselves to the pipeline and got water for next to nothing. As the Oliviers and we were last on the line, our share was thereby diminished and scarcely ever arrived. There was strange juggling with the municipal meter by which water was regulated. Subtleties in the payment of taxes also began to be revealed to me. When we bought our land, our fat notary of his own accord had registered half the price, 'because of the taxes', he explained: no one wrote down more than half, and the government, on this assumption, assessed double. Soon after, it imposed a capital levy, and I was walking into Ventimiglia to pay all at once, when I met the Orengo son, who explained how "the whole system of Italian finance is based on the fact that no one declares more than half. If you do so, you will pay your right amount. You are surely not anxious to pay *twice* what is due from you?" So I decided to do as the Romans and leave it to the government to get it right in the end.

There was a lawsuit too at this time. My Tuscan peasant's wife had become impossible and I had to go to law to get rid of them, and, after months of waiting, protested at the unwarranted delays. In a very short while, my lawyer explained that he "usually let these things go on for a long time, but you have such a good record with your peasants that I saw the judge yesterday, and we are going to finish it next week". The far better system of the country was to keep away from the law altogether, and to call in an 'arbitrator', a weather-beaten old countryman who settled every problem with commonsense and a knowledge of the customs of Liguria. The peasants were a constant worry; I was too poor to let them steal much beyond their wages, and that seemed to be the only basis on which anyone got successful service. The same was true of our house servants when we began to have any; I used to keep them for a certain time with blandishments and kindness, but it was difficult in a luxury region like the Riviera where they could get all they wished in an hotel in winter and rest at home in summer.

The children and Vera came down from Dronero to bathe in summer, and Mario's visits, less and less cordial, were borne because of them. There were four now. Little Paolo used to walk backwards into the sea so as not to be frightened by the look of it. Vera was settling happily in Dronero, and managed Mario in a quiet way so long as it did not mean anything in the nature of emancipation for herself. I went up now and then and Clot would take the chance of my being there to escape from her home and dash away on some cherished little journey, leaving her mother in my charge. This meant going once or twice a day to take the tottering old lady for a "constitutional" up and down the empty arcaded streets. She was considered feeble-minded by most people, but I think she was merely over-powered by her expressive family; she was very frail and plaintive and must once have been pretty before she wore a tightly curled and crooked little wig. She used to say a prayer every evening to St. Expédit to give her a comfortable night. I liked going to that dim old house, across the hall filled with carved chests, and portraits, and arms, into a boudoir plastered with small pictures in large frames on walls of red brocade, and chairs and sofas so stiffly upholstered that they seemed to be resilient when you sat on them: the tables were full of *bonbonnières* given by people at their weddings, and the windows never opened. The shutters were put back by a maid when visitors arrived.

At the back of the house was a library full of old good books, with vellum covers and titles handwritten on the back. At some time while I lived in Dronero I had thought to write a history of the region, which belonged to the Marquisate of Saluzzo through-out the middle ages, and I read Muratori in the library—chronicles in delightful latin full of ablatives. I still have the notes, and a chapter or two of this history put away, and it must be the first promising thing I wrote, for I showed it to W. P. and he read it and said nothing, but stood up and kissed me when he finished. I now had no time to write, but an indirect benefit came of my studies, for they had led me to visit the library in Cuneo, which was twelve miles away, and had accustomed me to bicycling the twenty-four miles there and back. The mingled smell of dust and acacia blossom still reminds me of those long, straight, scantily-shaded roads in the heavy air of spring, and one day especially, when Vera was with me, and we felt close together in the world.

The distance between Dronero and L'Arma was far greater—eighty miles or so—but I started early one morning and did it in a long day, looking round at each wayside halt, expecting to continue my journey by train; the train showed no sign of catching up, and I went from station to station till I reached the base of the Tenda pass still with some hours in hand, and bicycled through the tunnel at the top. It was two and a half miles long I think, lighted with electric lamps and full of noises as imprisoned echoes of lorries rolled lumbering by. Puddles dripped with dim flashes from the roof. As I rode down the other side I came off at every hairpin bend, for I only knew how to bicycle on flat ground and had never tried a hill before. Usually I bicycled for a part of the way only, or up and down the Riviera, and often arrived by the last motor bus in Ventimiglia and walked out about midnight, in moonlight that showed the white road and dim scented terraces of flowering stocks, and the glitter of the sea below. I once met a drunken man who lurched up out of the shadows and said: "Beware! the Others are coming", and left me anxiously wondering who the others might be. My mother, one night, in the same place—a lonely stretch under leaning olive trees—heard footsteps following; when she hurried, they hurried too, and at last she was relieved to see that they belonged to a very young carabinier who caught up with her and asked if he might walk beside her, as he was afraid of 'spirits' in the dark.

We went to and fro a good deal to Dronero during the first years, and spent Christmas with the children, and took the Oliviers up, rescuing Herbert whom they arrested for painting the old bridge (which was the central object of every picture card). The French frontier running to the west of all our country made things difficult for painters even then—and an artist guest at L'Arma was brought back to us between two carabiniers; he was uselessly trying to assert his innocence through the single Italian word he knew, which happened to be *oggi*—to-day.

The people whom we saw most of were the De Bottinis de Ste Agnès. Gabriel, the artilleryman, was not brilliant like his cavalry brother, but quiet, with a taste for travel. The Piedmontese are, I think, much more French in character than Italian, and Gabriel was very like the French *noble de province* one meets in novels of fifty years or more ago. He and my father during the war had tried to get a new bomb of his adopted by the War Office—and, having come to know us, I think he was pleased at the idea of marrying me but disliked Clot's exuberant way of settling it. These family alliances were matters of long negotiation in which the remotest relatives took a hand.

"What happens if I don't like the husband you choose or if he doesn't like me?" I once asked Clot before I had even met her brothers.

"What does that matter, if you are loved by all the rest of us?" said she—and went on to describe a world of affection in which everyone except the husband, even the housemaids, were included. It seemed natural to me, and pleasant, and I longed for Gabriel to make up his mind. I felt an inferiority complex at not being married, exasperated by a concert of Italian connections who had now adopted us and obviously thought me getting on in years. Everyone married by this sort of arrangement. I liked Gabriel and was constantly refusing other, even more unknown young men who were suggested. The Englishmen who came now and then all happened to be very dull, and agreed with everything I said—one of the unfortunate effects of being in love. I liked Gabriel far better: he had been away in North Africa for years, and had remained unsophisticated and direct. But he waited and hesitated for four years, and asked me when I was thinking of him no longer.

My mother longed to see me engaged to Gabriel, or anyone else, and felt it her own failure if I failed to become so. She welcomed all suitors indiscriminately, even the Baron who was so out of drawing that it was impossible to think of watching him at breakfast every day. I thought her suggestions excellent in theory for I felt humiliated at not being married—but I hated them when they became concrete, and shied away not from coquetry, but because I really could not tell beforehand. When one is in love, there is no shadow of doubt or hesitation: but when the imagination alone is engaged, and begins to meet the solid substance of reality, an invincible reluctance comes, in spite of oneself. If a man is impetuous enough, he can probably overcome it and make a happy marriage, but not, I feel sure, the happiest: that absolute willingness which comes so rarely to a woman is a feeling which nothing else can replace, perhaps the next in degree to the love of God. However this may be, my failure to find a husband made me frustrated and unhappy, for I felt it must be due to some invincible inferiority in myself. And what is worse, I thought my natural desires in this direction so extremely indelicate as to be hardly admissible, even to myself.

TO MY MOTHER FROM CLOTILDE DE BOTTINI DE STE. AGNÈS

7 Apr., 1919.

Tres chère, tu es un bijou, tu es exquise: je te fais une caresse très longue . . . merci de ne pas douter une minute que si Freya était souffrante aux Indes, je serai déjà sur le plus véloce trans-atlantique sans me retourner, comme la chose la plus naturelle comme s'il s'agissait de notre pauvre ange Amélie. Je ne puis dire plus. C'est vrai, uniquement, simplement *vrai*. Mais Freya *est une rose*. Moi je ne peux rien y ajouter ! ! !

Il y a une telle complication à l'heure présente pour mes projets. Ils sont tous soumis à mon frère qui je pense se decidera a *demander* à prendre une licenza et a nous arriver de Fiume. Je ne veux pas être dehors quand il rentre à la maison pour sa quinzaine. Et je ne puis donc rien préciser. Nous irions lui et moi à Menton et ainsi je verrai Freya.

D'autrepart, si Freya me jure la possibilité de me cacher chez elle, ce serait mieux pour nous jouir, car figure toi, *ma tante*, ma pauvre chère tante, *soeur de mon père*, ne pourrait pas sup-porter que je reste seulement une nuit hors de la villa . . . elle a fait une scène à Gabriel pour lui permettre d'aller a Nice et jouir chez mes cousins d'Adhêmar . . . elle est jalouse à nous étrangler. Ainsi je resterai tapie chez ma Freya, sans mettre le bout du nez dehors, puis je filerai à Menton avec mes robes et chapeaux comme si l'express de Turin me déposait haletante à la grille de la villa sous les platanes ou je me livre prisonnière pour *respirer, parler, dormir* boire et manger sans la possibilité d'un écart. . . . Ainsi! *juge! conseille!* Ah! ma chérie, presse Clot sur ton coeur . . . Ce n'est pas simple de combiner une escapade de ce côté là!! La *cavalerie* en sait quelque chose et l'itinéraire est sur une autre ligne vers la plaine Lombarde . . . *ou même* ROME!! Comme je languis trop de toi, écoute vite, faisons un geste gracieux toutes les deux—fixe un jour à Saluces du matin au soir. Je viens t'embrasser, nous parlerons, nous rirons, je connais une strega très intéressante, ce sera une journée délicieuse. . . . Réponds moi!! tous les jours sauf Dimanche et Mercredi car ces jours là je suis prise absolument. Pour toi je renonce un jour au manège et je ne puis t'offrir un holocauste plus incandescent . . . Toi renonce au sénateur S. Martin pour un jour . . .. Attends . . . à Dronero j'irai à l'assalto et je te le vole. Oh! comme c'est deux fois meilleur *l'amour volé*!! Quelle brigante je suis, et si perverse. Mais je t'aime si exagérément que j'écris des bêtises. . . . Maman t'embrasse et moi je te serre trop fort.

CLOT

TO MY FATHER

L'ARMA,
22 *May*, 1922.

Dearest Pips,

There is a beautiful peacefulness here since Herbert [Olivier]'s departure two days ago, so I am making use of it to write and tell you the news of this small corner—although I haven't had a word from you from Creston yet. You would like our climate now—I am sleeping up in the loggia, with the old moon looking in about two in the morning and the sunrise between Ventimiglia and Castel d'Appio, very comfortable to look at from bed. That charming Dr. of mine recommends *great laziness* in the morning: so I can have the luxury of being late and also feeling virtuous! You will be glad to hear that my queer bumps have gone since I have ceased being active— but it is rather sickening to see the lovely sea and not be allowed bathing, and no walking in the hills: I hope it may change pretty soon.

The trees are keeping right, and those new vegetables you put in near the *garofani* have put out about 8 inches of stem and leaves: but what happens then, and how and where do you eat them? I have just had all the mustard dug in; it became gigantic—but lucerne is a dismal failure, has all vanished away and only given increased activity to weeds!

When I have time, I go into the *vigna* to pick off the extra leaves that are now covering up the bunches and preventing their flowering. There ought to be such a vintage this year; Nicola calls me every morning to admire a new prodigy of a vine and says it is all his pruning; while I say it is my manure at last showing results. It is very pleasant now to sit in the vine rows and look at the sea across their leaves—the days are so still; Ventimiglia and the hill-side are reflected in the water, and the evening brings out the lovely pastel tints—and the fireflies.

Herbert's masons are all over the place, putting up and pulling down staircases, etc. . . . . I do hope he will not end in the bankruptcy court: we have given up any attempt at slowing him down. I feel I am going in the same fatal way: the cottage is very nearly built and looks less aggressive than might have been expected—when it is done I will send you a snapshot. I have also paid up for the land; it came to 6,670 lire and I reserved ¼ of the water of the big cistern, and the use of Herbert's pipes; also a mutual right of way and refusal of the property in case of sale: also the right to ¼ of the water of any cistern to be built in the future. It was hopeless to get H. to allow a bit of land for building a cistern of our own on (he made a last struggle to get back those olives from me!) so I thought that by keeping our right to the water in his tanks, it would always be possible to come to an arrangement when we want to build a tank of our own, as it would be to his advantage to give us an independent supply. I thought I should go mad at the notary's, what with Italian legal language and Herbert fussing over it. Then some imp of mischief prompted me to tease him by saying that of course we might still evict him unless he got the transfer of his property made out, and he spent nearly a day considering how he could prove in a court of law that the villas were really his!!

Viva and the Edwards have asked mama to go and stay for a while with them, and I think she may go and I shall remain here quietly and then go to meet Prof. Ker who has invited me to the hills: I am not to climb, but it will be nice to look at the snow even. I think Clot may come to look after me while I am alone, which would be very nice. She turned up here the other day and thrilled some English people who had dropped in to tea by explaining that we had been the first people to introduce the habit of washing into the province of Cuneo—all invented on the spur of the moment.

We are still worrying the municipality for the water supply, and reservoirs are getting very low: but now at last the first instalment of pipes has come and I suppose it will not be very long before they are laid down: but it is an awful country for getting things done!

I am reading the Aeneid in the afternoons on the loggia—there is such a fine boat-race in the fifth book, one feels as if it were going on just beyond the Punta; I don't think I have ever read any finer description. Arabic goes on, very slowly, too; but it is a disgusting language, and seems to get more and more difficult: and it is hard to concentrate on unpronounceable verbs when the sun is so hot.   Your

FREYA

20

Arabic. 1921-1923

I BEGAN to learn arabic in 1921. It was an optimistic thing to do considering how far my income was from the self-supporting state in which I proposed to leave it before I travelled. What actually started me I cannot remember, nor how I discovered an old white-bearded Capuchin to give me lessons in San Remo. W. P. was pained at my choice and would have preferred icelandic: but I thought that the most interesting things in the world were likely to happen in the neighbourhood of *oil*. This was in 1921 and the forecast has been accurate up to this day. It was a great effort to add arabic to my work. It meant an hour's walk into Ventimiglia twice a week; half an hour in the train eating my sandwiches: and then I walked to the monastery, to a little gate surrounded by all the ragged, maimed and blind who ate their bowl of soup at the monastery door. My old Capuchin, very benevolent, came to let me in; and we sat learning the elements, from an excellent primer used by the Italian missionaries, with waves of incense from the chapel nearby which made it hard to keep awake. When it was over, I climbed up the hill to tea with an old Scottish lady, Comtesse St. Amour de Chanaz; and had the same train journey and walk home to end up with. I did this through 1921, and by 1922 was beginning to read the Quran. My old monk had been thirty years in Beirut. His pleasure now was centred in Angora rabbits, which he showed me: he was a charming old man and by nature affectionate and friendly, but one could see him reminding himself at intervals that these were merely mundane affections, on a level with his Angora pets. The hours left over in San

Remo before the evening train were tedious, with nothing to do but to look at antique shops with no money to spend, a tantalizing pleasure.

Apart from all this, I liked my arabic days, as they gave me a world a little different from the vineyard and its problems. They brought Professor E. G. Browne, who came only once to L'Arma, but wrote to me as a friend until his death. He found a Persian teacher to stay with me for the Easter vacation in 1922, as a guest in exchange for work in the mornings—Dhabih Behruz, polite and small, with a cat-shaped face, and very sensitive. He never pushed his way, morally or materially, and we wondered how he secured a ticket or mounted a bus when travelling in Europe. On his journey out, he gave up his corner seat to a woman in Paris, who then asked if every Persian was 'coloured', by way of being polite. He was of course devoted to Edward Browne, and soon liked me and indeed told me that he 'venerated' me because I was 'unlike other Europeans'. This was lucky for he was very easily offended. His stories of Persia had an improbability which I now know was given by the town effendi's own ignorance of the country things he was trying to describe, of which he knows so little. We had anxious moments with him and his feelings at the frontier, where they told us that visas were required 'for Persia and all other British colonies'. He left with many expressions of affection, but I never heard from him again though I heard of him, for I met his brother in the town of Savah in 1931. I think what he liked best in the whole of his stay was the sight of the women kneeling in the white river bed of Ventimiglia, beating clothes with stones as they do in Persia.

One of the great advantages of my arabic was that it drew me more and more frequently to England. In the autumn of 1921, after the Alps and his stay at L'Arma, W. P. took me to London. He presented me with a first class-ticket, and we had a day in Paris. I led him to talk to the people at our table in the restaurant car, a thing he said he had never done before. One was an American school-teacher who 'had her photograph taken in Paris with Joan of Arc as a background', in the Rue de

Rivoli. In London he gave me a letter to Sir Denison Ross at the School of Oriental Studies in Finsbury Circus, and handed it to me, remarking that a friend of his had once composed a poem in a dream of which the last and only remembered line was: 'The red geese fly no more through Finsbury Circus'. I have often composed poetry in my sleep, but it has all melted away like Eurydice except for two lines in Italian:

> 'e nella notte nera
> Lacere van le nubi a la bufera . . .'

The red geese, though only imaginary, added their charm to Finsbury, where I now walked four times in the week, taking private lessons, as I had to crowd my learning into the shortest time. I thought, and still think, that a walk on the City pavement is one of the most romantic things in the world: the austere and unpretentious doors—the River Plate Company, or Burma Oil, or affairs in Argentine or Ecuador or Hudson's Bay—they jostle each other and lead away to strange places, and create a feeling of being all over the world at once among the messenger boys and top hats which were then still visible in Moorgate.

In the School, the names of those few who had taken degrees were written up over the stair in letters of gold and I wondered if I should ever be among them. Together with private lessons I joined a few small classes, and found a very different atmosphere from Bedford College—everyone was here because he or she wanted to learn, and Professor Thomas Arnold and Professor H. A. R. Gibb took this for granted, and made us learn as fast as we could. It was impossible not to love Professor Arnold— he was so gentle, so courteous, and apparently so convinced, when we made mistakes, that it was only through absent-mindedness and never stupidity: '*Please*', he would say: 'Please, Miss Stark,' and in his lucidity the intricacies of Arabic grammar melted away. Professor Gibb, who is a friend to-day, was much more alarming because he expected us to be intelligent, instead of being merely surprised if we happened not to be so. When I came again to London in 1922, and was examined by him, my

[278]

usual panic made me forget everything I knew; luckily I did this so completely that it appeared unnatural, and he gave me fifteen minutes to recover and try again. He talked kindly, the strange mental paralysis passed, and I was put into a class to work for the preliminary examination.

As we sat at our work, Sir Denison would trot in and out like a full moon dancing on the tips of its toes, or perhaps like a benevolent, but not strictly virtuous, Silenus; he would sit at our desks to look at our books—always beside the prettiest scholar, whose hand he liked to hold. I once asked our librarian why she chose all her staff so plain, and she told me that "it was better for Sir Denison". I liked him, and knew him well later on, and Lady Ross too; she was happy and devoted to him—which goes to show that a plurality of affections is not so bad, if there is enough to go round.

I had only a term at the School on this first occasion, and the tug of London made it hard to work—the ballet, *The Chauve-Souris, The Beggar's Opera*; and my father's arrival from Canada most of all. He came over again in 1922 and we met in London for an exhibition of fruit at the Crystal Palace, where his boxes of apples won the first prize for Canada and the second for the Empire. We went together to the Crystal Palace and superintended the arrangement of all the lovely fruit in pyramids. Gold and bronze medals came pouring in and everyone made much of him. My father looked really happy. He had let his hair grow a little longer, in a tiny curly wavelet over his ears. He loved Canada and the people, and spoke of a number of friends: and seemed to have slipped into a happy anchorage at last. I went with him to buy a new Burberry and admired that temple atmosphere of the Man's shop, the well-trained reverent way in which the beloved disreputable one he wore was lifted off him, its pockets relieved of string, matches, two cartridges, one or two specimen apples, and other bric-à-brac, and itself handed solemnly, not to the scrap-heap as I hoped, but to the cleaner.

When he left, he made me a present of ten pounds to travel

back to Italy 'in comfort', and I spent it on an aeroplane ticket to Paris, and chose a front seat beside the observer. The air service was still very young. They dressed me in sheepskins and (as it was hard to move at all, so wrapped up) lifted me across some part of the engine to the little double seat in front with all open except for a wind-screen before it. The observer sat down beside me, but there was never a thought of strapping in: when I noticed that the rush of the engine had lifted me on to my feet, and that the observer beside me was holding on to the screen in a determined way, I did so too. I have never enjoyed an air journey so much. The observer shouted out names of towns below, but they were blown away before they reached me; one could put one's head out from the screen a second, and feel as it were the rush of the world through space. When we reached Le Bourget, there was no place reserved to change in, and I was apparently expected to drive into Paris in my dishevelled state: I explained to the customs official that this was impossible: a mirror must be found. "It is only reason-able," said the French Customs. A mirror *was* found, and placed on the bench among the luggage—and I am probably the originator of the first thought for female comfort that ever crossed the mind of an air-line. Very soon afterwards, a lunatic shot the pilot of a London—Paris aeroplane from my little front seat, and it was forbidden to passengers.

After the Crystal Palace, my father left and asked me to look after the selling of a house in Torquay which had been let for many years. It looked as if it had been built, gardened and furnished in the 1880's, muslins and ribbons round every dressing-table, palms and begonias in the garden.

My father gave me either two or four thousand from this sale, and after this the problem of keeping alive gradually grew less difficult. I told him all that had happened, and how my mother was getting neither her own income nor the interest on his loan, and this perhaps made him sell; anyway he was very angry indeed, and told us to put the whole case into a lawyer's hands. The case was based on Mario's receipt, in his own handwriting; he had relied on my mother's weakness in all these years to ignore it. But though there could be no doubt about it, an Italian lawyer can postpone judgment time after time, by constant delays, and the lawsuit dragged on till 1926. It was decided just as my sister died, when we had no heart to think of money, and left most of it for the children. Mario was to pay my mother only for what she had earned by her own years of work in the factory, and had never been able to take out. He began to do this in small instalments which came for a time, and ceased. When she was alone in Italy in 1940, in prison and beyond the reach of anything from outside, he still made no effort to pay this sum or to help in any other way. The factory flourished through the war, and Mario died soon after, impervious to the end, so that I think even his own dishonesty came out of him unperceived. In his small way he was a dictator, and egotism made him feel that he had a right to all he wished, and to the end of her life, in spite of every proof, my mother believed in him.

Before I returned to Italy, about Christmas time in 1922, W. P. took me to Scotland with Olivia Horner, his god-daughter. We went in sleepers—the first time I had been in a sleeper—from which we descended under a cold starlit winter sky at Tarbet on Loch Lomond. We had a sitting-room to ourselves and big fires in the Tarbet Hotel. How enchanting it was! I had enjoyed nothing so much since the holiday at Cogne. We climbed the Cobbler in snow, and saw stoats in white winter fur. The landlady complained of the other guests; they came from Glasgow and asked for this and that—"but as for you and your friends, Professor Ker, sandwiches and the beauties of nature is all you ask for." We had sandwiches and the beauties of nature every day, and good weather generally, though we sat about in sopping bogs. There is always some green in winter all down the West of Britain, dull rust of bracken, and views of sea. Poldores, another adopted god-daughter and a doctor, was there with her parents, Dr. and Mrs. MacCunn, old friends of W. P's who lived at Tarbet. His sister Penelope came, white-haired and with the bluest eyes. She wore a wide blue cape and black hat, whose fashion never changed, and was deaf without her ear-trumpet, and unselfconscious about it in a happy world of her own. She and Margaret Olivier are the only persons I have known who could be called saintly, with a victorious goodness that keeps its young and shining tenderness to the end. I fell in love with her at once as everyone did, and she, and her elder sister later, and all these people, became my friends.

In 1923 a new neighbour, Mrs. Granville, came with an invalid son who had fallen in love with me at a picnic, and made his mother take a house close by belonging to our *Colonello*. She was smaller than I am, all hung about with little dangles of pearls and diamonds over Réville frocks, and she was county and clergy and had never met anything artistic in her life. When she was a girl, she told me, 'doctors were not asked to dinner in our neighbourhood any more than dentists are now.' She was charming in herself, artless, sensible, charitable and gay; no one could have settled more happily into our casual sort of life; and for her, it was a new horizon opening; she said she had never known how one could *enjoy* things before.

Another new friend was Venetia Buddicom, whose parents had a villa in Bordighera, and a garden carpeted with sheets of geranium under old olive trees. They were simple and charming, and liked us, which always surprised me—a complex bred by all the years of uncertain social status in Dronero. Venetia and I walked about together, and I loved her quiet reserve, her feeling for style in all things, and the beautiful carriage of her small head; she made me feel that my gaiety and general curiosity were not very dignified.

In the late spring, W. P. turned up from a tour through Tuscany with both god-daughters, Olivia and Poldores. He had become Professor of Poetry at Oxford in the interval and had to return to give his inaugural lecture, and I had my arabic examination in June. So we left the two girls with my mother, and travelled again to England, to meet in Macugnaga later. When I reached the Oriental School, I found that I had been given the wrong 'set book', by some mistake, and had about three hundred pages of arabic to read and know in the three weeks that remained before the examination. I did it, renouncing all enchantments of June in London, and the examination went surprisingly well: I was complimented by Professor Arnold on my brilliant pun: it seems that, in a bit of unseen translation, when asked to write in arabic that the king had defeated ninety of his enemies, I had managed to assert, by an only too easy confusion of terminals, that the queen had destroyed nine of her lovers: and the professor was far too pure a scholar to think that one could do this by mistake.

LETTERS TO MY MOTHER

THORNWORTHY,
CHAGFORD,
DEVON,
17 *Sept.*, 1921.

My dearest Biri,

There is a south-east wind and a drizzle after yesterday's beautiful sunshine—so I will take an hour before tea for writing to tell you of the journey. Until I actually woke up in London I felt this was all some kind of dream, the sight of that beautiful Kentish land of rolling meadow and trees could not make me realize that this was England; but it is sinking into me, and coming back hour by hour, and I am so happy to be in the dear country again and to hear English spoken in the lanes and in the streets.

We had a most agreeable journey—mostly eating and drinking—with a little sleep thrown in. From Marseilles to Avignon was sunset over the mouths of the Rhone, a clear gold sky on a sheet of cold and luminous water, with dark low hills and flaming lagoons in the foreground—and then the moonlight and a white road by the waterside: it was among the most beautiful things one can remember. We had breakfast on the

[283]

boulevard at Paris; then lunch on the train, already surrounded by travelling English. Our table, however, had a Frenchman (I think) and an American girl of the innocent kind who showed me a photo of herself standing with Joan of Arc (statue) in the background, and told me she had been in Paris six weeks and seen all of it except the Night Life. The crossing was sunny, with a breeze on the sea, enough to make me sedentary, but not sick: the Professor went for tea on board but I thought better not. At Dover there was a crowd and we thought we should be left behind when the Prof. got me into a gorgeous saloon with brown velvet arm-chairs and a Jewish family. I believe it was a Pullman, and I was much thrilled at the solemnity of the rich and their surroundings. And we went through Kent and a beautiful sunset till the lamps were lit and shone along the Thames, and we slid into London. Viva was there—told me I had put her out most dreadfully and it was quite useless to have gone, but I think she was really pleased—although they were only back that day from Tonbridge. Dear old Mr. Bale looks as well as last year and walks without pain, though still easily tired. It was such a joy to get into that house again: I might never have left it, it was indeed like a home-coming to those dear people. They asked after you and want you in the spring.

I had a tremendous day after that: in the morning to Victoria with the Prof. for luggage—and he has *not* let me pay for anything and I am not very happy about it. He took my trunk to Paddington and we walked back, and in the evening he invited himself to dinner and was so talkative and most pleasant (I told Viva that he would be easy to please as to cuisine after our course of education!).

Viva and I went to see caricatures of the Rossetti coterie by Max Beerbohm—great fun—and then for tea and ices at the Piccadilly. Maurice came to see me next morning before I went off and who should turn up at Paddington but the Prof. himself, with a book—isn't he a good friend? And I kept him without shaving water for ten days!

I travelled up easily and my vis-à-vis at lunch came from Palestine and was most interesting; and the West Country was in sunlight. Pud met me at Chagford and we walked on heather in the evening: it is like a dream to see it all again. To-morrow I shall ride. With lots of love, yours

FREYA

11 *GROVE END ROAD*,
21 *Oct.*, 1921.

My darling Biri,

Your letter has just come and I am much troubled over the absence of rain! Poor Nicola! You do not tell me if he is contented and happy? and Rosa too? I do hope so. Pips means to go there only after Christmas, I believe and I think it would be better for me to be there as far as harmony with Nicola goes, as Pips hates to have all the responsibility of arrangements.

I went to Finsbury Square this morning with Viva to see Sir Denison Ross, who was most amiable, tripping about with his round tummy and bulgy eyes and lively manner in a room hung with chinese inscriptions and arabic MSS. on the tables. I liked him—Viva, on the strength of the Professor's opinions, is beginning to like him too. He was in a great hurry, but seemed well impressed by my grammar, which I took with me. I told him I could stay only till Xmas and wanted coaching, and he went out and came back in two twinks saying: "You will have 4 hours a week here, two with a young Englishman, and two with an Arab from Mesopotamia(!!!)" Imagine my joyous feelings—so joyous that I forgot to ask the fee—I begin on Nov. 1st so as to have a free week first for Pips—I think I should get on fast.

Lots of love, dearest Biri, lots and lots of it from your

F.

11 *GROVE END ROAD*,
6 *Nov.*, 1921.

My darling B.,

I am so rushed for time with Pips here and 7 lectures a week of Arabic that I shan't manage a proper letter. It was so nice to get your two—after such an interval—and I am delighted about the dress and shoes. I hope they are all really nice ones? George I haven't yet been able to talk to properly, although

[285]

he came to the theatre yesterday. We saw 'Chauve Souris,' a Russian variety show full of the most delightful things and Pips enjoyed it ever so much, even after paying £3 for the tickets which is what amusements cost in this degraded age. He is back from the Moor, and will be leaving for Italy in a day or two. I shall leave here about Dec. 28th and will go to Droncro if you want me to—just as you like.

To-night we dine, Viva and I, at the Carlton with Prof. and Olivia—and the night before last I went to my first real dinner since the war, with some of Pips' grand friends, and had two glasses of champagne and felt very cheery and vivacious in consequence. So altogether I hope the rest of the week will be quiet to let me catch up with my work.

The Arabic is great fun. I am the most intelligent of my classes—the others all seem rather stupid as a matter of fact—but I have a good deal to catch up, being put with people who started a while ago. The Arab from Mesopotamia was a sad disillusion—a fat young man in a swallow-tail coat with purplish lips and a fat smile.

I have got myself good boots for country or ski-ing; also a cheap mac—and that is all I can do in the way of clothes although my poor old blue does look shabby—but it is only six weeks now, and on the Riviera I can wear white very soon.

It is lovely to think you may get over next year. I do believe the worst of our times are over. I think Pips is going to help too: he quite sees how hard it is to live nowadays on £200 a year! . . .

Must stop, lots of love, dearest Biri, your

F.

21

Alps and Pyrenees. 1923

IN July W. P. and I travelled out again, with our labours behind us, by the Simplon, along the Rhône valley where little towns and the gay and infant river sparkle under poplar trees. In the early morning at Vallorbe we sniffed the mountain air and tried to walk out while the train waited; a Swiss gendarme gruffly prevented us, and leant his huge truculent back against the door of our compartment: W. P. looked at it vindictively, and—speaking French to make himself clearly understood— told me how a discussion once arose as to which of all animals looks most nearly human, and a little man sitting in a corner suddenly said: "L'animal qui ressemble le plus a l'homme, c'est le Suisse."

My mother and the two god-daughters were already at Macugnaga, and we left our train at Domodossola to join them. There is a great pleasure in going to the same holiday place year after year: the circumstances vary and the background is the same, and it makes a sort of daisy chain through time. We were all well and happy this year. My mother sketched, and we three girls with W. P. walked out along the valleys, taking our luncheon, or up to Monte Moro—no serious climbing—and set out for Pizzo Bianco on the 23rd of July. There, when we had climbed to about nine thousand feet and were soon to be roped, W. P. gave a little sudden cry and died. The guide caught him— before any of us could get back to him his heart had stopped. Olivia and the guide went for help, and Poldores and I sat there for seven hours, until the village people came with a ladder to carry him down. We telegraphed, and his brother Charles came out, and Mr. Godley who was at Zermatt—but every arrangement had to be made at once, according to Italian law, and we decided to bury him in the cemetery he loved, under the ridge of Monte Rosa, with the guides. The Bishop of Novara, because W. P. had always gone to the little church on Sundays, gave his permission: and Charles Ker and Mr. Godley arrived, and approved. He was carried there in his old brown walking clothes with a bunch of wild strawberries in his hand, and the mountain people, raking in their hay, took their hats off as the small procession went through their fields. That summer scent has always kept, for me, a taste of sorrow.

*　　*　　*　　*　　*

Viva was at Zermatt at that time, and when my mother and I were left alone, she begged us to go to her. My mother went by train, and Tofi the guide took me across the pass over the Cima di Jazzi, and down the long snow slopes. W. P. had climbed the Matterhorn a year before: he had long wished to do it, and had written to me when he reached Breuil, and told me that he had felt me nearer to him than ever before as he walked those meadows. I was now drawn by a great longing to climb there also, and to have two days of that hill-solitude to get my strength again. 'I will lift up mine eyes unto the hills' is the psalm that has always been the truest word for me. So I spent a night at Zermatt and kept Tofi with a porter, and we walked up and slept till midnight at the Hornli hut, and looked out under an early moon shining yellow in the cup of snows, where avalanches were tumbling with their soft roar continuously into the night. I lay thinking 'why had I come' as one does so often: at midnight we had our breakfast and crept out with a lantern. There was a French party too, but they let us go first as we were making a traverse and going down the other side. Those great walls were like Dante's circles in the moonlight, but hard rock, safe and friendly. It took five hours to go up: I was always very slow up and very quick down, and the Frenchmen caught and passed us: at a little tiny upper hut we rested a few minutes and went on, and passed the Frenchmen in our turn where the rock became difficult, to Tofi's unconcealed satisfaction. When the day began it showed us uplifted in solitude: only Mont Blanc, Rosa, the lovely Weisshorn and a few others showed in our dawn—the rest lay dim in shadows far down. The top of the Matterhorn is a thin ridge, one side rock, one snow, but very narrow: I wanted to creep along it on all fours, but Tofi begged me to think of it as a street, and walk: I did this, and felt better: on either side you look down, Switzerland right and Italy left. The Italian descent is far more tremendous, though there are now ropes here and there to help. I was not in full training and as I was letting myself down one of the rope-stretches, my feet against the wall and Tofi paying out our own cord which tied me, my fingers suddenly refused to hold any longer: no will of mine could make them. I called to Tofi, who secured the rope and let me dangle, while I rested my hands: one swings like a pendulum and it is far safer than it feels. I was presently able to hold again and we went on, hurrying, for a storm was gathering behind us. It was so cold that my raw egg in its little aluminium case had pieces of ice floating in the white of it. We crossed back over the Theodule to Zermatt, reaching the Italian hut in so short a time that people were surprised. The usual thing is to sleep at Breuil, but I knew my mother would be anxious if I did not get home for the night: and we were back at five after a seventeen-hour day—not very tired either.

There was a street in Zermatt where the guides sat on benches, and a long central table at the hotel where only members of the Alpine Club were allowed a place while the rest sat around at separate tables and admired them—old mostly, but Olympian. The whole of Zermatt had a busy, prosperous temple-atmosphere, dedicated to the service of the mountains. Viva seemed to have nothing to do here, for she never climbed, but she walked about, and listened to concerts, and loved the atmosphere with a sort of vicarious pleasure from its social side. She was dear to us in our sadness. When I arrived over the mountains, she bought a silk dress and laid it ready for me on my bed, and there are few sorrows through which a new dress or hat will not send a little gleam of pleasure however fugitive. The grief for W. P. was not bitter, for he has never seemed far away or really separated by death.

* * * * *

I remember little of the summer after we travelled back to L'Arma, until September: then I went walking with Venetia in the Pyrenees.

I met her in Carcassonne, travelling third class, and wrote a series of letters to my mother describing the places we saw.

'Montpellier, Hôtel Midi,
4 p.m. Friday, 14.9.23.

'We had a fine morning in spite of rain at Marseilles. Went down to the old Port last night after dinner and saw notices of excursions for the Château d'If, so I thought it a good way to employ and not tire Ethel (a cousin who came as far as Marseilles). She is a lump to cart about; always thinking about the possible drawbacks and Mrs. Miller or equally irrelevant people. However she did develop gleams of liveliness. It was lovely dashing out into the wonderful bay, like an inland sea and beautiful even without the sun. It is all barren round slopes of tufa rock going down to the sea, a pleasant warm colour, and a feeling of nakedness about them. If is one of a little belt of islands. The best of the entertainment was the boatman catching stray dubious people along the quay and explaining what a desirable excursion it was and watching the look of interest or distrust dawning in their eyes. It was wonderful how clever he was: almost all those he snatched very soon came in meekly, having had no thought of it at all.

'It is worth while seeing the dungeons. Some are quite goodish rooms with fireplaces, but all with scarcely any windows and one tiny cell for the condamnés à mort with nothing at all and suffocating air even with the door open. A sad place. The names of the prisoners are written up over the doors: the Iron Mask and Monte Cristo, and the hole of communication, though I can't help having doubts as to its authenticity. As an anti-climax we were taken an extra bit along the coast to see the villa of Gaby Deslys.

'As luck has it this sunny country is deluged with a steady slanting rain—I wanted to go straight on to Carcassonne, but then saw what looked like towers here and thought I might as well stop. It is lovely country for a long stay: straight roads, open skies, olives and copses and patches of trees on uncultivated ground, the sort of things one gets to love, but nothing for sightseeing. The hotel has doubts about women, young, alone, but after scrutiny by an aged female decided I was respectable.

Later.

'I have been padding about and discovered the most attractive old provincial town. There is a big flat garden, Louis XIV style, with a kind of temple at the end and lovely clear water and two swans, trees and ramparts all round and a wonderful view of country that made me think of what you see from Richmond. And below that there is the Jardin des Plantes of Henri IV and a a statue of Rabelais with the inscription: "Vivez joyeux": a pleasant contrast to Chateau d'Îf—all shady trees, and a few professors sauntering, and students with books. The university itself is surrounded by narrow little streets, and good gateways, and dark with shops. The cathedral, I thought a huge bare ugly building till I came round the corner to the front which you see by the card is startling and very fine.

'*Montpellier, Hôtel du Midi.*
15 September, 1923.

'I walked over the university and saw the gown of Rabelais hung in a cupboard just behind the hall where they give the degrees. The spirit evidently survives, for just over against the door of that solemn apartment is a fresco with four pink students in blue striped bathing dresses drinking champagne by the riverside. I am quite sorry to go: it is real pleasant provincialism. All the people are fat and proud of being so; the dinner last night was a small kind of orgy and I was given a litre of wine without asking for it. They all realize that food and comfort is what one lives for and glory in it. The shops are innumerable, huddled in the smallest space, in tiny dark back streets, and you can satisfy every want of life in a five-minute walk. There is nothing austere about this delightful university: I wonder it has only six hundred students! When they die they send their portraits, and there are rows of them from A.D. 1300; the old custodian said to me: "C'est mieux d'attendre aussi longtemps que possible pour cela."

'I am glad to have seen the cathedral: I never met anything like it before. One tower is new and a whole bit has been added, and it is curious that although they have made it exact to the old stone by stone, the effect is quite different and says nothing.

'The place here seems good for priests, although the cathedral door had Vive la Révolution on it!

> '*Hôtel Bernard,*
> *Carcassonne,*
> *Aude.*
> 16 *September,* 1923.

'I meant to write last night but came home after a stroll round and round the battlements of the old town feeling inconceivably tired and only realized this morning out of the guidebook that the circuit is $1\frac{1}{2}$ kilometres. Venetia only turned up this morning early: Madame here was much relieved: she is fat with a turn-up nose, dressed in silk and the hotel is alright too, a dim place on a courtyard, entrance with pillars to support it, an aged waiter with a sense of responsibility, pretty chambermaids, an attempt at "confort moderne" which has had no influence at all on the nature of the house or inhabitants, and divine meals. The people all tuck their napkins over their stomachs. The French bourgeois has everything in life to make him happy except beauty in his wife, and that is a dubious happiness.

'We are in the new town—so to speak, for I believe it was

founded and laid out by the Black Prince in good straight streets, cobbled, and water running through them, a pleasant tinkle to listen to from one's bed. We have not yet explored it, except the pâtisserie which is all that you could expect in this country of epicureans. The town is full of country people in the mornings, and lots of booths—and they are a mountain race already, much keener-featured, with blue eyes often as not, and Basque in their speech I take it.

'I found my way to the old town, which is quite apart and grim and deserted on the hill. It is almost too good to be true. I do not love it, like Montpellier and the more human places; it is too like a monument and outside of real life, and one has to have guides and tourists all around—but I have never seen so wonderful a place. What would I not give to be transported for a day or two to its best times and see it with its own life and people. The country is wild and beautiful, not mountainous enough to hide the skies, and broken into vineyards and wild uncultivated places. It is a series of lovely open views from the battlements. Of course I should have brought Froissart; he travelled here and I never thought of him.

'Venetia and I went to hear Mass in the old church this morning and admired the red choirboys against those lovely pillars and glass. The choirboys did not live up to their surroundings and the poor old curé looked at them with pain all through the service. It was very pleasant up there.

'This hotel is clean—nothing smaller than a mouse which I discovered to our mutual surprise when putting my hand in my knapsack pocket for biscuits. But in the train yesterday a stout lady asked me to open the windows as she had a "punaise" in her hand—"elle est bien petite, mais, enfin c'en est une," and our carriage was overshadowed by a painful and suspicious silence.

'All this country has beautiful churches rising to immense high square towers above the townships round them, and visible like great symbols all over the countryside.

'I don't think we shall take a mule. It would be an awful tie.

'All the people here are vintaging. They wear black straw hats, or sunbonnets—the old women white caps with frills. All the country from Cette to this place is vine, not staked and tied like ours but loose like gooseberry bushes, and all dancing in the wind of the sea. Very good sweet grapes.

'*Hôtel Descamps,*
Les Cabannes.
19 *September*, 1923.

'Here we are on the edge of civilization, but rather shocked to find that a caravan of twenty-one English walked this way to Andorra before us. They sprained ankles however and had to be carried so we don't think much of them as forerunners. We have what looks like the most blood-thirsty brigand for a guide—a fisherman with an eye to business (asked fifty francs a day without a moment's hesitation)—and an adventurous spirit: his name is Antonine, but does not look like that, and the old lady here says he is "de toute confiance mais il ne faut pas écouter ses histoires . . .". The three ladies who run this place had just received their own snapshots from some English visitors, and the amiability so caused is all poured out on us. I have been sitting over the big open fire, made on the floor, with two little tree stems crossed and burning, and a wild black cat stretched out, and the two ugliest old women trotting round that ever existed outside of Rackham. It is a little summer place for fishermen, with a big stream of clear water and all green around, and the Pyrenees beginning most suddenly in abrupt rocks.

'We spent the day in Foix—with castle closing two valleys, and three old towers remaining where one can see over much hilly country. There are delightful rooms in the towers, with deep window-seats and "confort moderne" on most hygienic principles. Then we went to the Bibliothèque and met a charming man who became a friend. I told him to use Vaseline and preserve his old MSS—beautiful huge things of sixteenth or seventeenth century, illuminated, but all the good things cut out by nuns who gave them as prizes for good conduct. And what should I find in a huge old book but pages of arabic!

'We come here about 6 p.m. and spent the time, Venetia fishing and I asking for the guide. Have just been sitting now —after supper—in family circle in kitchen listening to nice but prosy old man lamenting the absence of anything masculine in our travelling outfit—même un beau-frère. We felt more and more depressed as we listened. We have taken tender farewells, and shall wake up with alarm clock and make our own breakfasts and be off by 6, I hope. Venetia now feels doubtful about walking, I doubtful about shoes—but there is no snow: only a night in a hut with the guide and no one for miles and miles as the old man repeated to us: but whether this was because we were behaving badly about the Ruhr I could not make out.

'We have lovely beds: we share the room and have an alcove each.

'*Fonda de Jean Torra,*
Andorra.
22 September, 1923.

'Here we really are, though it seems hard to believe—and I am talking Spanish of a sort and feel it strange to be for the first time in a country whose language is not familiar. Our guide turned up at 6 on Thursday and we started with the beginnings of dawn on a cold-looking grey morning with heavy dew. Antonine looked so remarkably unlike a guide and like a buccaneer that we had some doubts, and when we left a little village close to Les Cabannes we walked for the rest of the day in almost absolute solitude. They are not high mountains: one col was 2,600 metres—but long, long valleys, and no villages at all: nothing like the painted churches and towers of the Alpine valleys. Beautiful fishing, hunting—chamois, bear and wild boar, and quantities of birds—and a more beautiful valley than we followed I have never seen—we followed a good mule track near upon four hours through woods—le bois de Dendarme, and the sun came out and shone on the beech leaves and through the hazel trees on the deep pools of the stream, and then we climbed through a series of clefts from one hanging valley into another till we reached open pasture and the high ridge of cols —which here they call "ports"—which surround Andorra on every side. We met two shepherds with mules while we sat at lunch and that was all: their beasts were going down to winter quarters next day. They had no proper granges, only tiny cabins, turfed over and much like those of the ancient Britons on Dartmoor, I should say—and even Venetia's enthusiasm for sleeping in a hut was damped when she looked into them.

'We had no idea whether we could reach the first houses the other side before nightfall and walked all day with only two hours' rest. Had tea in a lovely upland by clear stream and made the kettle boil and then started on the last ridge—which of course opened out on to a large landscape with lonely lake in grass meadows, and folds of hills shining in the last light. We got to the ridge at 6 p.m. and looked over Andorra, all wild narrow ridges—and habitations nowhere—a most lonely beautiful country, and made for camping by one of the streams. We raced down and got to Serrat, where an auberge was promised. But that is only a summer place and the auberge was an old woman in a blackened room sitting by her cauldron—nice old people. The man came in later and we tried to talk in the patois. It is all Langue d'Oc, only with variations enough to prevent one from speaking. They had no candles, but lit up our supper with shreds of pine wood—the real old fashion—and talked of smuggling and the poor look-out now with the exchange. We slept on hay in the grange and the next morning took most cordial leave of Antonine who was going back to fish in the streams we had come up by. We loaded our packs and walked along feeling rather weighted by them. Venetia has carried so many things that I have to take *all* the food and it makes it a good deal heavier than when I have only my own affairs to think about. But it was an easy day, always following the stream down a mule path and the country getting more culti-vated—people cutting hay, mules at intervals balancing their packs, and little clusters of houses, all rough stone but with very neat slate roofs. The churches are old and simple outside, with gorgeous altar-pieces right up to the ceiling inside, rows of niches and wooden figures of saints in old dim gold.

'This is the main valley and we find there is a motor into Spain to Seo de Urgel (could any name be more alluring?)—where the bishop and the shops are. We are going to-morrow, but don't know what will happen as we had not counted on Spanish exchange, or on so long a way round: we are carefully portioning out our francs, and wondering. This is a pleasant little mountain village: all green, willows on the edge of the river and meadows sloping down, and the people prosperous. There is the Casa Comunale with rough frescoes, and the robes of the twenty-four councillors who govern this state: the two chief ones wear cocked hats when the bishop comes from Spain: the church is Spanish but the convicts are sent to France and so neutrality is preserved. The old woman who took us round showed us an evil old instrument for strangling the criminals (la garotte) but said with pride that it had not been used for fifty years.

'*Fonda Llebreta,*
Seo de Urgel.
24 *September,* 1923.

'I don't know whether this will reach you before we do, but it is such a joy to write this address and put on a Spanish stamp, that I am making the most of the excuse. We are leaving our hearts in this little town. As it is we ought not to be here, but Venetia yesterday was overcome by scruples and insisted on showing our kodak-permit to the douane; it was Sunday afternoon, the douane was sitting at the café, but came upstairs most cordially—white drill, diamond rings, and the most incomprehensible French you ever heard! He wrote out three sheets of government paper before we had time to wink and handed it to us saying we must deposit twenty pesetas and they would be returned when we left the country. We explained that we had only just over twenty pesetas altogether and poured our little all on to the table in front of him. He was most obliging: sent direct for the banker, explained that we were travelling "solas", yes, "solas", and showed our letter of credit. After many formalities Venetia wrote a cheque and got two pounds. And here we are for one day more. We leave to-morrow at eight, if, that is, we can pay our bill—because—feeling so rich, we have been buying cord shoes and nice little cakes with cream in them.

'We live in a delightful tavern: it looks villainous when you go in, but our room has a brick terrace with the river and hills and moonlight all in front of it, and big grapes on a trellis, and we have endless meals and polite people who greet us with new salutations each time. There is martial law in this country just now but no one would guess it—and this morning, as we wandered over the fort, the garrison posed to me for a snapshot: the gates were open, the walls crumbling, the courtyard planted with beds of iris: anything more peaceful you never saw. From there one looked up the valley and down, bright green meadows edged with willow and poplar, and the far bare lines of the hills closing in all round and beautiful in shape.

'The cathedral is very very early and all great columns of grey stone, square and simple, and here and there the high gilt edifice of the altars of this country; the high iron railing in front of the altar is topped with bunches of gilt iron beaten out and lovely against the grey. It is a seminary town: priests as thick as black-beetles and very like them. The soldiers are much more cheerful and look smart and neat compared to French or Italian. They have funny little hats looking like comic opera—high crowns of patent shiny leather with a pompon in front and other varieties.

'My Spanish gets on which is as well as nothing else is talked and the one or two who fancy themselves in French might as well talk Polish for all we can make of it.

'Did I tell you that as we walked down towards the frontier and thought of our plight if we were turned back penniless to Andorra, we sat on a stone and pulled out our passports to see if we could not write down Spain as one of the countries open to us, but after several attempts found that neither of us was really good at forgery. So we trusted to Providence, and found that the douanier had a passion for photography: he showed us his machine, and I photographed the corps de garde and we went on rejoicing. A pleasant, hospitable country—only I am getting so tired of their asking for the man who must be with us. Even an old unknown woman in the street hobbled up to me and asked me "no tienen hombre." Next time we must invent some decent reason: a pilgrimage, I think.'

Primo de Rivera was in the middle of his revolution, the place was full of soldiers, and the inhabitants forbidden to assemble in groups of more than three. But nothing could make Seo anything but an enchanted little sleepy town, with medieval wooden porticoes and the grey stone cathedral with its altars of dim gold. We liked the Spanish people we met: they were courteous, and rarely bothered us with curiosity and questions. We never saw women and came to the conclusion that they must always be kept indoors. The wine was delicious, rather sweet and heavy, tasting of grapes and sun, but the food heavy, and all meat. When we left Seo, we had so little money that we could only afford third class on the motor bus: no one in Spain goes so poorly except the soldiers. They put a ladder up to the roof of the bus in the public square and handed us up with grave but probably surprised politeness, to a little wooden seat which ran along the top. When we left the town by one of the long avenues of trees which line the roads, their branches swept the roof, and us on top of it; and we could not communicate with the driver below because a hood projected above his head and hid him: we held on for our lives, and after the avenue still continued to be shaken like dice till we reached the town of Puiccerda and were in France again.

From here we walked till dusk to Libia, and hit a fearfully dirty little inn with one room and one bed. In the dark I felt something, put my hand upon it and felt it large: I suppressed a shriek for Venetia's sake, but in about ten minutes another object settled upon me and I shrieked and rushed across the room for the light: the walls, so beautifully white when we went to

bed, were spotted all over with bugs. This was my first meeting
with such things, sadly familiar now, and we did not know that
one can stave them off by keeping a light on, so we had a bad
night. But the town was very attractive: it had a pharmacy
lined with painted Renaissance boxes—a little gem of a place—
and, in a round tower into which we wandered, we found the
Parish Council in session, who, seeing our interest in history,
went to a dilapidated old chest and pulled out document after
document with great red seals attached, seals of John and
Katherine of Aragon, priceless treasures. We left Libia walking,
and then went by train to Prades, where we had nothing but a
twenty-five centime stamp left us to pay the porter. But Venetia
got money in Perpignan, and we spent two days climbing Mont
Canigou, over shoulders of autumn-leaved blueberries, with the
Pyrenees in ranges stretched beyond. Lovely romantic names
are in all this country—Port des Craves, Fontariente—Provençal
that is neither French nor Italian and runs along the Mediterranean
from Piedmont to the Basques. The mountains seemed wilder
than the Alps, lapped round with forests rather than pastures—
stretches of uninhabited lands, more like Asia: we left them with
that Pisgah feeling all travellers know, of a view seen, not
visited, not forgotten.

TO MY FATHER

L'ARMA,
3 *Aug.*, 1923.

Dearest Pips,
    Your letter reached me in Zermatt, and cheered me up no
end talking about mountains and *grangie* and these good things.
We are back now, only arrived this morning at 2 a.m. in the
moonlight, the plain of Lombardy was like a steam-cauldron to
come into. It is wonderful what the hills do: I feel renovated

as soon as I get up over a thousand metres—and even with all the sadness of this time we are both feeling remarkably fit.

We went to Zermatt with Viva for a week after arranging everything at Macugnaga. Mama went by train and I up over the pass and it was glorious to get to the top of the wall and look over on all the giants, Mont Blanc with sun on him high above all the rest, and all the beautiful white shapes rising out of that immense field of ice and snow. You and I must go to Zermatt some time. It is a sort of meeting ground of all the old Alpine men: the most ancient sit at the head of the high table, the young ones discuss heresies at the lower end. You see nothing but axes and boots, and the ladies walk about in every variety of breeches, some looking very slim and elegant . . . others not!

It was wonderful blue clear weather and as I had the guide I could not bear to part with him immediately so we rested that night, and got a good Swiss 'porteur' and next morning started for Matterhorn. I wanted to go over the top and down the Italian side which is more difficult, and it appears that all the guides in Zermatt discussed the matter in relation to my fragile(?) appearance and betted against it: however we got to the Swiss hut, which is about 10,000 feet up at the bottom of the actual crest of rock, and there had a pleasant evening looking out on the wonderful ring of hills—Monte Rosa and all her group in snow and moonlight. There were four other caravans going up, but we had first start because of our difficult descent and I lay awake in my comfortable little room watching the moonlight and listening to the stones now and then rolling down the couloir, or the wind moaning round that gigantic corner. We started at one o'clock—with no lantern—a most mysterious feeling climbing up gullies and faces of rock in that uncertain light. One is much too busy to look down, but when we reached a little ledge about 4 a.m. and the daylight began to float in upon us and we sat down to drink tea, I saw that the whole side was one unbroken sheer slope, incredibly steep, and no place for giddy people. I was not in very good training of course and got breathless when hurried, so let the others go on ahead—but we caught them up when it came to the real rock-work. There is a terrific steep bit at the top with a rope to help you and just *wrinkles* of rock to hold you and a wind blowing like ice to get you off the top—and then when you do arrive there is a long ridge—about 15 minutes—with nothing at all on either hand: here you have an irresistible wish to crawl on all fours, but the guide informed me that I must "andare franca" so I just walked along and thought it very like life, with the abyss and the unknown on either hand, and there we left our companions and started going down the other most tremendous slope, I feeling rather like someone in the acrobatic kind of cinema. The other side has lots of ropes, and one overhanging place with a rope ladder down it, so that one's arms have more work than the legs all the way down. I was so tired in my arms that they would scarcely grip, but we got down remarkably quickly—2½ hours from the top to the Italian hut—and here rested one hour and I revived with tea and wine mixed —not a bad drink. It was a fine clear day: Monte Viso visible and every other hill in Europe as it seemed. We had more beastly ropes below the hut: it is unpleasant dangling in the air and looking down for miles into the valley. We met two Englishmen toiling up towards us, and passed the time of day, and by twelve o'clock we were on the Italian glacier. We did five more hours slogging mostly over softish snow, across the pass to Zermatt, and got triumphantly in—a long day's walk. The guides were so pleased, and want me to do all the really difficult things in the Alps now. They were nice people, both of them, and told me the miseries of taking people who have to be hauled up and down and cannot be moved along quickly when the *tormenta* comes.

I did no more climbing. It is so horribly expensive and I was only able to do this because Viva had invited us and we had no hotel to think of—but it is a grand sport. My dear Professor came that way two years ago, and I was thinking of him coming down into Italy, and it seems so strange that he should be on the other side when we feel him so near—I seem to be missing him more and more.

I will write in a day or two about things here, but I have not yet looked into them—except to examine the little trees Nicola is so bad about, and which seem at last to be recovering —after much spraying.

It is very very hot!

Lots of love to you my dear old Pips.   Are you going to be here in the autumn?   Yes please, Darwin tulips: their place is being dug next week I hope.   Also daffs if you have any.

Your own,

FREYA

PS. I thought you might like to see what I wrote the other day thinking of the Professor.

W. P. K.

On your good rest we laid the mountain flowers—
Rose-frilled dianthus and the dark bluebell,
And yellow lilies fresh with Alpine showers
And every name your love remembers well:—
Secretly, in your cell,
Their wild and tender fragrance will recall
The happiness of our adventurous morns,
While Rosa's shining horns
Receive the night and sunrise, and the fall
Of her loud streams is steady to your ear—
Rough mountain voice to soothe the mountaineer.

Here in the meadows where the pasturing cows
Turn their slow necks and move the collar bell
Your love will ever dwell
Beneath the lime-trees' shade whose flowering boughs
Greeted us with the daylight long ago
Beside the pilgrims way, the path we know.

The seasons in their sequence mild shall bring
Silence in winter and the shining snow,
Dumb voice of cataracts frozen—then the spring,
Quick thaw and sudden ecstasy—and lo!
Summer again when our wild roses blow,
And in their sober row,
Black gowns and kerchiefs bright,
The villagers to Mass or Vespers wend,
Or gather harvest in the clear sweet air—

Or, till night-shadows blend
The hills and heavens, must rake the flower-strewn hay;
All this was your delight,
And happiness to watch upon your way.

The sun is all about you yet, most dear.
In earliest radiance our hearts rise to you.
In the small brook's awakening voice we hear
Echoes of words, a memory to pursue.
Nor shall the granite ranges ever wear
Their coat of dawn, their earliest cloak of flame
But as a written signal, even your name
Glittering on Time and Space, who art beyond:
As on that day when we upon the hill
Kept through the hours our vigil sad and fond
And spake with you, and knew your heart was still.

22

Sickness. 1924-1925

IN the spring of 1924 my mother and I carried out a long-cherished project and visited Rome, with our *Colonello* and his brother to show it to us. As I was now working for my examination in arabic, I arranged to have proper lessons there on the set book (the history, al-Fakhrī, by Ibn aṭ-Ṭiḳṭaḳa) from a Mme. Veccia-Velieri, one of the small and excellent band of Italian Orientalists who produced the best review I know on current events of Islam. Rome and Carcassonne have the lovely sound of water in their streets and squares. We lived in a pension in Piazza Barberini, and I still think of the splash of the Barberini fountain in the night as part of the Roman magic. After my lesson every morning the *Colonello* took us sightseeing: the way we lingered among nude antiques worried him, and he wandered about with his eyes delicately fixed on the ceiling till we had finished. The two brothers would take us to dine at the Castello dei Cesari, or in some *trattoria* where huge Roman artichokes were fried in oil, crisp as potato chips and very good. I had a lovely dress (our income had increased and from now on the oases in the desert of clothes became more and more frequent): it was grey chiffon woven with a pattern of silver and gold, with a Turkish gold bolero and edged with fur, and it gave me immense pleasure: for the first time in my life I went to have my face made up and was much surprised and gratified by the result.

I loved the early Christian Rome, the churches with alabaster windows and the happy feeling of a religion that still saw Christ not crucified but as a shepherd lad carrying his lamb on his shoulders. We drove one beautiful day to Viterbo, with snow-topped

Soracte in sight, and back by the lake of Bracciano, across the Campagna flowering in yellow broom. We had an audience of the Pope, and went dressed in evening black with veils over our heads in the middle of the morning, and long gloves so that no flesh should be visible; and as I showed one inch of neck below my chin, a chamberlain dressed in red brocade offered a pin to close it up, while about twenty of us waited in a great salon with the guards in their Michaelangelo costume outside, and the gorgeous chamberlains inside. The small, round pontiff in white wool, with only an emerald on his finger for grandeur, came in —strangely impressive: and went round blessing us every one, and gave his ring to kiss.

My mother left at the end of three weeks (usual want of money), but I stayed another three because of the arabic, and continued to be taken about, and to wander by myself. Vera's brother-in-law and family were there and friendly, but the lawsuit was now in full swing and it was all very difficult, and anyway they still looked on us, rather unfairly since the money was mostly ours, as poor relations; so we saw little of them. We went to Nemi when the cyclamen were out; and I wandered often along the Appian Way, which had not yet been vulgarized by Mussolini, and flowed under its old paving stones and neglected graves, a river of poetry and time.

We had a sudden death when I returned to L'Arma. An elderly cousin came for a week-end and had a heart attack which killed her, in spite of all that the injections and the doctor could do. There had not been time to get a nurse, and her husband was away. This is the only time I have actually had to wash and dress anyone for burial. It was a shock and I was ill by now, a slow illness, nothing but accumulated worry and fatigue. They diagnosed it as gastric ulcers and were trying to cure it by diet and rest. For a week I was given nothing at all but white of egg, and for the rest of this year lived on milk, raw eggs, boiled macaroni and ham, and had to spend more than half my time lying down though in the other half I went about and even went ski-ing beyond the Tenda Pass, at Limone.

In June Penelope Ker, Poldores and Isobel Scott-Moncrieff went to Macugnaga to see W. P's grave, and sent me a ticket and invitation to join. All the Kers did this when they invited the generation of the godchildren. We spent a week there, with Monte Rosa heavy in snow over meadows in flower. Poldores stayed on with us into the summer and we went to Macugnaga again, and met Charles Ker there and a diminutive Glasgow business man with him called Mr. Beckett, who walked about in his tweeds like a small British tug in foreign tides, among the summer visiting Italians: he had little use for the Continent, and stuck to beer. Poldores and I made friends with the summer visitors and annoyed the well-dressed young women from Milan by carrying off the only good-looking Italian; he had come, he told my mother, to look for a wife. He never could decide which of us he liked better: and we took it, fairly, in turns to lure him from his parents to our table by a well-directed glance at lunch-time, when all the débutantes were looking on. Perhaps it did something to bring tweeds into fashion: sport then was only beginning to take hold of the Italian young men, and was unknown to the girls.

Poldores climbed the Cima di Jazzi, while I drank raw eggs and milk and rested. But the high air and the holiday absence of trouble were making me stronger: I found I was able to walk so long as I did not eat. I managed a flattish glacier, and presently began to toy with the idea of Monte Rosa, which I had longed to climb for several years. It had been done once from this side by a woman. We waited a long time for good weather: one needs three clear days for the ice to be suitable, and the climb can rarely be done more than once in a summer. At last all was right: I went with a Belgian and his guide, so as to share expense, and with Tofi, who had been with us at W. P's death the year before: Poldores and the young doctor came a seven hours' walk as far as the hut. It juts on a rock over the Marinelli couloir like a cliff at sea; far below, avalanches pour frothing like milk all day long: only at midnight when frost holds the heights, is there a lull, and that is the time when this dangerous couloir

[307]

can be crossed, with steps cut in its slope which is solid ice. This is where the three who first tried the climb were swept away. As the evening drew in, clouds began to appear: we had anxious doubts: one cannot risk bad weather, as one would be caught on the glacier with no way back. I had carried up my milk and eggs and the others sat watching their soup boil round the fire: at eleven Tofi called us; the stars were out; only a few wisps of cloud caught in the rock above: Poldores says that she heard my voice, lost in the couloir, saying "I think it will be clear" and wondered if that ordinary sentence was to be my last recorded word.

It was exciting to get on to that road of the avalanches, which seemed wide, like a rough slanting sea embraced in darkness. Tofi had cut most of the steps before calling us, and we could move quickly across in about twenty minutes. The chief danger of the climb was over. It is a big climb—twelve hours from the couloir to the top, up a face of tumbled ice. It is the guide's mountain: success depends on his ability to lead through the winding glassy crannies. Every now and then we stopped while he listened to tiny noises, crackings and breakings in the glacier, signals of danger. The ice here was in its own world: so steep that with a small lurch inwards one rested one's length against the giant face. For five hours Tofi or his cousin cut steps; the lovely swish of splinters slid past on the mountain of glass; we stood in small dents, big enough for the point of the boots, our ice-axes dug in above so as to hold in case of a slip, with time to look about us. Macugnaga and its valley lay in darkness; but above, in starlight, vague outlines of summits showed. It is not to be explained, how one of the things worth risking life for is to feel this mountain awe. After five hours of pure ice, we reached a long crocodile back of rock: then ice and the *bergschrund* where the glacier breaks from the rock, always a crevasse to cross, but filled with snow; it gave under me and I had a surprised moment, hanging by the rope, but was pulled out. My mother had been called to look at us through a telescope from the hotel: she saw me disappear in the crevasse, and a small cloud came and hid the recovery, so that she was left wondering and vowed never to look through telescopes again.

We reached the top in twelve hours exactly from the hut and then spent another three or four descending along the brow of Rosa to the Capanna Margherita, the highest in the Alps: there is a custodian there, changed every fortnight because of the loneliness of that high place. He got us a fine meal, and I forgot about my rules of diet and ate, but was immediately sick, feeling, even at the time, that it was rather impressive to be so on a balcony ten thousand feet above the ground below. Even when I am well, I need very little food above ten thousand feet and usually keep myself for a long time on lumps of sugar sucked at intervals. I returned to my milk: and felt better and better in the high air. It was my Belgian companion who gave out and developed mountain sickness in the night: he feared he could not face the descent, and decided to go down by the easy Swiss side while I returned with Tofi to Macugnaga—reluctantly, for with only two on the rope it became much more dangerous. Any slip on steep ice needs three people if it is not to be almost inevitably fatal. When we woke at 3 a.m. the world was all shrouded in mist: we started off and had no sooner descended a thousand feet or so than the mountain sickness passed completely in the strange way it has, and our party remained together. We came down by the Turlo pass, an easy way and the usual route for Monte Rosa from the Italian side, and reached Macugnaga for a late tea, dear Charles Ker running to meet us with his silk handkerchief as a present in his hand, so anxious to show his pleasure. The poor little Belgian wife looked quite thin, she had gone through agonies of anxiety, as apparently she did whenever her husband climbed.

This was the only really big climb of my life and we left Macugnaga a few days after. Tofi and I planned a new route up Monte Rosa by the Loccie glacier for the following season, but I became too ill to climb for many years, and the new route has now been done by someone else. The great listening glacier and its cracklings in the night are among the things I shall never forget.   Tofi ended sadly, for he and his cousin, who had accompanied us, were doing the same climb a year or two later with students from Turin: a stone hit the cousin in the forehead and pierced it, but did not kill him: they tied him on to a little platform of rock and left him, to bring help from the hut, for they were near the top.   To leave him alone was a monstrous thing, which no proper climber would have allowed.   The night came on and the man must have become delirious, or seized with panic: he got loose and was found weeks after in a crevasse. Tofi, of course, had his guide's book taken from him: he settled in his shop, with his plump cheerful wife and pretty little girl. He was the best guide I ever knew, and loved climbing passionately.   But he could not bear the sight of blood, and lost his head on that occasion.

Even without accidents the rolling of stones is one of the most sinister noises.   They hurtle like bullets as one climbs steadily and hopes for the best, and I have always imagined that a military advance across open country must give much the same feeling.   I have regretted the loss of mountaineering more than most things; it was the key of a world a little above the human world and beyond it, where one could always find a refuge from friction and time.

A little odd note-book belonging to these years shows in its jumble the sort of mixture my life was at the time: it is filled with dates for planting fruit trees and bedding out carnations, with scraps of poetry, English or Italian, which I tried to write, equally badly; whole lists of Arabic words; cooking recipes; my temperature, which showed a constant low fever and was supposed to be taken every day; and political extracts.   The fascists were in, and, like everyone else, I welcomed them with enthusiasm.   I remember passing a trainload of them at some station, young lads singing *Giovinezza* on their way to join the March on Rome—and I felt tears come and waved to them.   The Matteotti murder shook me: I told the Marchese Orengo how bad I thought the farce of a trial given to the murderers, and he answered: "You would not expect anyone to condemn their own side, would you?" a very typical Italian remark. I grew less and less wholeheartedly fascist, and realized I was against them in 1927 or so, when their military ideas began to show. My mother remained with them at heart for years, and it brought an added division between us.

These were unhappy years in this regard. My mother at last realized what Mario was like, but refused to face it, which made every step in the lawsuit a crisis. She resented having to do dull things like housekeeping, after the excitement and pride of all that old Dronero life. It must have been a bitter time for her, and I was too exasperated, and also too inexperienced, to realize it. I thought that if she would take charge of her own problems and trials for a year, I might get well again: and I was desperately ill now. My first note of going to a doctor was in April 1922; most of the four years after were spent on sofas, while carrying on my arabic, and trying, at intervals, to lead an ordinary life. I felt a constant sore grievance against my mother, and thought that she might at least try; and she did, but was psychologically unable to attend to things that bored her. She was full of affection, but not a concrete burden, even to the ordering of food, was ever lifted from me; and so much sentiment and so little assistance made me inclined to agree with Vera, who said that she hoped "mama is not going to turn into a mother *now*".

Nearly all trouble comes from mis-timing: the human relationships one longs for arrive too late, and unwanted. In the years that followed, all my mother's affection came to be concentrated upon me; but my own complete and happy devotion never returned. The self-centred feeling of having been wronged, and brooding on the wrong, went fairly soon; and perhaps illness had something to do with it—for I remember longing to get rid of it and being too weak to do so. At Asolo, a happy life smoothed things out, and it departed; and my mother came out of her storms and blossomed again. She still used to speak of my having done "a few weeks' housekeeping" while I was a girl (all those years of my youth), and wove her own backgrounds with no basis of ordinary facts: but as her mistakes had come out of the richness and not the poverty of her nature, she was able to turn away from them when she saw them at last. She grew in depth and love, with a nobility which all felt who knew her in her later years.

By the winter of 1924 I could not go on any longer and they said it was necessary to operate for gastric ulcer if I ever wanted to be cured. We were recommended to a surgeon who ran the hospital of St. Ursula in Aosta. I travelled lying down all the way; I had been doing this ever since Monte Rosa. It was January; Aosta was capped with snow, and the hospital was an ancient building belonging to the Order of SS. Maurice and Lazarus; the wards were arranged in vaulted halls, the walls were like fortress walls in thickness, the nuns padded up and down in their broad shoes on stone flags and wiped the thermometers on their voluminous skirts. I had a room in the more modern wing. While they were testing and examining me, we were able to explore the town, still marked by its rectangular Roman walls built by the legions, and Mount Emilius piled with snow on the south. We walked in the frozen beautiful country with quiet shapes of winter hills at every valley's end. With no Martha-work to be done, my mother was her natural self, full of enjoyment: she talked about painting to the surgeon, who used to sketch in his spare time—and so won his attention that they would both forget me till the very end of his morning visit, when I and my disease were treated in a rather cursory way. But as soon as I left L'Arma and all our troubles, I too began to recover, and was able to walk and feel less of the continual pain. I had had to make all business arrangements before leaving, in case I died, and had written to Vera to see if she could not induce Mario to pay a small part of his debts to help with the operation. Vera would not tackle him, but sent a thousand liras out of her own savings, and I remember being annoyed, forgetting that she had never done any more in the way of resistance for herself.

The operation was successful and my mother left a week later to look after things at home; she was almost immediately staying in Bordighera to look after a sick friend, and I heard this in the Aosta hospital with extreme exasperation. I felt that everything was going to rack and ruin—as indeed it was. It was a bad accompaniment to a serious operation: and we now added an epidemic of 'flu in Aosta. At the same time something went wrong in my wound which had almost healed; I think they let it close too soon. The chief surgeon used to go for two days a week to Turin and was caught and kept there by 'flu: his best assistant died of 'flu: and I began to have great pain and a temperature soaring up from one hour to the next. I asked the nuns to bring the other assistant, but they said he was a freemason: "We never use him for our best cases". I knew enough about nursing to realize that my wound *must* be opened again, and got the nun to bring the little silver probe and tried to hold her hand steady while she did it; the other nun was in tears at the foot of the bed: the wound had healed too much for anything but a knife, and after an attempt at which both their resolution and mine failed, they gave it up and begged me to offer up my sufferings to the Lord. I felt very profane and made so much fuss that they telegraphed to the surgeon, who left his own sickbed, arrived late at night, examined me, looked very serious, carried me down to the operating room, and let about a pint of septic stuff out of my poor body. He told me afterwards that I had a perfectly sound body, and that if one organ had been weak in any way I should have died.

After that I spent weeks in Aosta. The snows began to melt, the little willow shoots appeared, and slowly I saw patches of green—and still there I was. The surgeon was charming, a wonderful surgeon, but most casual. He took me to a ski-ing race on the Little St. Bernard when I began to get better, and remained standing for an hour or so in the snow watching the fascinating jumps: then turned suddenly, seized my pulse, looked worried, and laid me down in the car, back to bed in Aosta.

Our illnesses were always the most terrifyingly mismanaged affairs, but this I think was the worst. As I was getting better and tottering about the nuns' bare little garden, Gabriel arrived one day and proposed to me—as if anyone could think of any man at such a time! I was thinking of escape now and he was too late; but we sat cosily and talked in the sunshine. Soon after, I was allowed to travel; the surgeon drove me to Turin and put me into the train; my mother was to meet it at Brescia and carry me on to Asolo to convalesce: but there was some sort of an exhibition in Milan, every train crowded; she looked into one or two carriages at Brescia, where she could not see me because of the mass of people, and the train sailed away without her. I reached Vicenza at 10 p.m., was helped down from the tail of the train far beyond the station or porters, and sat sadly on my two suit-cases. I was far too weak to carry them. An engine came shunting along and I called to the engine driver: he shunted back into the station and sent a porter, who walked before me to a dingy little inn where the waiter brought coffee in a big bowl with his thumb held well inside it. I telegraphed, and took the train to Castelfranco next day, and saw Herbert Young on the platform and burst into tears. My mother came along a day after, full of affection, unconscious of having mismanaged anything at all, and delighted with the Renaissance monuments of Brescia.

Asolo was as always a home of peace, and this spring I learned from the needlework school there how to do the seventeenth century embroidery which has amused me ever since. It made the summer for me, for I had to spend the whole of it on my back. We took a peasant's house in the Dolomites—a place called S. Vito—where the doctor who was looking after me spent his summers. Viva came out, and we all went up together, stopping to let me rest at Belluno, while the others wandered about.

S. Vito was a fine open place, but I have poor memories of it: I never walked more than half a mile even at the last, and we had constant trouble with our peasant landlord and his wife who had expected to go on living with us and sharing the house and were furious at being turned out, and disagreeable all the time. Their ideas of letting a house were very primitive: they could not bear to see us change our visitors, and when Herbert and Viva left and Mrs. Granville and Bernard arrived, they first asked extra rent for new tenants, and then said that I was not respectable, accusing poor Herbert and Bernard, both equally improbable. I suppose my lying in bed all day was a new phenomenon to their peasant minds. They sent up two carabiniers to investigate, and Minnie Granville brought them to my bedside to talk italian, and I told them what I thought of the whole thing in such a decided way that they retired saying: "The signorina cannot be very ill; her voice rings with such energy", and handed on my messages to the monstrous old landlord. Our last sight of him, when we left, was with a saw in his hand, cutting up his winter wood in his own backyard with such obvious joy at being back in his house that one could not help sympathizing with him in spite of all. It was a very evil-minded place, for Venetia came and got a room in a farm nearby and they brought her no breakfast the first morning, because they "had seen her window open and concluded she had not slept in her room". All this made me dislike S. Vito!

Viva looked after me with great goodness for a while and then Minnie Granville took over. She showed her great worth this summer, for it was a horrid little uncomfortable house, and the landlord troubles were very upsetting for her: both her son and I needed constant care, and she was always cheerful and dealt with everything as it came. Viva was not kind to her, and Minnie, though friendly to all, could jangle her ear-rings and be quite fierce if attacked, so it was better when they separated. Between the two of them, every strain was taken from me, and I never forget their goodness at a time when it was needed so badly.

In the autumn I got worse again. This time the doctor delayed because he was getting married to an old love of thirty years before. They arrived at last: she looked quite hideous, just like a toad (a nice toad), and he adored her and called her pet names: he obviously saw her with the eyes of thirty years ago, and it showed that no woman need ever despair! He was so infatuated that he was useless as a doctor, and merely said there was nothing to be done and I would be an invalid for ever. Minnie got angrier and angrier; she went red when he came into the room. The snows were creeping down: it was September: one day we could bear it no longer, packed, left S. Vito, landlord, doctor and all, and came back to Asolo. I shall never forget the lovely feeling of being back in my own bed there. I was, immediately on arrival, given a strong injection and a strange thing happened to me. I fainted, and before I came to myself again, had a curious dreadful feeling of being outside myself, trying to get back, a lost feeling: I cannot describe it, but it has made it possible for me to imagine a state of separateness from the body, which has both added to and taken away from the fear of death.

In the autumn of that year the *Colonello* died of some unsuspected disease. It happened just after I returned to L'Arma and was a dreadful unforeseen trouble, and the beautiful old mother had to be got quietly to Rome without suspecting anything. Our whole life at L'Arma seemed different without the *Colonello*, with his walking-stick and big hat, passing by our doorstep every day.

LETTERS TO MY FATHER

OSPEDALE MAURIZIANO,
AOSTA,

25 Jan., 1925.

Dearest Pips,

You will be surprised with this address, but by the time this letter goes, I shall be well through an operation and on the way to spending a busy February here getting over it! The good doctor from San Remo came to the conclusion that it was better to cut away the ulcerated piece of my 'intestino', rather than face another six months of diet on my sofa with a chance of a relapse if ever I do anything energetic afterwards. We have come here because there is a particularly good surgeon whom he knows, and I expect that by the end of the week the ordeal will be over. It seems that the trouble has been there since 1918, a result of the typhoid and all the strenuousness of one kind and another since then. I shall have to take things fairly easy this year, and then I hope be as strong as ever again, as the cause of the trouble will have been removed.

We had some charming people at Mortola just before leaving —the son, a young man of 30, took his wife from Kashmir to Chinese Turkestan over more or less unexplored country, and spent four years in Kashgar as consul, the only Britisher in all that enormous country. He gave most fascinating accounts of a sort of Arcadian life; everything grows there—it is all highly cultivated, and well governed by the Chinese: no railways, telephones, etc., but a five-months' caravan trek to Pekin.—The most beautiful mountain ranges you ever saw, ending in the grassy steppes—if Europe turns to a wash-out, let us retreat and be happy in Central Asia!

There is scarcely any snow here, but cloudy weather, preparing for a fall I think. This is a medieval old place, beautiful arches and columns, and the black and white nuns flitting about make it look still more in character. There is a terrace with lovely columned parapet for when I get better: unfortunately it looks down the valley not up at the Grand Combin as I should like.

Bless you, my dearest—I hope to send good news and love you always.

FREYA

S. VITO,
12 *Sept.*, 1925.

Dearest Pips,

I sent your little note of questions to mama and hope you may hear from her. I am being kept out of all things in a little oasis, and know *nothing*, not even my bank account which I can't get out of her. I think, however, I shall have to go home pretty soon: it gets very cold up here and the snow is creeping towards us. I think as soon as I can take the journey, I will go to Viva's for the winter: the wretched doctor tells me at least a year of practically invalid life is necessary, and it is easier to manage in her comfortable house. Sometimes I cannot help feeling that it is almost better to have no life at all, but this is nonsense, and no doubt one day I shall wake up with the pleasant feeling that it is good to be in the world after all. I am really much better, only I suppose the 10 years of more or less constant strain have told more than I thought, and I cannot recuperate as I used. Doesn't it sound as if I were old and decrepit.

I have been walking a little—about a mile, and that is the limit I am not to exceed for the next year! It is extraordinary how much one comes to notice if one's walks are restricted: all the nice little things, beasts and flowers. Venetia had a good book, and I have the little one you gave me years ago at the Mauriziano—and between the two we have discovered a lot of things—a lovely little pink flower with silver leaves she found in the high rocks—*potentilla nitida*.

The snow is coming very near and much earlier than usual. There is just now a crowd of sheep pouring down from Pelmo after their summer season. I wish you were here to see the country again: I believe it would be good walking country. It is lovely to feel the soft turf underfoot.

Viva has sent me the *Arabian Nights* in Arabic and I am waiting to get to my dictionary to tackle them.

Lots of love darling Pips. I do hope something comes of Venetia's farmer friend.

Your own
FREYA.

FROM MY FATHER

BROKEN HILL RANCH,
CRESTON B.C.,
7 *Jan.*, 1926.

Dear Freya,

I am owing you two if not three letters, so there is a lot to say to you. Xmas has gone and we are in another year of toil and unknown quantities. I hope it will mean a complete restoration to you of your own self—that is the best of all wishes we can offer to you and it is, I feel, sure to come after all your patience if there is any reward for virtue in this wicked but at the same time very nice world. Now about the ranch. I am not very eager to get rid of it at the present time in its somewhat dilapidated condition after the storm. Anyway, £8,000 would be a preposterous figure to ask for it. £4,000 at the outside would be as much as I'd expect but it may improve as time goes on and recovery taken place. I was harder hit than I thought and shall have to replant perhaps 4 acres of orchard. This will mean time and patience. I will send you another lot of photos. I quite understand the difficulty of placing younger sons in the colonies who are without experience. In fact, I should myself be scared to death if I had to go through it again, now I know something of the many pitfalls, both natural and human, laid ready for newcomers. The greatest I think is coming into a new country and the inability of gauging the probabilities of success when one has only the experience of the old country to guide one. They are absolutely useless, conditions being so diverse; in fact, they are more likely to lead astray rather than help as I have seen happen time and again out here. The trouble too with most young Englishmen is their inordinate love of sport—or at least the ones who are attracted to this country—which is an ideal sporting country; it becomes paramount with them out here to the neglect of their real practical interests. However, given a healthy young fellow with determination to get on and an interest in the sort of life he intends to take up and with *some capital to back up his efforts*, given time for a few years to feel his feet, and a mentor back of him, there is every probability of success coming. At the same time he is living in one of the healthiest countries of the world. One of the most essential things for a young man is to have a good knowledge of some trade before he starts. If he is a good mechanic, a good carpenter, a good horticulturalist and can always pay his way at a pinch, he is safe. A good motor mechanic is a fine outfit; a carpenter can save half the cost of fitting up his ranch and so on.

Wheat growing in the prairies it now again to the fore, and seems to offer good opportunities. Vast tracts in B.C. of cattle and wheat lands are likely to be opened up soon. Dairying in the west is going ahead; poultry-farming in B.C. is progressing. In fact, B.C. has got ahead of all the world and we are actually exporting breeding stock to England. Down on Vancouver Island, south end of it, horticulture is leading. Sweet pea growing is extending rapidly. All the English firms now send out here for seed, probably if you are growing some in your garden this year and it's extra fine stuff, the seed will have come from B.C. Tulips and gladioli is now their branch industry. I'm going in for tulips myself as a sort of second string to my bow and it promises well. I started with 2,000 three years back; have increased my stock to 20,000; shall have 50,000 next year, and when I get 100,000, I shall begin selling. The bulbs increase 100 per cent to 150 per cent every year and sell for 12/- to 30/- per hundred, so there is a good margin. The sweet pea growers get $1.00 a lb. for their seed and contracts ahead with the English seedsmen for all their output—a pretty good proposition. So you can see there are many possibilities if a young fellow knows how to choose and *knows his own mind* and has some guidance to begin with.

Well, that's enough about young men: now we'll turn to old ones. That is myself. I shall be 73 before very long and I am still full of fight, in spite of some hard knocks and feel I can keep going, perhaps for a few more years, bar accidents. I'm just getting round from a bad chill (a bit of carelessness on my part) but otherwise have been keeping fine. Work with me at present is not much, being mid-winter, but we shall soon be in spring again. . . . I feel that if I gave this up, I should soon drop to pieces. The life suits me, especially when I am digging all day long. The elevation is absolutely necessary for me (just as if I had T.B.). The long hot summer is ideal and in winter with tons of firewood off my own land handy, I can keep my cottage as snug and warm as any place I've ever been in; in fact, my life is worth many more years here than elsewhere. When I am past work, then it may be another matter.

By the bye, I see there is just inaugurated a line of new steamers (Motor steamers Italian) with direct service between Genoa and Vancouver with accommodation for 12 passengers. This would be an ideal route for me or for *you* to and fro. If only that storm hadn't come along I should have been across this autumn, as I should have made at least £1,000, but must wait now. But keep that intelligence in mind for some future occasion. I think perhaps such a trip would do you good and you'd see what a colony looks like and it would interest you. We are not altogether serious minded. Once or twice a month we have a dance in which your Pa joins, and then an evening's bridge, generally Sundays. Occasionally I have been known to go through till the next morning and after a ten-mile drive and breakfast, start in for a day's work, but it's only to you I indulge in such confessions. . . .

Tante cose

PIPS.

PS. Send me an odd paper occasionally.

23

Arabia in Sight. 1926-1927

WHEN I returned to Viva in London I went to see a
Harley Street specialist. He said there must probably
be another operation, and I walked back along Wigmore
Street with a feeling like lead inside me. He gave me a letter
to a surgeon and we went, and I was examined, and the verdict
was *no* operation: the nurse who dressed me said it was nice to
see people glad of such news; usually they were "so disappointed."
We now abandoned the specialist and Viva brought her own
G.P., a sensible man who finally cured me. He told me that
the whole trouble had been carelessness in childhood and strain
later on, and that my last year's relapses could have been avoided:
I must spend several months in bed. This was the fifth year of
illness and the third of almost constant lying down; I was very
tired of it all. Viva looked after me and spoiled me, for she
liked having me safely in bed in her own hands to be an object
of devotion. She longed pathetically to possess the people she
loved, and later on could hardly bear me to blossom out into
independence, and felt it unhappily if anyone young or gay
invited me, until it finally led her to suffer if any success or
pleasure came. I think it was the difficulty a beautiful woman
often has in facing old age, and would have passed in time. I
came to be torn between my gratitude and affection and this
unreasonable curb. It was almost absurd, for if I was asked out
to dine at the Savoy, Viva's only comment would be: "It is
a long time since you have been to Highgate to visit your grandmother", and goodness knows I had not had a surfeit of

dissipation in my youth. Now, however, I was safely tucked in bed and arabic my chief distraction.

On my arrival in England, before seeing the doctors, I had gone down to the School of Oriental Studies and arranged to have lessons from a young Egyptian with a head as bald as an egg called Abd el Qadir. On the day he was to come I was already in bed, but I had no intention of losing my lessons. Viva promised to come back in time to chaperone, and a chair was put for him at the bedside. Viva was late, and he tried to escape; but I held him resolutely to his task and handed him the *Arabian Nights* of which, I soon discovered, I happened to have the unexpurgated edition: he was obviously relieved when Viva came. Olivia Horner told this episode to Guy le Strange, who sent me an edition of the *Arabian Nights* expurgated by the Jesuit fathers, and opened a friendship which lasted till his death. He was a charming old man; although nearly blind, he was learning Italian so as to read Petrarch. He was run over by a bus when close upon eighty (I think), and wrote to me saying: "This is not likely to happen to me again." When he was young he had travelled "post" in Persia, as much as seventy or eighty miles a day, changing horses, and had visited Lady Ellenborough's husband, the Sheikh of Palmyra.

My illness had again brought time for reading: Charles Doughty, Gibbon, Dante, Horace Walpole, Mme. de Sévigné, Montaigne, Balzac, Trollope are the landmarks of these years. With my teacher, a nice quiet man, I studied the Pre-Islamic Mu'allaqat, and this helped me through the months. Everyone thought it a good sick-bed occupation, but to me it was far more than that—it was escape. Our income was slowly rising: I have a little note-book where it is marked year by year—£90, £150, £200: and I had promised myself years ago that when it reached £300 I would leave all this toil and go, with my mother provided for. I had continually a miserable sense of being a failure. I was thirty-two and had done nothing except house-keep: in writing to someone whom she wanted me to marry, my mother once said that I was good with servants—the only

inducement that came into her mind. I studied arabic with
the hope that at some time it might lead me out of the endless
Martha lane into some sort of fairyland of my own. But it was
such a fragile hope, and so dear to me, that I never mentioned
it to anyone.

A nurse came every day, and a nice woman for massage who
used to tell incredible stories of the *nouveaux riches* she attended—
one especially, who had a dark water-line because she never
washed below her decolleté. In the spring I got better; I remember very little of it beyond the arabic. The St. John's Wood
of my childhood seemed to have faded: dear old Mr. Bale had
died some years before; his cherry tree still blossomed but
in the gardens all about us flats were shooting up on every
side.

I was well enough in the spring to go to Asolo and L'Arma,
where all seemed to promise well. A pleasant summer party
gathered—Poldores, David Horner, Venetia, Mervyn Arnold
Forster who had met me in England and became a dear friend—
and Gabriel's younger brother the cavalry officer. In the middle
of all this came news that Vera was ill.

I had seen Vera very little during the lawsuit, which in 1925
was decided in our favour; it had not spoilt our affection, and
Vera, in spite of all difficulties, came in the spring of 1926 to
Asolo for three days. She came looking terribly thin but pretty;
her eyes were like dark brown stars and she had heavy long hair,
so heavy that she had to cut part of it off because it could not
be coiled on her head: her cheeks were still pink as in our childhood. Poldores was staying and we had a happy time, and
wandered about our childish bits of garden and the walks we
used to know. We spent a day in Padua and were turned out
of St. Antony's church because Vera had sleeves only to the
elbow (as if an *elbow* could ever lead anyone astray). We
arranged another meeting one day in early summer half-way
between Dronero and L'Arma; because of the lawsuit, Mario
would not let her come down to us any more. She was
still thinner and I was disturbed about it. She was going with

the children to the seaside, to a place called Varazze. There she fell ill with septicaemia, the result of a miscarriage. I can never pass Varazze in the train now without a horrible tightening of the heart. I went to her. Her sister-in-law was there, and Mario half distracted. We struggled for two months: she had a wonderful constitution, like mine, and time after time seemed to have conquered, till the disease found some new form. If penicillin had been invented, she would have been saved. They cut off her lovely heavy hair. She accepted it all with the same quiet detachment with which she had faced her life. We had long heartfelt talks at that time and she thanked me for the years of happiness she had with Mario since we had gone from Dronero: if she had not been left alone there, she would have run away and got divorced she told me—and might be living now. How can one tell what one does? Mario was really devoted: he nursed her, and brought a specialist from Turin, and was up night after night. After some weeks she seemed better. I returned to L'Arma while my mother came to take my place. On the 23rd of September she died. I have known two great sorrows, the loss of Guido and of Vera; but the one has long since healed and is ordinarily forgotten, and Vera's death is still as harsh as ever and will be as long as I can feel. I cannot help believing that if she had wanted life more, she could have held it: but she was not interested, and accepted death as she had accepted her marriage and her baptism, and no one outside her could help. In her last years she was happy in a quiet way, but never knew the radiance which alone makes life worth living, even if it comes for only a short gleam and disappears.

I went to Dronero to be with the four children who were cheerful and beautiful and fond both of my mother and me. Everyone was very kind, and thought that we would live there. For a time I thought so too and tried to face it. Dronero, now without Vera, filled me with horror. They put her in a family vault, an underground cell with coffins in rows—little Leonarda, the old Contessa, Mario's brother Angelo—all the people we had known 'lapped in lead': one went down steps with a hideous

[325]

weeping monument above. I did it once, and have never been near it since: it seemed a blasphemy against death.

In the early months of this year, when I was in England, I received a letter from Herbert Young.

ASOLO,
15 Feb., 1926.
(S. Valentine's day would have been more appropriate.)

My dearest Freya,

I have a proposal to make you, but don't be alarmed, for it is not of a matrimonial kind. Put very briefly it is this: Do you think you could carry on this Asolo property after I have gone permanently? I mean making it a home? If so I shall be delighted, because then I shall be sure that this dear place, where I have lived such a long time, and which is, in a sense, my creation, will not fall into unworthy hands, and be destroyed perhaps—a contingency that revolts me. It has been offered to my brother Fred, but he says he couldn't live here—and I quite see his reasons for saying so. My dear Cousin Molly, to whom I turned after Fred's refusal, has reluctantly found herself obliged to decline the offer: and her reasons are also very reasonable. I have had you, my dearest, in mind for some time past, but thought that my brother and Molly should have first refusal, so to speak. My other relatives don't count, because, (if for no other reason) none of them could make a home in Asolo.

To be quite clear, I propose to make a will in your favour, leaving all my Asolo properties to you, i.e. houses and garden and furniture, etc., etc. Of course I don't want to tie you down here for always and always—don't I go away myself pretty often? But to have it and keep it as a home: not a place to sell —unless circumstances oblige you to part with it. I think that is clear, isn't it? It isn't necessary to go into details until I have your affirmative answer, which I hope to get speedily, for I am all impatience to settle this matter. You, my dear, seem to me indicated as quite the most proper person to inherit this "earthly Paradise," as some enthusiasts have called it. You have very early associations with Asolo. When first I saw you, you were crawling about on the floor of my studio, an inarticulate infant, and I know you love the place. If there are any objections, let me know and combat them.

Yours most lovingly

HERBERT.

I thought it over, and accepted, and it was a happiness for us all, for Herbert, my mother and myself. To them, it gave companionship and to me, for the first time since early childhood in Ford Park, it offered a home, a place that goes on whether you are there or not, that you come back to and find waiting with a welcome. This would have had to be given up if we stayed in Dronero. It was so difficult a decision to make. I waited, and walked with the children, scrambling for blackberries, climbing the cliffs above the river, all the time trying to see the way clearly. The children, delighted to have someone to play with them, grew fond of me: and as soon as this became obvious, Mario began to be jealous; he talked about the dangers of their becoming English. This settled the matter. I knew he would always pull the other way if he saw that they loved us; and it became clearer and clearer till we finally decided to let them grow up with undivided feelings, little Italians, to come to us later when inevitable troubles with Mario began for them. My cousin Mary returned to Dronero and looked after them for many years, until war scattered her and them—her to an exile where Mario left her destitute and she tried to commit suicide; and the two boys—one to be lost in Russia and one to die as a partisan. One niece remains, who looks and laughs so like Vera that I sometimes mistake, and think my sister there.

By the autumn of 1926 my income reached the desired three hundred pounds. It went through vicissitudes, for Mexican Eagle Oil, in which I had five hundred, collapsed. I told this sadly to a friend, who hesitated a day or two and then said: "I ought not to mention it, but as you have had a loss, it may be useful to you to know that Canadian Grand Trunk Railways are going to rise very soon." They were engaged in a lawsuit and would either go steeply down or up according to the verdict, of which she must have had some inkling. I thought this good enough, scraped together every penny I could lay hands on, practically the whole of my capital, went to Barclay's Bank in Monte Carlo, and invested it in Grand Trunk, in spite of a mild protest from one of the managers whom I knew. I subscribed to the *Financial Times* for a few weeks to follow the operation. The shares remained steady, then began to go down, day after day. I felt I should get frightened, and resolved not to look at my *Financial Times* for a fortnight: at the end of that time the shares were rising: they rose from thirty-five to fifty-one, and I sold; I think they began to drop again at fifty-two or fifty-three. When I went to the bank, two managers came out and congratulated me: they said that I had shown such confidence that the whole staff invested. This was my only success in gambling, but it made my journeys to the East possible.

I was in England that autumn. I had come to the conclusion that a degree in arabic was not necessary to me: what I wanted was the living language and to go out and practise it in its own habitation. I made various enquiries—from Mr. Wellcome, the archæologist, from Professor Newberry, who was charming but discouraging, and in September 1927 from Col. Moore who had been in Kuwait. I travelled to Marseilles to meet him and he tried to help me to join the missionaries on the Persian Gulf, but failed. In July, 1927, I was told of a chance to go as governess to the princesses in Bagdad and travelled to London for an interview: my wish to learn arabic was not an asset and I was rejected; and finally Sir Thomas Arnold gave me a letter to Dr. Manasseh in the Lebanon and I decided to go out and study there alone.

My last winter in England was happy. I spent Christmas with W. P's two sisters in the Campsie Fells, a house unlike any other, whose doors were always open—and the only one I know where a second hot-water bottle was brought to one's bed with the early morning tea. No one ever wanted to leave the Miss Kers—the maids, cook, gardener, were all old: and children, friends, good works, books and correspondence flowed through the house in a mixture of commonsense and kindness, lighted and corrected with emotion from Penelope, and a pleasing nip of acid from Car. They took me to see Edinburgh for the first time—the Firth of Forth shining in frosty sunlight and a military funeral with pipers passing by. And then I came down through the pleasant west to stay with W. P. James in Cardiff, and drive over the Beacons to Brecon, and by the Usk the most romantic of valleys, through the lands of King Arthur and his knights and the dreams of my childhood. The mining crowds did not look friendly: I have seen their look since on faces in Eastern crowds, and know what it means: unemployment was bad at this time. From Cardiff I went to Venetia's house at Nannerch in Flintshire. Tucked into high moors, it looks across a gentle valley; a long avenue of beeches leads up to it; and it is full of that charm of a country house loved and cared for, a sense of stability, and gentle living. Venetia was detained unexpectedly in London by some trouble, and I was alone three days with the housekeeper who stood, starched and forbidding, behind my chair at meals. I cannot bear this speechless grandeur even now, and made her talk about Welsh grammar; but she never really relaxed, though one felt she would have liked to. We had a day with hounds when Venetia came; and then I was back in London: Stanley Spencer's *Resurrection*, the Russian Crown Jewels at Christie's, Olivia Horner's wedding, *The Constant Nymph*, the Royal Geographical Society and the posthumous story of Gertrude Bell's journey to Hayil—and in April Milan again, and an hour or two at the Poldi Pezzoli, before the Venice train. I got out at Vicenza and found Herbert and my mother there to meet me, and we sat at a café in the Palladian square, as we were to do often in later years.

The summer was passed at L'Arma. Herbert Olivier's white elephants of villas were let to pleasant people: the children came down and we had Gabriel's brother with another cavalry officer and Gustino, our *Colonello's* brother, with his Russian fiancée.

We spent the whole summer on the beach or under olive trees, in a pleasant, lazy and friendly way, and watched the fireflies sparkling at night or phosphorus dripping from the oars at sea. I had got a new man and L'Arma looked well cared for, its little plots of vines and flowers were in good order; I was always afraid bits of the house might fall off, as it had been so economically built, but as a matter of fact it has turned out to be quite solid, and has survived bombing, shelling, mining, and the visits of fascists, Germans and Senegalese. It had a charm which everyone felt who came there, because it was unpretentious, like an old car with no paint left on it—you can do just what you like with it.

We went back by Dronero to Asolo, where my mother started a new life by building up a little handicraft industry for the weaving of silk. She became contented, joyous and serene as all her later friends have known her: the resentment of those years after Dronero vanished, and she and I settled with permanent happiness into that most difficult relationship of parent and child.

I was busy getting ready for my great adventure when a telegram came to say that my father had had a stroke. He fell down in the street of his Canadian town and was carried home, recovering consciousness enough to say "I want no doctor and no parson." I got ready to go out to him. But he recovered and telegraphed to me to continue on my journey. He was able to move about his cottage and to write letters.

BROKEN HILL RANCH,
CRESTON B.C.,
5 Oct., 1927.

Dear Freya (This is for you and mamma),

If you got them, I'm afraid my telegram and Dr. Henderson's have given you a scare. I hope you refused to submit to that condition long.

I am to-day, I am glad to say, getting slowly round, only crippled on the right side, but with aid of two sticks when my guardians are out of the way, able to walk outside and stroll in the Ranch. I don't think you should upset your own plans in any case. If I don't pull round, no human good would have been done, as you could not get here for some time, if I have a relapse; better just "carry on" with your own plans.

I'm well looked after and am in my own home and don't worry. I've fixed up with Dr. to be cremated, and so there will be no trouble in future and you will be able to dispose of the ashes as you may think best amongst the Gentians and Edelweiss in your garden—that's all plain sailing. Do just as you like.

It's just five days since I telegraphed and no reply come. I don't know whether you are getting any news. I hope not, so you won't be worrying. Give my love to the kiddies.

I got knocked over by a "stroke" in town after talking to some friends. Found myself leaning up against a telephone post and wondering how my walking [stick] had got on the ground and the difficulty of retrieving it, just the experience of any drunk and disorderly. Then a friend got hold of me and whisked me off to Dr. in his car "and so home" like Pepys. Dr. is pretty good to me, and friends, and all round.

I was telling him just now of the custom in Piedmont when a man is in extremis of preparing as good a banquet as possible to set before the victim by which the poor fellow realizes his condition. I told him I should expect the same treatment, and, if he appeared one day with a roast goose and sucking pig followed by ices, with two or three bottles of wine, I should know what to expect, but he'd best be sure of his diagnosis beforehand. I'm afraid I rather shocked him. Well, I must close. My love, and all my love to you as you know.

Ever your

PIPS.

Mr. Allan Imperial Bank is good and safe. Littlejohn, a Scot, a good friend, would help with all possible advice.

I ought to have given up everything and gone to Canada, and have it always as a remorse when I remember that I did not do so. I seized on his telegram and deceived myself with it, and only went to him a year later, and spent two winters with him before he died. I think it was wrong, yet he got much

pleasure out of my travels, for they were the things he would
have loved to do himself. When later I was ill in Persia in 1931
I remember thinking: "I must not die before him, it will grieve
him too much"; but he died a week or so before, and I knew
nothing of it until his last letter reached me in Teheran, full of
a happy courage. He kept his interest in politics and art to the
last. When he went out to Canada at the age of fifty-two and
lived so rough a life, he said to a friend who asked if it was not
too much for him: "I always like to try to do a little more than
I can."

I have often wondered what share my two parents have in
me. To disentangle the threads of circumstance and heredity
seems to me more fascinating than any mystery of fiction. I
think I am a normal sort of person, a meeting ground for my
parents' extremes, for they were both extraordinary in their way.
My father was the original mind of the two, though few people
who knew them realized it: his thoughts were always independent, though he kept initiative in action for rare occasions.
Vera inherited his character, original, observant, and slow. My
mother had fewer ideas of her own, and the playing with ideas
bored her: but her marvellous energy seized on any material that
was given her, and worked it and transformed it, so that all the
world and she herself soon considered it her own. She had a
wonderful life-giving quality; her arrival lit up any gathering
and she became its natural centre; she had a splendid presence,
and scarcely ever knew an illness of any sort; and she had an
impetuousness and generosity which made her throw herself into
anything that anyone asked of her, with little discrimination, and
ever listening to him who asked the loudest. I think she never
looked inside herself until after Vera's marriage, when the world
which she thought so smooth and unproblematical, opened in
rifts and chasms about her: in those years her resentment against
us both, unconscious but real—for by our existence we forced
unpleasant facts upon her—gradually changed to the perception
that in family life she had not been as successful as in her other
activities: she became ardently Catholic and would have liked

to become ardently maternal. With Vera it was too late even for any surface affection, and I think that my mother's clinging to small and social satisfactions was a refuge from a feeling, perhaps unrecognized by herself, that she had missed more important things. It took her many years to see that her road was a mistaken one, but having seen it she did what few have the courage to do—she changed her direction, regardless of what it cost her. In Asolo she began to return to the values known in our childhood and neglected for so many years: and the affections which she had not had time for, came back. I think she would have liked to go on from where she left off, twenty years and more before. But I was thirty-four years old, and had been more alone than most of my age; and had faced in those years all those problems from which she turned away. Possessive love is no good to one except in early childhood, and even then I cannot help thinking that it is safer to tread very delicately so as not to give that feeling of suffocation which is so often produced by the affections of women. Our lives, branching off into different zones, became as happily arranged as they could be; my mother, in the centre of her own picture, was able to love wholeheartedly without the obligation or weight of responsibility, which was more than she could bear; and I came to think of her as one human being should think of another, independently of social relationship—as the most vital, loving, generous, and delightful companion.

On the 18th of November, though I was still very delicate, with a blood pressure of only 78 instead of 130, I sailed in the Lloyd Triestino for Beirut—and my travels in the East began.

*   *   *

This story of my life, up to this moment, was written for Sydney Cockerell at his request, during a short lull that came to me in the war years, in Cyprus, and I have not altered it except to rearrange and tidy it up for publication—and to add a few letters and extracts here and there. The end of the MS. said:

'I have brought this record up to my departure for the East, and the rest you know. The opening out of the world, the enchantment of that journey, you can imagine. Nothing could spoil it, not the shadow of my father's illness, not my own body which racked me with pains for days every week through that winter. I had made up my mind that I would rather die than go on living as an invalid; I paid no attention to the pain, and it gradually gave in and went away. When I had asked my doctor in London if I could go he said: "If you were a soldier, I should not pass you as fit: but if I were in your place, I should do just as you are doing." He was a sensible man. I feel now that every one of these last fifteen years has been worth five years of ordinary life—so that would give me a long span even if I were to die to-morrow . . .

'Ever so many things that I have omitted keep on coming into my mind as I write: our visit to Naples, in 1906 probably, as children, when we stayed at the Hotel Luna in Amalfi and watched the people fleeing from the cholera epidemic, driving in open carriages along the coast road, and seized by carabiniers who stood with a sort of watering cart filled with disinfectant and sprayed them as they passed . . .

'Our attempts at acting when our cousins were in Dronero, in 1905, and Vera's hatred of it and her appearance as Margherita in *Faust*, saying only: "I must die: what a pity," and lying down and doing so with a sigh of relief.

'Sleighing down the tortuous ice-covered hill-paths in winter, and learning to ski later, when my father brought us skis—somewhere about 1907 or 1908: we never learnt well: we had no teachers. And Mr. Geddes who came out from England to become a partner in the factory—lasting a very little while, and called Chopin's Funeral March "very jolly" when my mother played it, and found us so highbrow and dull . . .

'In 1925 I was baptized a Presbyterian. I did not wish to die outside the Christian brotherhood, and I knew my operation was to be a risky one. The Thirty-nine Articles seemed to me more than anyone could accept as an adult and so I spoke to the Presbyterian padre at Bordighera and he baptized me quietly one morning . . .

'I have now come to the end of my holiday. I leave in two days and have just managed to finish this record. If I have time I will read it through, but there is no time to improve it from what it is, a bare jumble written with no arrangement of words or style or matter; the facts are all true and I have tried to give them as fairly as I could—the only inaccuracies I think may be dates here and there when I have forgotten the sequence. As you see, it is a very private history: I am glad to have written it for you. I felt a great reluctance, for I try to forget and indeed have long succeeded in not thinking of the unhappy things among all these memories—but now I am happy that you know them, and I realize that it was rather a burden to have them all entirely to myself. I do not think I regret anything except the coming into our lives of Mario—the only person of those with whom we were deeply involved whom I could truly dislike: it would be unfair to all the good and splendid people who have been our friends, if I did not do so. As a matter of fact even he was not unmitigatedly objectionable: he loved Vera and was making her happy at the last, and he never looked at anyone else while she lived. He also loved the children with his jealous love, which, alas, led to anger, malice and all horrors when they grew up to want souls of their own. The moral of it all seems to be that everyone develops his own soul in the world, and the crime of crimes is to interfere with this process in those you are responsible for; perhaps that is what is meant by Christ's word about children? Some lives, like my mother's, are terribly expensive in the lives of other people: yet she had something to show for it in her own richness, which gave out as much sunlight as it absorbed. But the deepest love of young people goes, I think, to those like my father, and W. P., and yourself, dear Sydney, who feel tenderly about the "living space of other human souls."'

ASOLO

Index